THE FUTURE OF ETHNICITY, RACE, AND NATIONALITY

THE FUTURE OF
ETHNICITY, RACE, AND
NATIONALITY

Walter L. Wallace

 PRAEGER

Westport, Connecticut
London

Library of Congress Cataloging-in-Publication Data

Wallace, Walter L.
     The future of ethnicity, race, and nationality / Walter L.
     Wallace.
        p.   cm.
     Includes bibliographical references and index.
     ISBN 0–275–95831–0 (alk. paper)
     1. Intergroup relations.   2. Acculturation.   3. Human evolution.
     4. International relations.   I. Title.
     HM131.W35   1997
     303.48′2—DC21   97–8865

British Library Cataloguing in Publication Data is available.

Library of Congress Catalog Card Number: 97–8865
ISBN: 0–275–95831–0

First published in 1997

Praeger Publishers, 88 Post Road West, Westport, CT 06881
An imprint of Greenwood Publishing Group, Inc.

Printed in the United States of America

The paper used in this book complies with the
Permanent Paper Standard issued by the National
Information Standards Organization (Z39.48–1984).

10 9 8 7 6 5 4 3 2 1

Copyright Acknowledgments

The author and publisher gratefully acknowledge permission to use excerpts from the following:

Stephen Castles and Mark J. Miller. 1993. *The Age of Migration*. New York: Macmillan. Reprinted by permission of The Guilford Press.

Thomas Sowell. 1981. *Ethnic America*. New York: BasicBooks. Copyright © 1981 by BasicBooks, Inc. Reprinted by permission of BasicBooks, a division of HarperCollins Publishers, Inc.

Malcolm Waters. 1995. *Globalization*. London and New York. Reprinted by permission of Routledge.

Max Weber. 1978. *Economy and Society*. 2 vols. Edited and translated by Guenther Roth and Claus Wittich. Berkeley, CA: University of California Press. Reprinted by permission of University of California Press.

What? What?

CONTENTS

FIGURES

ACKNOWLEDGMENTS

First thanks first: to Sarane Boocock, all-around sine qua non. Thanks, too, to Chaim Adler, Miguel Centeno, Frank Dobbin, Howard Taylor, and Charles Westoff for comments on various versions of the manuscript; to Paul DiMaggio and Tom Espenshade for pointing me to a couple of specialized literatures; to Valera Mamedaliev for comments on an early version, and especially for computer expertise in preparing camera-ready figures and helping me prepare camera-ready pages (and thanks to people at the CIT Help Desk in the latter regard); to Donna DeFrancisco for expert and thoughtful secretarial help all year around; to Blanche Anderson for compiling the index of names on short notice; to Cindy Gibson for being generally helpful; and to Marilyn Brownstein and Nina Duprey of Greenwood Publishing for their indispensable assistance in getting the manuscript into public print.

Especially in an analysis of such sensitive subject matter as ethnicity, race, and nationality, it is essential to make clear that notwithstanding the enormous help I have received—from all those mentioned above, and of course from the many authors whose work is quoted or referred to here—I bear sole responsibility for writing, or quoting, everything that appears in this book. I do, therefore and hereby, make at least that one thing perfectly clear.

1

INTRODUCTION

A large percentage of the news carried by the mass media these days, probably everywhere in the world, is about relations between ethnic groups, racial groups, and nationality groups. Something really important is happening in this area of life just now. But *what is it?*

In order to answer this question sensibly we have to call up some other points in time with which to compare our "now." If we want to understand what is happening now, and if we want to make reasonable guesses about what is likely to happen in the future and make plans around these guesses, immersing ourselves entirely in the here-and-now would be a big mistake. We need to lift our heads; look around; get our bearings. Then, as Abraham Lincoln put it, "If we could first know where we are, and whither we are tending, we could better judge what to do and how to do it" (1971:40; see also Durkheim 1984:14).[1]

This book, then, will try to explain where we are, how we got here, and whither we are tending—but it will stop short of making detailed judgments about exactly what to do next and how to do it. Although such judgments are what Lincoln and all of us are ultimately seeking, we all know it would be a great help in working them out if we had a sense of *going somewhere* (a star to steer by, as someone must have said), and therefore some way to tell whether a given judgment of what to do and how to do it would put us more on-course or not. That *going-somewhere* sense is what I am after here.

But when it comes to lifting our heads and looking around to see where we are, how we got here, and whither we are tending, the biologist Richard Dawkins warns that "our brains are built to deal with . . . processes that take seconds, minutes, years or, at most, decades to complete"—implying that we may be constitutionally unable to lift our heads very far. Immersion in the here-and-now may be pretty much all we humans are capable of doing.

Undaunted, however, Dawkins himself proceeds to set forth "a theory of cumulative processes so slow that they take between thousands and millions of decades to complete" (1987:xi; see also 3, 181). That is my predicament, and my project, here, too. Despite the strong pressures we all feel to let ourselves be swallowed up in the often baffling and infuriating particulars of daily news (no wonder we call it the daily press), I shall try to draw attention to processes that cannot be detected by comparing one day with the next, or one century with the next, or even one millennium with the next—and not by examining any single part of the world, or any single ethnic, racial, or nationality group all by itself.

In a word, then, the focus in this book is the forest, not the trees—and the forest here is the whole human species over the past couple hundred thousand years, and into rather more than a couple hundred thousand years of what seems to be its likely future—not just the United States last week, this coming Friday, and next Monday.

One way of appreciating what this means is to compare two perspectives on, say, a single drop of water: that of a close-up snapshot and that of a movie-from-a-distance. The close-up snapshot can show us only the particular drop of water in which we are interested, plus whatever background happens to be there at the instant the shutter clicks. For some purposes, of course, that is quite enough.[2] But in the movie taken from a distance we may discover much more about our drop—for example, that it and many others may make up a river flowing in some general direction. We may also spot a waterfall marking the river's passage from one relatively calm state up-river, through a short phase of mad turbulence, to another relatively calm state down-river.

I choose the movie-from-a-distance perspective here because if one is in a canoe trying to navigate that river (and not merely surveying it from a safely disinterested distance), it can come in very handy to know the waterfall's location and dimensions, and it can be reassuring to discover that it takes up only a small part of the entire river.

There is one other reason, too, for my choice: Every other analysis of ethnic, racial, and nationality relations of which I am aware is a close-up snapshot. Taking a different perspective from the rest of the pack can lead to seeing things one might not otherwise see, and even if the reader thinks the particular things I happen to see are whacky (or wacky)—which is always a possibility—the perspective itself may be worthwhile.

This book also departs from the ordinary by explicitly including nationality groups, as well as ethnic and racial groups, in its subject matter. One well-established empirical ground for this inclusion is that the earliest known nations (ancient Sumer and ancient Egypt) were not ethnically and racially homogeneous populations but regional consolidations of many different local populations.[3] McNeill tells us that "from the beginning of recorded history, a mixture of peoples occupied the valleys of Mesopotamia. . . . [But] it is usual to call the earliest civilization 'Sumerian'; for the oldest written records were made in that tongue, and the first fully developed cities clustered . . . where Sumerian-speakers were most numerous." And of the Old Kingdom of ancient Egypt he says, "The extraordinary confusion of the Egyptian pantheon reflected the existence, survival, and elaboration of diverse local cults" (McNeill 1963:32–33, 75)—and different local cults were apt to belong to different local ethnic groups. Needless to add, taking in (whether by hook, crook, or mutual choice) persons who belong to different ethnic, and racial groups has remained a prominent feature of every nation from ancient Sumer and Egypt to the present day.

Nationality groups are connected with ethnic and racial groups in another way as well. Although, as chapter 2 will argue, nations rely on their members' belief that they share a common *destiny*, nations also steal some of the thunder of families, kinship groups, ethnic groups, and racial groups— namely, their members' belief that they share a common *descent*—when they invoke ideas like "motherland," "fatherland," "founding fathers," and "patriotism." In this and other ways, nations, while being actually heterogeneous, strive to smooth over their heterogeneity with claims of being potentially homogeneous—that is, as being ethnic groups and, to a lesser extent, racial groups in-the-making.[4] Similarly, when ethnic and racial groups aspire to nationhood they attach a destiny orientation to their characteristic descent orientation and claim to be nations-in-the-making.

For both these reasons, then, this book will treat nationality groups as local and regional *consolidators of ethnic and racial groups*; that is, as way-stations on the road to the eventual consolidation of all ethnicities into *one global* ethnicity, all races into *one global* race, and all nationalities into *one global* nationality—an eventuality that I shall call global species consolidation.

And with that, I have tipped my hand: I do *not* believe that the many past and present "diasporas" (of Jews, Chinese, Muslims, Europeans, Africans, Asians, etc.) were disasters and should be reversed. I do *not* believe that "the biggest disservice we can do to ourselves is to reiterate, to reconfirm, to reconstruct the notion of the melting pot metaphor. We didn't melt. We shouldn't melt. It wasn't a good idea in the first place."[5] At the same time, however, one must admit that a greatly off-putting problem with the whole idea of global consolidation is that it can be used as a velvet glove masking the iron fist of *global dominance* by some particular ethnic group, some particular racial group, or some particular nationality group. I shall have more to say about this, and about a closely related topic—namely, multiculturalism—in the closing chapter, after the intervening chapters have prepared the way.

Setting this problem aside for a while, then, I argue that the melting pot is working (albeit in fits and starts, with occasional backward steps as well as mainly forward ones—and always painfully) and that it has been working, worldwide, for the better part of ten thousand years. As far as its working in the United States is concerned, this is certainly no new idea. Ralph Waldo Emerson argued, as early as 1845, that "in this [North American] continent . . . the energy of Irish, Germans, Swedes, Poles, and Cossacks, and all the European tribes,— of the Africans, and of the Polynesians,—will construct a new race, a new religion, a new state, a new literature, which will be as vigorous as the new Europe which came out of the smelting-pot of the Dark Ages" (quoted in

Gordon 1964:117). John Dewey, too, addressing the National Educational Association in 1916, remarked that

the fact is, the genuine American, the typical American, is himself a hyphenated character. . . . He is international and interracial in his make-up. . . . Pole-German-English-French-Spanish-Italian-Greek-Irish-Scandinavian-Bohemian-Jew and so on. . . . When every [school] pupil recognizes all the factors which have gone into our being, he will continue to prize and reverence that coming from his own past, but he will think of it as honored in being simply one factor in forming a whole, nobler and finer than itself (quoted in Gordon 1964:139).

In addition, here is the view of a leading student of American ethnic groups in our own time—a view he applies only to "ethnic groups with European origins" but I shall extend it to other groups, including other racial groups, though not all to the same degree:

When one considers the profound changes that have occurred among American ethnic groups over the past century—the loss of the mother tongue and most other core elements of immigrant culture, the dispersion of immigrant communities, the considerable economic and occupational mobility over several generations, the erosion and atrophy of ethnic cultures, the decline of religion which once buttressed ethnicity, the cultural convergence of the various ethnic subsocieties, and the accelerating rates of ethnic and religious intermarriage—it is difficult to avoid the conclusion that what we have been witnessing for several decades is the melting pot in the making (Steinberg 1989:73).

Many American authors have stressed the exceptionality of the United States (see, for example, Lipset and Raab 1995) and have, more or less on this basis, limited the scope of their analysis and their melting-pot forecasts to this country. (Actually, U.S. exceptionality seems to be only a matter of degree; the whole world is moving in the same general direction but, as with ethnic and racial groups inside the U.S., not all parts of the world are moving at the same speed.) Martin Luther King, Jr. took a more global view: "Sooner or later, all people of the world will have to discover a way to live together in peace. . . . This faith can give us courage to . . . [live] in the creative turmoil of a genuine civilization struggling to be born" (1992:109, 111).

It is Malcolm X's statement, however, that is most to my liking: "I'm a human being first and foremost, and as such I'm for whoever and whatever benefits humanity *as a whole*" (1966:366, italics in original).

So the bottom line of this book will be that ethnic, racial, and nationality melting has been working, is working, will go on working and, what's more, *should* go on working, not only on a national but a global scale. To those who claim "East is East, and West is West, and never the twain shall meet," then, I counter with Naisbitt's view: "How rich [and I would add survival-strong] the world will be when both the cultures and the economies of West and

East converge" (1996:256) and, above all, with Palmer's view that "broadly speaking, one sees a change from a time when primitive tribes recognized only fellow tribesmen as 'men,' which is to say that they had no abstract conception of 'man' at all, to a time when all human beings are seen as variants of a single mankind" (1973:139), and Robertson's view that "it is the world, or 'humanity,' as a whole which becomes the dominant survival unit" (1992:117).

In fact, it seems to me that everybody already knows, if they have thought about it at all, that global species consolidation has been working and is still working, despite *everything*—and note: despite surges of separatism, too, for all separatisms (with the sole exception of mass suicides) propose something less than complete and permanent separation, and so at least leave the door open to eventual consolidation. The watershed difference, then, may fall between people who do and do not think global species consolidation *should* be working—which is to say, between those who are looking for ways to reverse it and those who are looking for ways to facilitate it.

I belong firmly and enthusiastically to the "facilitate it" camp, on what seems to me to be the unassailable ground (to be elucidated here) that global species consolidation will dramatically improve our species' chances of survival.

Note that this ground is not an appeal to what is usually called morality.[6] It does not claim that global species consolidation is the morally right thing to do. In fact, I shall neither assume nor propound *any* particular morality as justification for global species consolidation. My standpoint in this book (and my professional strength, such as it is) is not that of preacher or moralist but social scientist. Furthermore, moral rightness or wrongness seems logically secondary to species survival: without survival of the human species there can be no human behavior to call right or wrong, and no one to call it that.[7]

It follows from my focus on the survival of the human species that this book will have a strong future-orientation, as reflected in its title. Such an orientation, however, does not mean the book will pretend to prophesy. In a strictly scientific view, *nothing* in the future can be regarded as certain—no, not even death and taxes. At the same time, however, there are compelling scientific reasons for regarding some future events (like death and taxes, or tomorrow's sunrise) as much more *probable* than others. I hold that global species consolidation, in addition to being highly desirable on species survival grounds, is also highly probable in this scientific sense.

Two different analogies will help convey the basic structure of my thinking about this probability.[8]

First, imagine a large number of small ponds forming from rains falling in the highlands somewhere. Imagine these ponds overflowing, and small streams starting out from them. Driven by the force of gravity, and totally without knowing what they are doing, all these streams will do exactly the same thing in different ways and at different speeds—namely, head downhill. At first, they trickle slowly, erratically, meanderingly. But little by little they pick up momentum and consistent direction—merging, splitting, merging again, looping around or washing away high points in their path, backing up and collecting in marshes and lakes from which, sooner or later, they issue in rivers that grow wider and wider—until, eventually, there is almost no stopping them. They all pour into the same single global ocean basin and mingle so intimately there that no one can tell from which highland pond any single spoonful started.

For the second analogy, imagine a large number of kids all in the same small room and all blowing up soap bubbles that expand at different rates. Given breath and time enough, an absence of evaporation (and ignoring several other things—like the space that the kids themselves take up, and possible interruptions by peers, parents, and pets), these bubbles will eventually make contact with each other and merge into a smaller and smaller number of larger and larger bubbles. Finally, they will merge into one single bubble filling the entire room.

Of course, even the best analogies (and these two are certainly not in that category) fall flat on their faces when confronted with the hard fact that nothing is anything other than itself. Populations of living human beings are neither ponds and streams nor kids' soap bubbles. Nevertheless, the special usefulness of an analogy lies in the light it can cast not on the whole complicated and ultimately unique thing in which one is interested but on some particular aspect of that thing. The above analogies are meant to highlight the following aspects of global species consolidation.[9]

First, both analogies highlight the role of *equifinality*—that is, the principle expressed by "All roads lead to Rome" and "There's more than one way to skin a cat."[10] In the case at hand, both analogies point to the strong likelihood that different ethnic, racial, and nationality groups will wind up in the same place in the long run, no matter how complicated and varied may be the paths they follow to get there. Then, when considered separately, the analogies highlight the two different kinds of forces that explain *why* this common convergence is occurring: forces that originate outside human societies, and forces that originate inside them.

The ponds-and-streams analogy, by stressing the parts played by gravity and the way Earth's surface is shaped in bringing all the different waters together, underscores the idea that the future of ethnicity, race, and nationality depends heavily on conditions that lie outside human societies. Chief among these is the simple fact that the Earth is a gravitationally closed near-sphere from which most humans will be unable to escape for a long time to come and which—as our numbers grow and as we move and message across it—compels us, sooner or later, to make contact with each other. The soap bubble analogy, on the other hand, by stressing the rising air pressure inside each individual bubble, emphasizes that there are certain engines *inside* human societies driving them not only toward contact but toward consolidation after contact. (One is tempted to call these internal consolidation engines—and to note that their operation involves, as we shall see, a good deal of internal combustion.)

Once again, the world's ethnic, racial, and nationality groups are not nearly as simple as these analogies would make out. Still, the analogies do have something going for them. Humankind (with all the devastations it has suffered in its 200-to-400 thousand years so far) has managed to accomplish what amounts to a gigantic, multifaceted, growth and increasingly global consolidation of its survival forces. That is to say, humankind is today much more populous, more spatially extensive and mobile, more physically powerful, more knowing of its environment and of itself—and it is more globally interdependent, more ideationally communicative and syncretistic, and more ethnically, racially, and nationally mixed and mixing—than it has ever been.

There is nothing new in those conclusions; many other observers have said the same things:

A succession of technological developments is breaking down the walls of isolation everywhere. . . . People who neither look alike nor think alike are being brought together in transactions of all kinds, direct and vicarious (Shibutani and Kwan 1965:8, 9).

The expansion of the media of communication, not least the development of global TV, and of other new technologies of rapid communication and travel, has made people all over the world more conscious of other places and of the world as a whole. . . . [E]nvironmental concerns have enhanced this sense of shared fate. From a different angle, we can point to the ways in which the Cold War, with its shadow of nuclear disaster, also heightened that sense of the world being one (Robertson 1992:184).

Various trends from global warming to twenty-four-hour-a-day trading are transnational . . . reminding us that the earth, for all its divisions, is a single unit. [These trends] are largely out of the control of the authorities of the traditional nation-state (Kennedy 1993:130).

Environmentalists, development professionals, human rights activists, information specialists [and members of various religious groups]—whose commonality depends less on co-residence in "sovereign" territorial space and more on common world views, purposes, interests, and praxis . . . [are] constituting a "world politics" (Rudolph 1996:26).

The minorities question in all parts of the world is coming to be more and more indivisible as internal disturbances in any one country become a threat to the peace of all and as the ideals and ideologies originating in one group are soon shared by others in remote corners of the earth (Wirth 1945:347).

These are strong testimonies to the progress of global species consolidation. But it would be foolish to wink at the murderously parasitical trends that have hitched rides on the back of that consolidation, or at the trends that run so determinedly against it. Among the worst of the parasites are ·the trades in debilitating drugs, and in women's bodies. Regarding the globalized drug trade, Stares tells us that

the global diffusion of technical expertise and the internationalization of manufacturing have made it possible to cultivate and refine drugs in remote places of the world and still be within reach of distant markets. . . . The growing integration of the global financial system . . . has also provided traffickers with many more opportunities to launder money and invest in other activities—licit or illicit. . . . And finally, expanding personal mobility and . . . the growth of the mass media and global telecommunications have undoubtedly increased the global awareness of drugs and propagation of drug fashions around the world (1996:5–6; see also Caplow 1996).

And regarding the globalized trade in women (a trade that was the likely precursor of the slave trade in men and children as well as women [see Lerner 1986: 76–100] which will be discussed in chapter 5), Barry says

The international prostitution market of women's bodies for sex is perpetuated by organized crime, operated through multinational conglomerates that include tourist agencies, hotel chains, airlines, international traffickers. . . . Under rapid industrial- ization, state, community, and family economies become increasingly dependent on prostitution industries both as a source of foreign exchange through sex tourism and as a means of siphoning women off from the developing labor force (1995:163).

High on the list of trends running directly counter to global species consolidation, of course, are the many ethnocentrist, racist, and nationalist movements of the world—especially when one takes into account the increasingly monstrous and sophisticated weaponry that the more rabid groups of this kind are likely to have at their disposal. Perhaps less dramatic, but even higher on the list are the steadily rising population and other pressures our species brings to bear on the planet's biosphere, pressures that produce rising global temperatures and that pollute or exhaust natural resources. In addition (and in the long-run, most important of all), there are the many catastrophes that the natural environment seems sure to lay on our doorstep from time to time. These include climate changes, collisions with asteroids and comets, and far more virulent microbiological epidemics than we have experienced so far—not to mention your usual floods, volcanic eruptions, and earthquakes—and some of these catastrophes could terminate humankind altogether.

In principle, at least, we could try to cope with all this by reversing the now well-established globalization processes (discussed in chapter 2). That is, we could try somehow to rewind history to the small, localized, hunter-gatherer type of societies in which humankind lived for hundreds of thousands of years before the Neolithic Revolution. But it seems impossible to do that and still manage to keep alive anything like our present world population of nearly six billion, and equally impossible to do it permanently—that is, without eventually coming around to repeat the same processes that have brought us to our present state of globalization. Moreover, it seems very likely that the most dangerous future challenges to our species' survival can only be met by a fully globalized human society (see chapter 6).

So when all is said and done, Benjamin Franklin seems to have been right on the money: "We must all hang together, or assuredly we shall all hang separately." I believe hanging together is the more likely possibility, but that likelihood does not mean we can passively fold our hands and wait for global consolidation to come to us. Indeed, the general sense of urgency expressed by Alexander Hamilton—when advocating the same regional consolidation as Franklin—seems as essential in our own time as in his:

A man must be far gone in Utopian speculations who can seriously doubt that, if these States should either be wholly disunited, or only united in partial confederacies, the subdivisions into which they might be thrown would have frequent and violent contests with each other. . . . To look for a continuation of harmony between a number of independent, unconnected sovereignties in the same neighborhood, would be to disregard the uniform course of human events, and to set at defiance the accumulated experience of ages (Hamilton, et al. 1961:54).

Now it should be clear that although the main target of this book is the future survival of the human species, its argument must trace a path through the past and present—because we have first to assess where we are and how we got here before we can start thinking sensibly about whither we are tending. Consequently, the next four chapters, roughly 70% of the book, will be devoted to assessments of the past and present (although I shall not resist drawing some whither-are-we-tending conclusions along the way). On the foundation proposed by these chapters, the closing chapter will offer the book's most explicitly future-oriented discussion.

With that, and to bring this Introduction to a close, here is a quick chapter-by-chapter preview of what lies ahead.

Chapter 2 will introduce the idea that the entire history of humankind fits a model that I call the Grand Cycle. It comprises four overlapping stages: (1) starting some 100 thousand years ago, slow dispersion of the human species outward from what was its point of origin in eastern Africa to all the major landmasses of the world; (2) a successively sociocultural, ethnic, and racial differentiation of the relatively isolated populations that resulted from dispersion; (3) starting with the Neolithic Revolution and the invention of agriculture roughly ten thousand years ago, the gradual development of contact among those differentiated populations; and (4) first local, then regional, and now a growing global consolidation of these in-contact, vigorously competing, often warring, but (believe it or not) increasingly cooperative populations.

Chapter 3 will try to demonstrate the fit between this Grand Cycle and the broad facts of human history so far, and will also introduce the principal institutions (the internal consolidation engines referred to above) inside each human society which have driven that history—namely, the economy, the polity, science-education-technology, and religion.

Chapter 4 will concentrate on the contact stage of the Grand Cycle. It will discuss invaders, refugees, slaves, and immigrants as the principal types of migrants through which contact has been made among different ethnic, racial, and nationality groups; it will examine the roles of wealth, power, knowledge, and honor (prime products of the institutions mentioned above) in determining relations between those migrants and their hosts; and it will take a brief look at migrants' tendencies to migrate further, beyond their ports of original entry, inside their hostlands.

Chapter 5 will focus on post-contact events. Here the basic strategies that host and migrant groups use when competing for wealth, power, knowledge, and honor will be analyzed—including stereotyping, prejudice, discrimination, segregation, genocide, and slavery. In addition, and most important, the chapter will consider how competition engenders cooperation—that is, coalitions among competitors that can grow bigger and bigger until they become global and species-wide.

Chapter 6 will offer some guesses about the future—formulated as responses to some questions that may have arisen in the reader's mind while reading the preceding chapters, and some inferences about conditions in society (specifically, in those internal consolidation engines mentioned above) that have to be met in order to complete our ten thousand-year-long drive toward global species consolidation and embark on our *next* (bigger) turn around the Grand Cycle.

NOTES

1. Similarly, and with specific reference to the subject matter of this book, Gordon says "intergroup relations work in the United States proceeds like a race horse galloping along with blinders. He doesn't know where he's been, he doesn't know where he is, and he doesn't know where he is going" (1964:9). Schermerhorn, too, argues that "a comparative study requires a view of ethnic groups in a macrosociological perspective" (1978:50), but unfortunately he does not extend that perspective to the level of global human society.

2. As Simmel puts it, "We obtain different pictures of an object when we see it at a distance of two, or of five, or of ten yards. . . . [A] view gained at any distance whatever has its own justification. It cannot be replaced or corrected by any other view [from] another distance" (1950:7–8).

3. With the claim that these ancient societies were "nations" I depart from those scholars who argue that "The nation-state is a construction *specific to the modern era*" (McNeely 1995:149, italics added; but compare 3).

4. Lieberson and Waters' discussion of "unhyphenated" White Americans, and Alba's discussion of "European Americans," examined in chapter 5, would confirm the ethnic group in-the-making aspect of present-day America.

5. Anna Deavere Smith, quoted in a 1993 WGBH Educational Foundation poster. See also Daniels 1990:8.

6. It may be claimed, however, that ultimately the species survival ground is itself moral—insofar as it assumes an arbitrarily high value for the human species and the generalized intelligence that it manifests.

7. Note that no claim whatever is being made in this book for the genetic, phenotypic, esthetic, moral, intellectual, or any other superiority of *the individual*

members of an ethnically, racially, and nationally consolidated human species—such as seems to have been made by José Vasconcelos in his writings on "la raza cosmica" (see De Beer 1966:290–314). The superiority claimed here is exclusively for the sociocultural organization of such a consolidated species.

8. Neither my forecast of eventual global species consolidation, nor my wish to facilitate it, is unanimous among scholars in the field. Here are some leading opinions on both sides.

Marx (1818–1883) sums up his forecast of consolidation as "the new world" of the future which will embrace a "universal intercourse founded upon the mutual dependency of mankind" (Marx and Engels 1978:663). Simmel (1858–1918) shares this view: "The very universality of the processes which belong to human society, whether looked at from the point of view of religion or trading or logical thinking, at least opens the door to a universal society; and, in fact, these tendencies all express themselves where the social development has gone far enough to make it possible" (1950:284). Durkheim (1856–1917) too, says "a social life of a new sort is developing. . . . As it extends, the collective horizon enlarges; the society ceases to appear as the only whole, to become a part of a much vaster one, with indetermined frontiers, which is susceptible of advancing indefinitely" (1965:493). Freud (1856–1939) agrees: "Civilization is a process in the service of Eros, whose purpose is to combine single human individuals, and after that families, then races, peoples and nations, into one great unity, the unity of mankind" (1961:77). Although Spencer (1820–1903) does not make a succinct prediction of consolidation, his basic argument is that "Social growth proceeds by . . . compounding and re-compounding [different societies]. The primitive social group . . . never attains any considerable size by simple [natural] increase," and, by way of indicating that such larger, compound, societies are generally superior to smaller ones, he claims "increase of mass is habitually accompanied by increase of structure. . . . [and exhibits] that integration which is the primary trait of evolution" (1898, I:466, 471).

Despite the prominent contribution his work makes to the consolidation argument of this book—Weber's view of the future globality of that consolidation is overwhelmingly negative. True, Weber (1864–1920) argues that "the international division of labour is a normal corollary of expanding capitalism," that "the rising significance of fixed capital will gradually bring about a situation in leading nations whereby interest in stabilization of mutual trade relations will gain a constantly increasing force" (1989b:214, 213), and he speaks of the possibility of "a unified God of the entire world" (1946:333). But Weber quite clearly regards a future global consolidation of human societies as undesirable. To the end of his life, Weber believed in the superiority of German national culture and was a strong advocate of defending it against merger with other cultures. "The deadly seriousness of the population problem," Weber argued, is the crucial factor because "it prevents us from believing that elbowroom in this earthly existence can be won in any other way than through the hard struggle of human beings with each other " (1989a:198).

Tocqueville (1805–1859), too, takes a dim view of consolidation—but for explicitly racist reasons (in contrast with Weber's nationalist reasons): "We should almost say that the European is to the other races of mankind what man himself is to the lower animals: he makes them subservient to his use, and when he cannot subdue he destroys them" (1945, I:344). Tocqueville's conclusion regarding global species consolidation along the dimension of race is quite unambiguous: "I do not believe that the white and black races will *ever* live in *any* country upon an equal footing" (1945, I:388–389, italics added). And in specific reference to the United States, Tocqueville tells us "Those who hope that the Europeans will ever be amalgamated with the Negroes appear to me to delude themselves. . . . I see that in a certain portion of the territory of the United States at the present day the *legal* barrier which separated the two races is falling away, but not that which exists in the manners of the country; slavery recedes, but the *prejudice* to which it has given birth is *immovable*"(1945, I:373; italics in original). (Yet Tocqueville also claims that "In some parts of America the European and the Negro races are so crossed with one another that it is rare to meet with a man who is entirely black or entirely white; when they have arrived at this point, the two races may really be said to be combined, or, rather, to have been absorbed in a third race, which is connected with both without being identical with either" [1945, I:389].)

Among contemporary writers, Alexander is prominent among those who argue against consolidation ever playing a significant role in ethnic and racial relations. He proposes, instead, that ethnic and racial differences (and discrimination on these grounds) are permanent. Thus, Alexander distinguishes between what he calls "primordial" and "civil" ties (see Tocqueville's distinction between informal "prejudice" and the formal "legal" system, mentioned above): "By [primordial] we refer to the seemingly natural ties that structure solidarity—race, territory, kinship, language, even religion. . . . To the degree that people share any one of these traits, so they will feel direct, emotional bonds. . . . Civil ties . . . are more mediated and less emotional, more abstract and self-consciously constructed. . . . They refer to ethical or moral qualities associated with "social" functions and institutions" (1980:8). On this basis, Alexander, like Tocqueville, then discounts the likelihood of even national, let alone global, ethnic and racial consolidation: "Every national society exhibits an historical core . . . [which will] necessarily establish . . . the pre-eminence of certain primordial qualities. While members of the non-core groups may be extended full legal rights . . . their full membership in the [primordial] solidarity of the national community may *never* be complete" (1980:10, italics added). Smith (who also accepts the idea that nations are built upon, and necessarily retain, "core" ethnic groups—see 1986), argues for the indispensability (and, therefore, the permanence) of nationality differences: "the myths, memories, symbols and ceremonies of nationalism provide the *sole basis* for such social cohesion and political action as modern societies . . . can muster" (1995:155, italics added). Reich, too, rejects global consolidation—for reasons that involve his opposition to what he calls "impassive cosmopolitanism": "Without strong attachments and loyalties extending beyond family and friends," Reich argues, cosmopolitans with a global perspective "may never develop the habits and attitudes of social responsibility. They will be world citizens, but without accepting or even acknowledging any of the obligations that citizenship in a polity normally implies. . . . Without a real political community in which to learn, refine, and practice the ideals of justice and fairness, they may find these ideals to be meaningless abstractions" (1992:309). If one wonders why a national political community should be more "real" in this respect than a global one, and why the "strong attachments and loyalties extending beyond family and friends" that generate social responsibility should stop short at national boundaries, Reich's answer merely asserts that "We learn to feel responsible for others because we share with them a common history, we participate with them in a common culture, we face with them a common fate. As the social philosopher Michael Ignatieff has written, 'We think of ourselves not as human beings first, but as sons, and daughters . . . tribesmen, and neighbors'" (1992:310). One cannot help wondering what can be the basis for Reich's, and Ignatieff's, belief that we do not already share a common *human* history and a common *human* fate, and why they cannot believe that some people do indeed—and, more important, that all people *can*—think of themselves as human beings first.)

In contrast with Reich, Hannerz traces the last half-century's shift from national to global cosmopolitanism as follows: "The cosmopolitans of the town were those who thought and who lived their lives within the structure of the nation rather than purely within the structure of the locality. Since then, the scale of culture and social structure has grown, so that what was cosmopolitan in the early 1940s may be counted as a moderate form of localism by now. 'Today it is international integration that determines universality, while national culture has an air of provincialism'" (1990:237). On Reich's side of the issue, however, Smith claims that "the differences between segments of humanity in terms of lifestyle and belief-repertoire are too great, and the common elements too generalized, to permit us to *even conceive of* a globalized culture" (1990: 171, italics added)—an unfortunate conceptual inability, however, that Smith fortunately soon tones down when he says "the project of a global culture . . . must appear premature for some time to come" (1990:180), for the achievement of such a culture is, of course, premature for *some* time to come but that is not the same as for *all* time to come. Barth emphasizes that "cultural differences can persist despite inter-ethnic contact and interdependence" (1981:199), but he does not consider whether such differences can persist *indefinitely*, nor whether there are conditions that efface them. McNeill, however, sees the origin of such conditions in civilization itself—whose beginnings go back some ten thousand years: "Marginality and pluralism," he says, "were and are the norm of civilized existence" (1985:6). DiMaggio and Ostrower describe one instance of such marginality—namely, the "bicultural competence" among black Americans, especially those in the middle class, as manifested in their "dual engagement . . . with both elite Euro-American and historically Afro-American art forms. At the century's turn, Du Bois wrote of the 'double consciousness' of black Americans adept at functioning in two different worlds" (1990:774, 773, italics removed). By way of justifying his own rejection of global species consolidation, van den Berghe asserts his "basic argument" that "ethnic and racial sentiments are extensions of kinship sentiments. Ethnocentrism and racism are . . . extended forms of nepotism—the propensity to favor kin over nonkin" (van den Berghe 1987:8, 18). Then, unaccountably overlooking the Greylag geese so famously imprinted on human males as their "mother," (see Lorenz 1970:124–126), van den Berghe claims that nepotism is a "genetically selected propensity" (1987:8)—clearly implying that ethnocentrism and racism (and nationalism?), too, are "genetically selected" and therefore biologically advantageous propensities.

Such opinions notwithstanding, some recent writers—like Shibutani, Kwan, and Steinberg (all quoted elsewhere here)—do share my view that ethnocentrism, racism, and nationalism are neither permanent nor biologically advantageous, and that the global consolidation of our species is now a clearly foreseeable potentiality. This view, however, is often expressed with marked ambivalence. Thus, on the one hand, Featherstone insists that "the formation of a world state [is] a highly unlikely prospect," but on the other hand, he admits that "It . . . may be possible to point to . . . processes which sustain the exchange and flow of goods, people, information, knowledge and images which give rise to communication processes which gain some autonomy on a global level" (1990:1). Similarly, Smith says "national cultures inspired by rediscovered ethno-histories, continue to divide our world into discrete cultural blocks" and "Even in . . . distant scenarios, it is hard to envisage the absorption of ethno-national cultures [in a global culture]," but he also says that "At the same time, the partial mixing of cultures, the rise of lingua franca and of wider 'Pan' nationalisms . . . have created the possibility of 'families of culture' which portend wider regional patchwork culture-areas. Such culture-areas may perhaps serve as models in the more long-term future for even broader inter-continental versions" (1990:180, 185, 188; see also Huntington 1996). Bauman is less ambivalent, but does not go far enough toward actual global species consolidation: "the continuous re-drawing of boundaries typical of contemporary (post modern) culture and the easiness with which they are crossed in the absence of state-hired border-guards renders the antagonisms somewhat more shallow, short-lived and less venomous or radical. With the state declaring (and practising) its indifference to cultural and ethnic pluralism, tolerance stands a better chance than ever before" (1990:168).

9. Note that both analogies employ an "eventually" claim. It has been argued that "it is both dubious and unfalsifiable . . . to argue that groups which have not assimilated are nevertheless definitely *going to* assimilate—ultimately" (Barth and Noel, 1972:336). Against this, however, consider that no one is likely to call "dubious and unfalsifiable" an argument that a certain pot of water which has never yet boiled will eventually boil—provided that the right processes of heating and/or pressure and/or volume changes are known to be present in and around the pot. Indeed, it is only after we have specified the nature of such processes (which this book tries to do for global species consolidation) that it makes sense to bother even looking into the question of *when* the eventuality in question may be expected to occur.

10. Equifinality has also been called functional equivalence, structural substitutability, and convergent evolution (see Wallace 1983:410–413, 1988:30–31, 1994: 220–221, 286–287), and it has been mathematized in the Boolean concept of "basins of attraction" (see Kauffman 1995:78). The complement of equifinality (i.e., that alternative effects may flow from the same cause) has been called equioriginality (Wallace 1983:410). Pennisi and Roush describe an example that combines both concepts: "all embryos must pass through a narrow developmental bottleneck called the 'phylotypic' stage. . . . For example, all vertebrate embryos at a certain stage . . . have the same body plan. . . . Yet before this stage, embryos may look very different, and afterward, their development takes them down a variety of paths to finned, feathered, or footed adults" (1997:37).

2

THE GRAND CYCLE

This chapter discusses the four stages of the Grand Cycle of human prehistory and history: dispersion, differentiation, contact, and consolidation.[1]

In brief, our first turn around the Grand Cycle has gone like this: After some four million years of prehominid and early hominid evolution in eastern Africa, our own species, Homo sapiens, emerged—somewhere between 400 and 200 thousand years ago. Then, beginning about 100 thousand years ago, this species slowly dispersed out of eastern Africa to inhabit, as we do today, all the major landmasses of the planet. Adapting to the different territories in which they settled and to their own internal peculiarities at that time, these largely separated populations grew increasingly different from one another. In time, they organized themselves in different ways, came to speak different languages, developed different arts and technologies, venerated different ancestors and worshipped different gods, and looked physically more or less different from each other.

Then, starting about ten thousand years ago and continuing up to the present—after ninety thousand years of dispersion and differentiation—a formidable change in direction has taken hold: More and more human societies have been making closer and closer contact with one another, thereby turning away from further species dispersion and differentiation and heading toward species consolidation (or, of course, one might say *re*consolidation while making sure to emphasize that this time the consolidation is global rather than locally east African).

The numbers in that paragraph make the essential point that populations of the human societal universe spent at least *nine times* as many years flying apart as they have spent coming together. This suggests that although for many reasons to be discussed here, global species consolidation is not likely to take nearly as long as did the original global species dispersion and differentiation, it still seems sure to occupy many future generations (another one or two thousand years?—a mere drop in the bucket) before it can be completed.

My speaking of one or two thousand years as a drop in the bucket is not frivolous. It is meant to underscore the kind of time scale that is required for the argument set forth here to make sense. As Dawkins indicates (see chapter 1), most of us reckon the future in terms of our own expected lifespans; anything much beyond that is apt to be classed as fantasy rather than future. For most of us the future is tomorrow, or next year, or a few decades from now at most.

Yet, if we stop and think about it seriously, we know that we are living 200-to-400 thousand years after the first few people like us evolved in eastern Africa—people who must certainly have reckoned "the future" only in terms of *their* expected life-spans. From our present vantage point, however, we know that the species to which those ancestors of ours belonged actually had a future far longer (and more fabulously successful) than any of those ancestors could possibly have imagined.

More important than that, however, is the fact that over the thousands of lifespans that have intervened between our first ancestors and ourselves human knowledge of the past and present of many things has increased enormously, and with that increase has come some more modest but nevertheless significant increase in our ability to infer something about what our future is apt to look like.

This is what I have in mind when I invoke a timescale that treats one or two thousand years—in either direction, past or future—as a drop in the bucket.

Let us, then, examine the 200-to-400 thousand years of humankind's first turn around the Grand Cycle, with special attention to the circumstances of our species' differentiation into ethnic, racial, and nationality groups.

DISPERSION

Almost all modern paleoanthropologists agree that every human being now alive can be traced back through the fossil and genetic records roughly in the following way:[2]

The hominid lineage diverged from the chimpanzee lineage at ~6 Ma [million years ago], and it evolved exclusively on the African continent until the emergence of *Homo erectus* somewhat before 1.7 Ma. . . . Shortly after its emergence in Africa, *H. erectus* spread to other continents. Fossil remains of *H. erectus* have been found in Africa, Indonesia (Java), China, the Middle East, and Europe. . . . The transition from *H. erectus* to *H. sapiens* occurred around 400,000 years ago (Ayala 1995:1935; see also Klein 1989:100, 102, 137, 183, 204–206, 223, 344–410; Marks 1995:17; Fagan 1989:81–120; 1990:15, 20).[3]

Ayala's figure of 400,000 years has recently been challenged by molecular biologists who claim the figure is nearer 200,000 (see Wilford 1995). But in any case, the main implication is clear: Counting generations as averaging twenty-five years, if we could trace Homo sapiens back somewhere between 8,000 and 16,000 generations (depending on whether we accept 200,000 years or 400,000 years as the elapsed time), we would come to the few Homo sapiens women and men from which every single one of the nearly six billion humans now alive is descended.

All humans, then, are Africans in origin, and except for those of us whose ancestors never migrated outside that original homeland, we all belong to the African diaspora—whether in one of its early or late phases, and no matter how we identify ourselves ethnically, racially, and nationally now. It is an essential fact of history that no one has known the time and place of this common origin until the present century because neither oral histories nor written ones reach back nearly far enough. Only the remarkable work of paleoanthropologists on-site in eastern Africa and geneticists in laboratories has assembled the physical evidence (see Klein 1989) needed to establish this signal twentieth century discovery about our species (a discovery whose perspectival significance stands alongside those, also made in the twentieth century, regarding the size and age of the universe as a whole).

Exactly why some of our ancestors migrated out of Africa while others of those same ancestors did not is probably an unanswerable question. But judging from the factors that often lead other species to divide into leavers and stayers, one may reasonably speculate that different climate fluctuations in different locations may have forced groups in one location to leave while groups in other locations stayed where they were.[4] Alternatively, climate fluctuations could have made food supplies in a given area of eastern Africa first increase (leading to an increase in population), and then decrease (leading to food shortages and sharper and sharper competition), with the weaker groups being driven out by the stronger. Both scenarios are consistent with Gamble's claim that "the dispersal of the first Ancients . . . from Africa about a million years ago [resulted from] continuous selection pressure to extend range as one route to longterm survival" (1993:117).[5] How descendants of these hypothetical early leavers and stayers experienced dramatic reversals of fortune—through what I shall call territorial luck (the "luck of the territorial draw")—will be taken up in the next chapter.

There are two presently contending hypotheses regarding the exact sequence of events leading to the worldwide dispersion of Homo sapiens.[6] Both hypotheses agree, however, that generations-long migrations out of eastern Africa eventually colonized one land area after another: southern, western, and northern Africa; and—via the northern extension of the Great Rift Valley (i.e., across the Sinai peninsula and up through the Jordan River valley)—the Near East and Eurasia; Japan, Australia, Polynesia; and finally Siberia and the Americas (see Klein 1989:406, 388, 395, 391; Marshall 1990; Fagan 1990:90, 141, 201–203; Gamble 1993:179–240). Figure 2.1 portrays, schematically, the main highways of this dispersion (see Fagan 1990:234–235).

Figure 2.1
Global Dispersion of Homo Sapiens

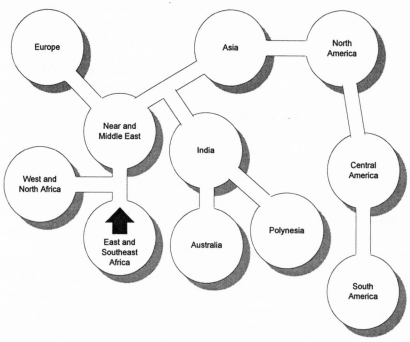

Stages of Dispersion

Let us imagine ourselves part of some group that, for whatever reason, migrated out of the original homeland. What would happen to our group? Schwartz has examined "thirteen postmigration communities" that migrated in modern times to areas not already occupied by others. "Following a migration," Schwartz says, "communities may be said to proceed through three stages of organization: pioneering, [formalization], and stabilization" (Schwartz 1985:235, 236).[7]

The pioneering stage "usually covers the initial two to four years following the colonization of a new area. During this time, the community directs its major efforts toward survival." The "structuring" process takes place when, "after the first or second successful harvest, more permanent shelters are constructed, a common building may be added, and the settlement begins to move past the feeling of impermanence." Then, during the stabilization stage, "the community settles down to develop along lines not directly related to the resettlement" (Schwartz 1985:237, 238, 240). At this time, however, "there is often a strong attempt to retain the old ways . . . [and] deviations from the norm [may be] explained as 'temporary adjustments,' implying the intention to return to the 'real' ways at a later time." In other cases, however, "a strong feeling begins to emerge that the people need no longer be bound by norms dictated during the pioneering phase, and consequently they become receptive to culture change at an earlier time" (Schwartz 1985:238–239)—that is, change in a different direction from that experienced in their homeland.

Schwartz adds that "During [the pioneering and structuring stages], factionalism can break the community apart and lead to part of the group either moving back to the mother community or establishing a new settlement, which would begin a new pioneering phase in another location" (1985:237). That is to say, a given dispersion may be followed by a back-migration or by a re-migration—courses that (I would add) may be taken during stabilization as well as during pioneering and structuring.[8] Figure 2.2 summarizes.

It is important to note that the global dispersion of our species continues to this very day with the increasing human penetrations of rainforest, tundra, and desert areas, and the many crisscrossing and overlapping migrations of members of different ethnic, racial, and nationality groups across the face of the planet. Indeed, Castles and Miller tell us that "international migration has grown in volume and significance since 1945 and most particularly since the mid-1980s. The perspective for the 1990s and the early part of the next century is that migration will continue to grow, and that it is likely to be one of the most important factors in global change" (1993:3–4).[9]

So, obviously, a second dispersion model has to be added to Schwartz's, one that focuses on migrations of groups into territories that are *already occupied* by others. Castles and Miller propose that such migrations typically proceed in four steps: (1) "temporary labour migration of young workers, remittance of earnings and continued orientation to the home location"; (2) "prolonging of stay and the development of social networks . . . in the new environment"; (3) "family reunion, growing consciousness of long-term settlement, increased orientation towards the receiving country, and emergence of ethnic communities"; (4) "permanent settlement which . . . leads either to secure legal status and eventual citizenship, or to political exclusion, socio-economic marginalisation and the formation of permanent ethnic minorities" (1993:25). Figure 2.3 summarizes with modifications that allow for back-migration and re-migration (as in Figure 2.2).

DIFFERENTIATION

Two principal types of factors are likely to have accounted for the population differentiation that followed species dispersion. The first factor is a combination of what we may call "sociocultural founder effect" and "sociocultural drift" (adapted from Wilson 1992:81–82). The "founder effect" idea here is that the sociocultural structures of any two subgroups of a parent or "founder" group are likely to differ from one another in some way (even some very small way). The basic statistical reason for this is easy to see: Absolute identity of any two things—at least above the molecular level—is, in principle, virtually impossible because out of all the vast number of different relationships that the

Figure 2.2
Dispersion Processes to Territories Not Already Occupied by Humans

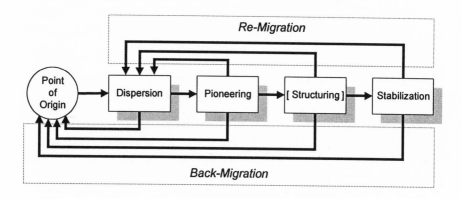

two things could have with each other, only *one* is identity. The sociocultural structures that descend from different "founder" sociocultural structures, then, are likely to differ, and to differ more and more as time goes by—just as a very small difference in the headings of two ships will take them farther and farther apart. The "drift" idea here is that the sociocultural structure of a group of individuals is more likely to change (again, even if only in some small way) from some initial state than to remain completely and permanently fixed in its initial state. The basic reason for this is also easy to see: Out of all the vast number of states that a given thing could be in at any given moment, only *one* can be identical with its state at the immediately preceding moment. The net result of founder effect plus drift is that dispersing subgroups of an original group will grow increasingly different from one another, but the differences will not have any particular direction.

The second factor (I shall call it "the luck of the territorial draw"—see chapter 3) gives directionality to those differences. The basic idea here is that no two geographical locations can be absolutely identical in their terrain, ecology, climate, and so on; therefore, each subgroup, in adapting to its own location, will become different from the others, not in randomly selected directions but in directions set by the differences between their territories.

Stages of Differentiation

The first stage of differentiation among human populations that are dispersing from each other would be sociocultural. This refers to differences in the subgroups' physical activities (who does what, when, and where) and in their norms, values, and beliefs (who thinks—and experiences emotionally—what, when, and where). And needless to say, in cases where the initial isolation of a

Figure 2.3
Dispersion Processes to Territories Already Occupied by Humans

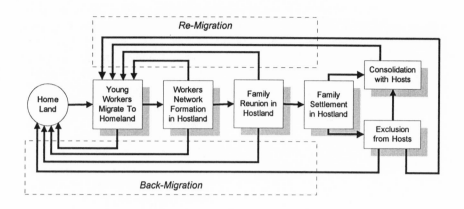

group is soon reduced or eliminated by immediate back-migration, differentiation would not go beyond the sociocultural stage and would soon disappear.

Here is a graphic illustration of the sociocultural stage of differentiation. After the social psychologists Sherif and Sherif had divided their twenty-four male summer campers—all of whom were "close to twelve years of age, . . . from settled American [i.e., European American] families of the lower-middle-class income group in the New Haven [Connecticut] area [and] were Protestants" (1953: 238)—into two separate bunkhouses, sociocultural differentiation between the bunkhouses set in immediately. "Along with the formation of a more or less defined group structure . . . each group developed strong ingroup feelings of loyalty and solidarity" (1953:260). Such feelings were enhanced by members' agreement on special names for the groups ["Red Devils" and "Bulldogs"] and special names for some of its members, its own preferred songs (into which members "inserted their own group's name in a glorifying fashion"), and their own way of punishing those who violated their group's norms (see 1953:248–270). In addition, "those members [of each group] who continued to mingle or who wanted to mingle with boys in the [other group] . . . were branded as 'traitors' and even threatened until they saw less of the boys with whom they had been friendly [before the division into separate groups took place]" (1953:260).

Then, after a period of separation and its resulting sociocultural differentiation, Sherif and Sherif brought the two groups of boys back into contact under conditions deliberately planned to bring about intergroup competition. Each group could receive "a certain number of points or credits for winning athletic events . . . and for excellence in performing camp duties, such as camp cleaning, K.P., etc." (1953:271–272), and as the competition went on, rivalry and hostility between the Red Devils and the Bulldogs intensified to the point of physical violence and the brandishing of knives.[10]

Where intergroup isolation persists for many generations, a second, ethnic stage of differentiation between the subpopulations would be added to the sociocultural stage. And, given the inbreeding that such isolation implies, each new generation's gene pool would diverge from that of corresponding generations in other groups (under influences of genetic founder effect plus genetic drift, and genetic adaptation to geographical location—see previous discussion, and see Molnar 1992:25, 184; Kottack 1987:43–50). There would first arise such genetic differences whose physiological expressions one can now observe between, say, Swedes and Italians, or north Italians and south Italians, or the English and Turks, or Yoruba and Makonde, or Han, Mongols, and Tibetans. Then, with continued generations of population inbreeding, the differences often called "racial" (e.g., skin and eye color, cranial and nasal indexes, hairiness and hair texture, resistances and susceptibilities to specific diseases, etc.) would come into existence by an accumulation of small and large steps.

Although, to my knowledge, no experiment has yet simulated the effects of ethnic differentiation, a persuasive demonstration of some effects of simulated racial identification alone—as carried out by Jane Elliot, an elementary school teacher in the United States—is reported by Peters (1971). In this demonstration, a group of European American elementary school children were divided into groups according to an explicitly stated and directly visible anatomical criterion: each subject's eye color, as augmented by a special colored collar worn so that it could be seen from all sides.

"Today, I [Jane Elliot] told the class, the blue-eyed people will be on the bottom and the brown-eyed people on the top. . . . What I mean is that brown-eyed people are better than blue-eyed people. They are cleaner than blue-eyed people. They are more civilized than blue-eyed people. And they are smarter than blue-eyed people.". . . When a brown-eyed child stumbled in reading aloud, [Ms. Elliot] helped him. When a blue-eyed child stumbled, she shook her head and called on a brown-eyed child to read the passage correctly. . . . The brown-eyed children took a special joy in baiting their blue-eyed classmates. None invited their erstwhile [blue-eyed] friends to play with them at recess. . . . At recess, [one blue-eyed girl] walking disconsolately across the playground, was struck across the back by the deliberately outstretched arm of a brown-eyed girl who the day before had been her best friend. "You got in my way," challenged the brown-eyed girl, "and I'm better than you, so you have to apologize" (Peters 1971:21, 24).

When the roles were reversed and the teacher treated the blue-eyed children as superior to those with brown eyes, "a number of blue-eyed girls gloated visibly at the prospect of revenge. . . . Within minutes, [the brown-eyed children] had become nervous, depressed, resentful" (1971:30–31). Similarly, Moskos reports on the training of equal opportunity instructors in the U.S. Armed Services: "What is most vivid in the memory of . . . graduates is the 'shock treatment' [involved in] role playing, whites seeing situations from the standpoint of a minority member—or minorities taking the viewpoint of majority members" (1991:19).

If population isolation and inbreeding persists over hundreds of thousands of years, the adaptive gene pool differences modelled by Jane Elliot would increase until they resulted in *species* differences between populations.[11] It is a crucially important fact, however, that such isolation did not persist nearly long enough for species differentiation to occur in Homo sapiens. Today, we— all nearly 6 billion of us—remain members of a single species, capable of interbreeding freely and producing fertile offspring (see Smith and Layton 1987), even though, as Marks points out, "If one compares people from [widely separated] places, one finds them, unsurprisingly, looking very different. . . . This is not to suggest that there are three clear biological categories of people: only, rather, that three populations from widely different parts of the world can be distinguished from one another" (1995:158–159).[12]

So it seems altogether reasonable to expect that when separated groups that have grown socioculturally different (as in the Sherif and Sherif study) and ethnically different, and also anatomically different (as in the Elliot demonstration) come into contact with one another under circumstances where one or more of the resources and rewards of social life are scarce, the normal first (but not necessarily final) result will be sharp competition and often bloody conflict between the two sides (see Huntington 1996:67). Moreover, inasmuch as the probability that any two such groups will bring to that competition precisely the same strengths and weaknesses is virtually zero (especially given the widely different territorial luck the various dispersing human groups have experienced, a point discussed in chapter 3), one of the groups is almost certain to achieve competitive dominance over the other in one or more ways.

Before turning to an examination of the nature of ethnic, racial, and nationality differences as such, note that the dispersion and differentiation of humankind was, on balance, strongly beneficial to the species (but see Roberts 1992 for a discussion of how the costs of isolation in a small population had escalated by the nineteenth and twentieth centuries). Geographical dispersion reduced the species' liability to extinction from localized causes such as floods, droughts, fires, freezes, earthquakes, volcanic eruptions, hurricanes, tsunamis, micro-biological and insect plagues, and the like. And differentiation dramatically increased the species' store of sociocultural, ethnic, and genetic diversity— and thus its fitness for survival across a wide variety of natural environments and changes therein (see Diamond 1992:218; Dawkins 1987:267; Leakey and Lewin 1992:57, 85, 213).[13] Indeed, species dispersion and differentiation were no more disasters than is the presently unfolding species consolidation; each serves the species' longterm survival, given its state of sociocultural development at the time.

Ethnic and Racial Differentiation

The sociological theorist Max Weber (1864–1920) provides an insightful starting point for identifying the essential qualities of ethnic and racial groups: When, through "migration or expansion, . . . groups of people that had previously lived in complete or partial isolation from each other [as a result of dispersion from a common origin, but this discovery was made after Weber's death] and become accommodated to heterogeneous conditions of existence came to live side by side. . . . the obvious contrast usually evokes, on both sides, the idea of blood disaffinity, regardless of the objective state of affairs (1978:392). Now such ideas as "*blood* disaffinity" are special because they refer to differences in ancestry or descent, and this implies *unalterable original* (that is, "unalterable" prior to the invention of genetic engineering) differences between groups. However, as previously indicated, all the evidence indicates that if we look back far enough no such differences can be found; all lines of human ancestry converge, objectively, on the same tiny prehistoric human population in eastern Africa.

But, obviously, objective fact is not the point here; it is *subjective belief* that counts in groups' judgment of each other's descent, and such beliefs may may not coincide with objective fact. This is why Weber says,

We shall call "ethnic groups" those human groups that entertain a *subjective belief in their common descent* because of similarities of physical type or of customs or both, or because of memories of colonization and migration. . . . *It does not matter whether or not an objective blood relationship exists.* Ethnic membership differs from the kinship group precisely by being a presumed identity (1978:389, italics added; compare Durkheim 1965:122).[14]

So let us say that both kinship and ethnicity pertain, in different ways, only to subjective judgments about biological descent, and both use such judgments as means of establishing individuals' group memberships and loyalties. In other words, on the tacit (and often patently erroneous) assumption that "Blood is thicker than water," judgments about a person's kinship and ethnicity are taken to indicate which *side* that person belongs to in the often life-and-death struggles over wealth, power, knowledge, and honor—the resources and rewards of human life.

Now genetic tests (which are currently the only known objective way to determine a person's descent) have been available only recently and can only be performed in controlled laboratory conditions. So the question arises: How have ordinary people in ordinary life assessed whether some other person does or does not share their particular line of descent?

Eyewitness Certification and Naked-Eye Insignia. Consider, first, familial and kinship descent. In these two relatively simple cases, assessment is apt to be based on the testimony of someone who claims to have been there (or of someone who claims to have been told by someone else who claims to have been there) when key kinship-determining events occurred. This, indeed, is the significance of the almost universal requirement of eyewitness certification of descent-relevant events like marriage, birth, adoption, inheritance and disinheritance, emigration and immigration, and death.

The situation, however, is quite different in the case of ethnic and racial descent: No one can claim they were eyewitnesses to the key events that determine ethnicity and race because such events are uniformly mythical or legendary, or at least so deeply ancient as to be beyond the reach of reliable written records. Although eyewitnesses (e.g., the attending physician or midwife) may certify that a particular child was seen to have been born of a particular mother, any certification of that child's ethnicity or race depends on presumptions about the mother's (and/or father's) ethnicity and race. These, in turn, depend on presumptions about *their* parents' ethnicity and race, and so on, back beyond any eyewitness certification. Therefore, although family and kinship group descent rest on eyewitness certification, ethnic and racial descent are unavoidably presumptive.

But precisely because eyewitness certification cannot be used in ethnic and racial descent-assessments, we have to ask: What other techniques are used to make such assessments?

Whatever may be their details, we should expect these techniques to specify certain easily-perceived-from-a-distance—let us call them "naked-eye" —insignia that all members of the ingroup should display. A good analogy is the way armies teach soldiers how to identify friendly troops: by easily spotted flags, uniforms, rank-insignia, and the like. Given this expectation as a guide, we see immediately that the insignia employed in the assessment of ethnic and racial descent fall into two types.

The first type is *behavioral*; such insignia specify certain things that one should be able, from a distance and without any special observational equipment, to see and/or hear the other person do.[15] For example, s/he will wear a particular kind of clothing, a particular kind of amulet, and/or body decoration; speak a particular language or dialect, and will stand a certain distance away when speaking to someone else (see Hall 1966); s/he will use hand gestures sparingly or profusely; laugh, or cry, or become appropriately solemn, at the telling of certain jokes, stories, and maxims; express appreciation or ridicule of particular kinds of music, dance, plastic art, and theater; eat particular kinds of foods in particular ways; worship particular deities in particular ways; and so on.[16]

Such behavioral insignia are the determining character of *ethnic* identification, and they are presumed to be reliable outward manifestations of invisible inward thought patterns, emotional and behavioral dispositions, and abilities. For this reason, they are used not only as descriptions of past and present behavior, but as predictors of how any individual displaying them will behave in the future. Such predictions, of course, are what is meant by "counting on" one's friends and "anticipating" one's enemies' moves.

The second type of naked-eye insignia of descent is *anatomical*, and this is the determining character of racial identity (although, as Weber says, "physical type" or anatomy often plays a role in ethnic identity as well—for anatomy is often a good clue to behavior).[17] Anatomical insignia specify how the body of the other person will appear, visually, if s/he shares one's own presumed common descent, regardless of how s/he behaves. For example, s/he will have a particular skin color; a particular bodybuild; a particular eye shape and eye color; a particular nose shape and lip shape; a particular profusion, distribution, color, and texture of hair, and so on.

Such anatomical insignia, too, become freighted with inferences about the invisible "underlying" traits for which the outward insignia are taken as reliably predictive as well as validly descriptive indicators.[18]

Note that naked-eye insignia of presumed descent can be, and often are, presented (or mis-presented) as though they were eyewitness certifications of actual descent. For example, part of the information given in a modern passport may describe the bearer as having such-and-such family surname, given name, birthdate, and birthplace, while another part no less matter-of-factly may describe the bearer as belonging to such-and-such ethnic and/or racial group. No acknowledgment is given of the fact that the first items of information are confirmed by eyewitness certification, while the second items rely only on presumptive naked-eye insignia as assessed by the subject, or by others. Thus, in the latter connection, Simpson and Yinger report that in 1978, "the Office of Federal Statistical Policy instructed [all federal agencies] to use 'the [ancestry] category which most closely reflects the individual's recognition in his community'" (and one wonders whether it was intended that agencies should conduct community surveys to ascertain this recognition), whereas "the general practice of those administering government programs and of college admissions officers is to accept a person's *own* declaration of his racial or ethnic identity unless it obviously conflicts with reality" (1985:28–29). "Reality" here can only mean the admission officers' assessments of the person's anatomical and behavioral insignia.

In an attempt to assess the error to which the naked-eye anatomical insignia of race are liable,[19] Stuckert estimates that 23.9 percent of Americans who were classified as "white" in the 1970 U.S. census had some objectively African ancestry (i.e., persons eyewitness-certifiably born in Africa) acquired in their family histories sometime after 1750, and that 80.5 percent of Americans who were classified as "Negro" in that census had some objectively non-African ancestry (i.e., persons eyewitness certifiably born outside of Africa), also acquired after 1750 (see 1976).[20] On this basis, Simpson and Yinger conclude that

if 43,368,000 "white" persons had some African ancestry [acquired after 1750] in 1970, the majority of persons with African ancestry [were then] classified as white. According to these figures, some 64,000,000 persons (42,000,000 Whites and 22,000,000 Blacks), or approximately 29 percent of the population of the United States have some African ancestry. These data show that racial purity in the white race is a myth (1985:298).

Williamson adds that at one extreme of Black-White mixture in the United States during the nineteenth and early twentieth century, "invisible blackness" produced "passing," which "meant crossing the race line and winning acceptance as white in the white world. Now and again, light mulattoes would simply drop out of sight, move to an area where they were not known, usually north or west, and allow their new neighbors to take them as white. . . . [But] passing was not limited to mulattoes who were very light. Darker mulattoes could pass easily enough by moving to a proper locale and taking Spanish, Portuguese, or other Latin names that explained their color and features" (1980:100–101).[21]

Finally, one notes that although the insignia of presumed racial descent are everywhere anatomical, the cutting points applied to those insignia vary from place to place:

Whereas the United States maintains an essentially biracial system in which people are classified as either white or black, Brazil's multiracial system provides for more than two categories. There are three major groupings recognized in Brazil, but the boundaries between them are neither rigid nor clear-cut. *Branco* (white), *prêto* (black), and *pardo* (mulatto) are the most encompassing terms, but Brazilians employ literally dozens of more precise terms to characterize people of various mixed racial origins, depending on their physical features. Racial terminology is strongly localized, and from region to region, and even community to community, standards of classification vary (Marger 1991:410).[22]

Ethnic, Racial, and Nationality Identity and Joint Political Action

Again, identifying *another* person ethnically, racially, and/or nationally can be a matter of life and death in the competition and conflict between strangers. (I recall a scene in the movie "Lawrence of Arabia," when two members of different Arab ethnic groups catch sight of each other around a desert waterhole claimed as its exclusive possession by one of the groups; one man kills the other without a moment's hesitation.) But one's own *self*-identity in this respect also carries great weight, for it confers life-enhancing prestige, esteem, worth, dignity, face, *honor* on oneself: "The belief in ethnic affinity. . . . affects the individual's sense of honor and dignity. . . . The conviction of the excellence of one's own customs and the inferiority of alien ones [is] a conviction which sustains the sense of ethnic honor" (Weber, 1978:391; see also Patterson 1982:10–11, 79–81; Smith 1990:182).[23]

Moreover, "behind all ethnic diversities there is somehow naturally the notion of the '*chosen* people'" (Weber 1978:391, italics added), and individuals' beliefs in their having been chosen for special honor (i.e., blessed, protected from misfortune) by their groups' deity or deities—from whom they typically regard themselves as descended—greatly enhances their morale. This, in turn, strengthens the vigor and self-confidence of their joint political action when contending with other groups. As Durkheim says, "The believer who thinks he feels the regard of his god turned graciously towards him . . . is in moral harmony with his comrades, he has more confidence, courage and boldness in action" (1965:242, see also 402).

Consequently, "every permanent political association had a special god who guaranteed the success of the political action of the group. When fully developed, this god . . . accepted offerings and prayers only from the members of his group" (Weber 1978:413).[24] Moreover, since "the tribe . . . soon adopts the whole symbolism of blood-relationship. . . . tribal consciousness usually has a political meaning: in case of military danger or opportunity it easily provides the basis for joint political action" (Weber 1978:393, 394), whether in defensive or offensive war.

Thus, belief in common descent (whether based on behavioral or anatomical insignia) enhances both joint political behavior and joint religious behavior, and these, in turn, enhance belief in common descent.[25] The result is a powerfully self-amplifying spiral leading directly to group closure, both territorially and reproductively. Accordingly, one would expect every ethnic and racial group to become more and more completely pinched off from all the others.

In other words, and employing an analogy drawn from modern cosmology, one predicts an ethnic and racial "big bang" involving fragmentation of the species into descent-oriented groups that flee into deeper and deeper isolation from each other. Indeed, after their prehistoric dispersion into certain geographically special areas of the world some of those fragments did maintain their closure well into modern times. Diamond, for example, quotes a New Guinea highlander saying that before 1930 "we had not seen far places. We knew only this side of the mountains. And we thought we were the only living people,"[26] and Diamond goes on to estimate the high degree of ethnic differentiation under these circumstances as follows: "New Guinea, with less than one-tenth of Europe's area and less than one-hundredth of its population, has about a thousand languages" (1992:229, 232).[27]

It would therefore be difficult to overestimate the significance of the fact that an ethnic and racial big bang has *not* occurred on anything like a global scale, as seems very clearly indicated by the fact that the New Guinea highlander mentioned above is quoted by someone (Diamond) who was born far beyond "the other side of the mountains."

What happened to reverse the course of the initial dispersion and differentiation of the human species?

The next three chapters are devoted to answering this question, but it will help set the stage for that answer if I now introduce a concept that will play a key role in it. The concept is *coalition*, and it refers to any alliance, for any purpose whatever, between two or more participants—whether these participants be individual persons or groups of persons. With that definition in mind, consider Figure 2.4 and its schematic summary of the inclusiveness (or, more technically, hierarchical) relationships among several types of coalition.

Here, a family group is defined as a sexuality coalition between individual adults and/or a parenting coalition between one or more adults and one or more children. A kinship group—often called a clan or lineage—is a coalition of two or more families. An ethnic group is a coalition of two or more kinship groups. A racial group is a coalition of two or more ethnic groups. (And as already indicated, family and kinship group coalitions rely on eyewitness certifications of membership; ethnic and racial group coalitions rely on naked-eye presumptions of membership—ethnic coalitions relying on behavioral insignia, while racial coalitions rely on anatomical insignia.)

Now it is essential to note how Figure 2.4 changes its argument at this point. That is to say, in constructing the next higher type of coalition—namely, nationality groups—the pattern of successive inclusion of whole entities that characterizes the steps from individuals to family groups, to ethnic groups, to racial groups, is changed. Nationality groups are coalitions that may wholly include familial, kinship, ethnic, racial, and alien-nationality groups but that, more typically, *cut across* such groups and thereby manifest the turn, starting slowly with the beginning of the Neolithic Age some ten thousand years ago, away from further differentiation of the species and toward species consolidation.[28]

It should also be clear, however, that although nationality groups represent a different type of coalition, they are, nevertheless, coalitions. In this sense, all the types of coalitions shown in Figure 2.4 are stepping stones arranged hierarchically (i.e., according to their increasing inclusiveness) up from the individual toward the ultimate human coalition—namely, global species consolidation. Simon offers the following argument for building almost any kind of complex structure in just such a hierarchical manner:

One can show on quite simple and general grounds that the time required for a complex system, containing k elementary components, say, to evolve by processes of natural selection from those components is very much shorter if the system is itself comprised of one or more layers of stable component subsystems than if its elementary parts are its only stable components. . . . [For example, imagine] two watchmakers [assembling] fine watches, each watch containing ten thousand parts. [Suppose the first watchmaker] has organized his total assembly operation into a series of subassemblies [where] each subassembly is a stable arrangement of 100 elements, and each watch, a stable arrangement of 100 subassemblies. The second watchmaker has developed no such organization. [Now suppose that] each watchmaker is interrupted frequently to answer the phone, [that] the average interval between phone interruptions is a time long enough to assemble about 150 elements, [and that] an interruption causes any set of elements that does not yet form a stable system to fall apart completely. By the time he has answered about eleven phone calls, the first watchmaker will usually have finished assembling a watch. The second watchmaker will almost never succeed in assembling one (1973:7; see also Wallace 1983:162–170; 1988:37–38).

Figure 2.4
Inclusiveness Relations Among Family, Kinship, Ethnic, Racial, and
Nationality Groups

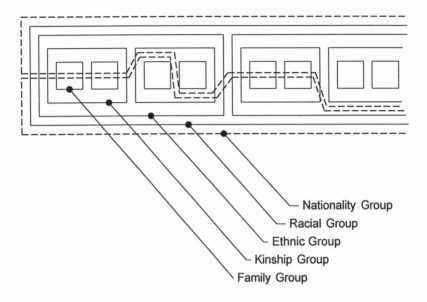

On this ground, two inferences seem justified. First, the series of stepping stones shown in Figure 2.4 is not a result of chance alone; natural selection, driven by the imperatives of species survival, has operated to bring them about; and second, the particular stepping stone called "nationality group" is, in Waters' phrase, "both a globalized and a globalizing phenomenon" (1995:136).

Nationality Groups

Seeing nationality groups as coalitions of ethnic (and, increasingly, racial) coalitions facilitates our recognizing that, for example, the present "Chinese" nationality includes Han, Kazakhs, Mongols, Tibetans, Uygurs, and others; the "French" include Basques, Bretons, Burgundians, Provencales, and others; the "Germans" include Saxons, Thuringians, Bavarians, and others; the "Nigerians" include Hausa, Djerma-Songhai, Igbo, Fulani, and others; the "English" include Celts, Romans, Angles, Saxons, Jutes, Danes, Normans, and others; the "Italians" include Neapolitans, Sardinians, Syracusans, Istrians, Calabrians, Tuscans, Lombards, Slovenes, and others; the "Americans" include individuals having all of the above ethnic, racial, and nationality origins (and more besides)—and so on.

But a nation does not merely paste its brand label (like "American") across all the diverse ethnic, racial, and nationality groups it incorporates. It also creates new labels that bring some groups there into especially intimate relations while holding other parts more separate from each other. Thus, Enloe points out that the American "state employs ethnic categories to suit its administrative-political ends. In so doing, it requires individuals subject to certain laws to respond as 'Hispanics' or 'Indians' or 'Filipinos'" even though each of these designations lumps together many ethnicities that formerly thought themselves unrelated. Given enough time, Enloe says, "this state practice may encourage individuals to see themselves as part of not just an artifial state category but as a group which shares important common experiences: oppression, deprivation, and also benefits" (1981:134; see also Massey 1993:7–8).

So it was that "at the threshold of the nineteenth century" when the men who governed the United States "defined democracy as a caste system organized by conceptions called race. . . . the mixed immigrants from Europe were arbitrarily [named] 'white' regardless of the multitudes who had hacked and spawned their ways through Europe from Asia and Africa in centuries gone by" (Jennings 1993:309). Similarly, Enloe notes that "the American state has legitimized 'Blacks' as an ethnic category in law, despite the variety of ethnic groups from which Afro-Americans derived" (1981:134; see also Jones 1963:13).

In summary, then, "modern nations are an amalgam of historical communities which possessed a fairly clear sense of separate identity in the past but have been brought together by various economic, social and political developments" (Birch 1989:8; see also Gellner 1983:139–140; and Tilly 1975a:42–43). By way of acknowledging the large role of conquest in this amalgamation, Said tells us that "Imperialism consolidated the mixture of cultures and identities on a global scale" (1993:336).[29] Portes describes one way that consolidation has been achieved in our own time: "The North American expansion into its immediate periphery . . . altered the makeup of [the penetrated] societies to the point where many would-be migrants were acculturated into North American ways even before setting foot [in North America]." In a word, "The social, economic, and cultural institutions of the sending areas are . . . remolded until migration to the hegemonic center emerges as a plausible option." Similarly, "workers in Third World 'runaway' industries are exposed to the modes of production and cultural patterns of the advanced West. Their employment is short-lived, however, leaving them with new skills and consumption aspirations but without the means to implement them. . . . Emigration emerges as a solution" (1995:20, 21).

Ethnic Descent and National Destiny. Reflecting on this profoundly consolidating property of nationality groups, Weber observes that "the concept of 'nation' . . . certainly cannot be stated in terms of empirical qualities common to those who count as members of the nation. . . . [Nevertheless,] the concept undoubtedly means, above all, that it is proper to expect from [nationality] groups a specific *sentiment of solidarity* in the face of other groups. Thus, the concept belongs in the sphere of *values*" (1978:922, italics changed).

But what is the nature of this sentiment of national solidarity which can unite people who are convinced that they are *originally* different, being products of altogether different ancestral lines of descent?

Weber answers: "above all, national solidarity may be linked to . . . [belief in] a common political *destiny*" (1978:923, italics added; see also his reference to "responsibility towards succeeding [not preceding] generations" at 921); and "The earliest and most energetic manifestations of the idea [of a nation] . . . have contained the legend of a providential '*mission.*' Those to whom the representatives of the idea zealously turned were expected to shoulder this mission" (1978:925, italics added).[30]

Thus, a specifically *national* solidarity lies not in its presumption of some line of past descent that its followers already share but in its prediction of some future destiny that they will share. John Quincy Adams put the difference succinctly: Immigrants to America, he said, must "look forward to their posterity rather than backward to their ancestors" (quoted in Gordon 1964:94).[31] In other words, as chapter 1 has indicated, where the rallying-cry of families, kindship groups, ethnic groups, and racial groups is descent-oriented ("Blood is thicker than water!") the rallying-cry of nationality groups is destiny-oriented ("Toward a better future for all!").

Note that these two organizing principles look in different directions: one looks toward the past and the other looks toward the future. A nationality group, then, need not ask its citizens to drop or deny their different lines of presumed past descent; it only asks them to regard these lines as irrelevant when the group is confronted by threats (from within or from without) to its predicted future destiny. In this way, nationality's woof weaves its various ethnic (and racial) warp lines of descent together into a single future-oriented fabric. For this reason, nationality groups constitute a *new* type of stepping stone toward global species consolidation—one that adds considerations of sharing a common future to considerations of sharing a common past.

There is, of course, a powerful connection between the presumption of common descent that sustains ethnicity and race and the prediction of common destiny that sustains nationality. The first answers the question Where did we *come from*? while the second answers the question Where are we *going*? Together with the answer to the obvious third question, namely, Where *are* we now? they make up the core of a group's *identity*. Not surprisingly, therefore, nationality groups typically combine notions of common descent ("founding fathers") with common destiny ("to secure the blessings of liberty to ourselves and our posterity") with common territory ("from sea to shining sea"), and seal the whole package with common divine grace or honor ("one nation under God"). Thus, Pan tells us that

to be really and truly Chinese, it was commonly believed, one had to trace one's ancestry to the progenitor of the Chinese race. . . . [who] was, and still is, held to be the Yellow Emperor Huang Ti, one of the culture heroes of Chinese mythology. It doesn't much matter that his existence is a matter not of attested fact but of misty legend; the Yellow

Emperor still has his burial place in Huangling, a small town beside a Yellow River tributary in the ancient Chinese heartland (1994:10; see also 11, 19).

But just what is the nature of this "mission," this "common destiny," around which nationality groups so successfully rally their heterogeneous and otherwise warring participants? In Weber's phrase, it is *the glory of power over other communities*" (1978:911, italics added; see also 925)—a phrase that desperately needs generalizing beyond "power" to *pre-eminence* over other communities, in order to allow for superiority in wealth, knowledge, and honor as well.[32] Thus: *"Deutschland über alles*," "Rule, Britannia," and "And conquer we must" (in all cases, "when our cause it is just" is taken for granted—for what nation ever regards its cause as unjust?).[33]

Moreover, it should be noted that some of those "other communities" which nationality groups are devoted to dominating are "domestic" and lie inside them (see Figure 2.4 and chapter 5), while others are "foreign" and lie outside them.

War. One especially powerful means for dominating both the communities inside a nation and the communities outside that nation, is war. The power of that means derives largely from the fact that in war "the individual is expected ultimately to face death in the group interest. This gives to the political community its particular pathos and raises its enduring emotional foundations." Therefore, "The community of political destiny, i.e., above all, of common political struggle of life and death, has given rise to groups with joint memories which often have had a deeper impact than the ties of merely cultural, linguistic, or ethnic community. It is this 'community of memories' which . . . constitutes the ultimately decisive element of 'national consciousness'" (Weber 1978:903).

Such memories include, in the very first place, dead comrades— friends, colleagues, lovers, spouses, brothers and sisters, daughters and sons, infants, children, adults—for whom the survivors of war painfully seek some justification and some assurance that "these dead shall not have died in vain." The need for such assurance may cry out especially when the dead in question died fighting against members of their own ancestral family, kinship, ethnic, racial, or nationality groups on the other side—as was prominently the case, for example, of Americans on both sides of the Civil War and in both World Wars.

The key justification may be the survivors' dissonance-reducing rationalization that the nation on whose behalf their comrades gave "the last full measure of devotion" *must* be morally superior to, and more worthy of honor than, all other groups; otherwise, all those dead did indeed die in vain.

In this way, citizens' shared valuations of the honor of their *nation* are greatly enhanced relative to the honor of its ethnic, racial, and alien-nationality components. Sooner or later, then, nearly all survivors of every nation's wars become patriots, pledging that "from these honored dead we take increased devotion to that cause for which they gave the last full measure of devotion"; sworn to the conviction that "who for his *country* dies has lived greatly"; and ready, even eager, to die in their country's cause. Thus, the British poet Rupert

Brooke, on the way to battle (which he did not live to fight) in World War I: "If I should die, think only this of me: That there's some corner of a foreign land that is forever England." Note: not forever Brooke family land, or forever ethnically Anglo-Saxon land, or racially Caucasoid land, but forever *England.*

And note that a war-losing nation fares almost as well as a war-winning nation with respect to the national loyalties the war generates: "It matter little who wins. To make a people great it is necessary to send them to battle" (Mussolini 1955:926).

It seems no accident, therefore, that the directors and administrators of nation-states (whether appointed or elected) assiduously nurture their nationals' readiness to die in wars by dedicating public war commemorations of all kinds—wreathed monuments in virtually every town and village the world over; tombs, glass-walled ossuaries, perpetually impeccable cemeteries; medals and citations for personal bravery on the field of battle and for sacrifices on the homefront; holiday fireworks, parades, solemn public eulogy; verse after verse in national anthems; and the blood red in most nations' flags.[34] That is, all this is no accident if Weber is right that "feudal lords, like modern officers or bureaucrats, are the natural and primary exponents of this desire for power-oriented prestige for one's own political structure. Power for their political community means power for themselves, as well as the prestige based on this power. For the bureaucrat and the officer, an expansion of power means more office positions, more sinecures, and better opportunities for promotion" (1978: 911).

It is altogether striking, too, how equal opportunity to offer up their lives and limbs in the nation's wars has been a nearly universal demand of ethnic, racial, and alien-nationality groups seeking full citizenship in that nation. Sherif and Sherif note that "hostility toward the out-group is one manifestation of in-group identification and loyalty" (1953:284), and "the last full measure of devotion" in such hostility is regarded, on all sides, as a dues payment more deserving of a full measure of ingroup membership than any other. Thus, when in 1703 the Province of South Carolina felt threatened by war with the Yamassee Indian tribe, the slaveowner legislature promised that "as a reward for killing or capturing [a Yamassee] enemy during battle, the slave would 'have and enjoy his freedom'" (Moskos and Butler 1996:16–17, see also 18–20). Similarly, "the first and most important test of the status of the Negro during the Civil War was concerned with his employment as a soldier. At the opening of the War the services of free Negroes were refused by the Secretary of War. . . . It was only after the Emancipation Proclamation and the pressing need for Union troops in Louisiana that the enlistment of Negro soldiers became a definite policy of the North" (Frazier 1957a:105–106), with the result that some 186,000 Black Americans fought in the Union Army, sustaining a "casualty rate [that] was 40 percent higher that the white rate, [and] until 1865, all blacks were paid half as much" (Moskos and Butler 1996:23; see also Sowell 1981:196).

It is difficult to believe that the thirteenth, fourteenth, and fifteenth Amendments to the Constitution of the United States would have been adopted as soon as they were (in 1865, 1868, and 1870) without these African-American losses in the Union cause.

Weber formulates the general point as follows: "War makes for an unconditionally devoted and sacrificial community among the combatants. . . . These feelings break down all the naturally given barriers of association" (1946:335).[35] Thus have the boiling blood pots of war helped to melt down many ethnic and racial groups into one nation, indivisible (see Tilly 1975a:42, 73–76; 1975b:623; Arnold 1991:10; Bennet 1997).[36]

But when one notices the dogged persistence of anti-Black racial discrimination in the Union armies during the Civil War and in civilian life long after, one returns to Weber's implicit qualification that although fighting on the same side, and even on opposite sides, in wars "*makes for*" community among combatants, it certainly does not *guarantee* such a community. Dippel cites another example: "Of the 100,000 Jews who served in the German military [during World War I], 35,000 were decorated, and 12,000—or 12 percent—died. . . . [But] instead of fading away, anti-Semitism was revived by the war: Jews were branded war profiteers. . . . Second, their sacrifice in blood was gainsaid. Just when they thought they had made the final payment for entrance into German society, the Jews found more doors being rudely slammed in their faces" (1996:20). The dangers to which the middleman role (which Jews have often played) is so often exposed (see chapter 5) helps account for the failure of Weber's hypothesis regarding the national group's construction of a barrier-breaking "community of combatants" in this case. Similarly, differences in wealth, power, knowledge, and honor—traceable to what the next chapter will call the luck of the territorial draw, between African-American former slaves and European-American former slavemasters—helps account for the failure of Weber's hypothesis in the case of post-Civil War race relations in the United States.

Despite these exceptions, however, it still seems fair to say that whenever national loyalty does show the ability to override long-standing ethnic and racial (and previous nationality) differences, this ability resides largely in the effects on the survivors of their comrades' deaths in combat. Here, indeed, by way of conclusion, is Abraham Lincoln's familiar expression of this point on the battlefield at Gettysburg:

But, in a larger sense, we can not dedicate—we can not consecrate—we can not hallow—this ground. The brave men, living and dead, who struggled here, have consecrated it, far above our poor power to add or detract. . . . It is rather for us to be here dedicated to the great task remaining before us—that from these honored dead we take increased devotion to that cause for which they gave the last full measure of devotion—that we here highly resolve that these dead shall not have died in vain.

And on the foundation formed by this destiny-based type of human group—this "nationality" group, invented as a result of the Neolithic Revolution and capable of cutting across and consolidating all descent-based types of groups—a new

Figure 2.5
The Grand Cycle

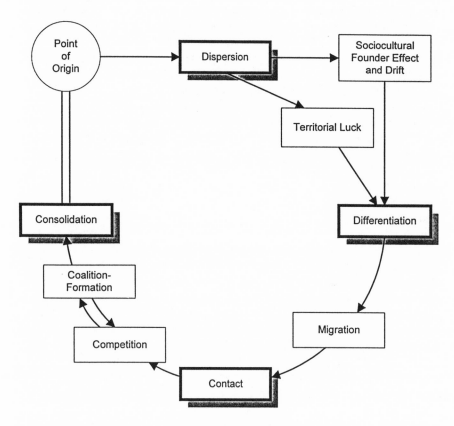

step toward global species consolidation is already nascent in the coalitions of various kinds that nations form among themselves.[37] (Chapter 5 will address the seeming paradox of the melting pot idea—namely, that a succession of *cooperative* coalitions can be born from the fires of *competition and conflict*.)

Now, before closing this chapter, it will be useful to consider the general summary of the Grand Cycle (and the further preview of chapters that are to follow) that is represented by Figure 2.5. The four primary processes in the Grand Cycle are schematized here: dispersion, differentiation, contact, and consolidation.[38] Dispersion, by definition, can only occur from some given point of origin and an evolutionary locus, or a consolidation that has been produced by a prior turn of the cycle, may constitute such a point. Between any two adjacent primary processes there are secondary processes that account for the transitions from one primary process to the next. Thus, a combination of sociocultural founder effect and drift plus territorial luck accounts for the transition from dispersion to differentiation; migration accounts for the transi-

tiation to contact (discussed in chapter 4); and the interaction and hierarchical development of competition and coalition formation (discussed in chapter 5) accounts for the transition from contact to consolidation.

The next chapter has two goals: first, to flesh-out Figure 2.5 with more historical facts; and second, to examine the nature of the "engines" *inside* each human society that, together with *outside* geographical and ecological forces, have been driving human history in its first turn around the Grand Cycle.

NOTES

1. Robert E. Park's "race relations cycle" is still the best known theory of race relations. In brief, Park argues that "the race relations cycle which takes the form . . . of contact, competition, accommodation and eventual assimilation, is apparently progressive and irreversible. Custom regulations, immigration restrictions and racial barriers may slacken the tempo of the movement; may perhaps halt it altogether for a time; but cannot change its direction; cannot in any way reverse it" (1950:150; see also Park and Burgess 1921:511). Park and Burgess clarify the "accommodation" phase as "the natural issue of conflicts. . . . [wherein] the antagonism of the hostile elements is, for the time being, regulated, and conflict disappears as overt action. . . . [However, it] is only with assimilation that this antagonism . . . is likely to be wholly dissolved" (1921:665). There are some important differences between Park's "race relations cycle" and the Grand Cycle of dispersion, differentiation, contact, and consolidation, that is proposed here. To start with, of course, the Grand Cycle explicitly includes ethnic, and nationality, groups as well as racial groups. Second, whereas Park calls the race relations cycle "progressive and irreversible," no such deterministic claims are made for the Grand Cycle. Third, Park refers to "assimilation," but this term's implication of one-way flow (i.e., an assimila*tor* assimilates the assimila*ted*) is rejected here in favor of "consolidation" because it indicates what is inevitably a *two*-way merger in which one side or the other may be dominant but never exclusively so. Fagan's remark that "world history during the past six centuries has not been the history of western expansion, but of thousands of diverse human societies *interacting* with one another" (1984:12, italics added) conveys this mutuality well, as does Kishore Mahbubani: "The real success of the Pacific community [of Asian societies and American societies] will come when the learning process in the Pacific becomes a two-way street rather than a one-way street" (quoted in Naisbitt 1996:248; see also Moskos and Butler 1996:43). Compare, for example, Gordon's more strictly one-way, assimilator/assimilated, discussion (1964:68–72, but see 109–110). Despite his terminology, Park seems clearly to have *intended* the mutuality adopted here. For example, Burgess and Park say, "Assimilation is a process of interpenetration and fusion in which persons and groups acquire the memories, sentiments, and attitudes of other persons or groups, and by sharing their experience and history, are incorporated with them in a common cultural life" (1921:735–736). Similarly, Park, writing alone, defines assimilation as "the process . . . by which groups of individuals, originally indifferent or perhaps hostile, achieve [a] corporate character . . . [the latter being a] practical working arrangement, into which individuals with

widely different mental capacities enter as co-ordinate parts" (1950:207). Note also Park and Burgess's inclusion of "amalgamation" as as "aspect of assimilation." Thus, "while [amalgamation] is limited to the crossing of racial traits through intermarriage, it naturally promotes assimilation or the cross-fertilization of social heritages" (1921:737). My use of the term "consolidation," then, is meant as a more explicitly two-way replacement for "assimilation" when both sociocultural merger and gene pool merger (amalgamation) are indicated. Note that the mutuality I have in mind does not imply that the influences from different parties must carry equal weight, or that they must weigh in proportion to their population sizes, as determinants of some given feature of the merged entity (see Gordon 1964:124). It implies only that in all intergroup contact there is *some* exchange of influence, whether equal or lopsided. Fourth, although Park claims the race relations cycle "tends everywhere to repeat itself" (1950:150), he does not hypothesize a succession of increasingly extensive repetitions, such as is proposed here (see chapter 6). Fifth, and perhaps most important of all, the initial species dispersion and differentiation are claimed here to have taken place prehistorically—prior to Park's contact stage. Indeed, Park's "race relations cycle" seems best understood as a claim about how consolidation, and *only* consolidation, unfolds, whereas the dispersion-differentiation-contact-consolidation cycle is a claim about how human history in its entirely (i.e., prehistory, history, and likely future history) unfolds.

2. Life's evolution on Earth reminds one of the branching growth of a tree, of which the Grand Cycle represents the way the Homo sapiens branch has grown, with its substitution of an unusual but not unique consolidation stage in place of a new speciation branching. (I say "not unique" because although Ridley says "Normally . . . [the extremes of geographic variation within a species] never meet each other" [1993:412], he does cite instances of this happening among non-human animal species [see 1993:412–415, 423–526]). The basic growth pattern involves different populations of a species dispersing from a single point of origin into new environments as they pursue more and better life resources (see Gamble 1993:77), and note that new ecological environments do not necessarily require *geographically* new territories insofar as the same territory can contain a large variety of environments ("niches") for life (see Ridley 1993:409–410). These populations then become increasingly adapted to their respective environments and increasingly different from each other until the differences become species differences—that is to say, great enough to prevent the breeding of fertile offspring across populations. From that point, the dispersion-differentiation cycle repeats itself. Darwin expressed this idea as follows: "There is grandeur in [the] view of life . . . having been originally breathed into a few forms or into one; and that . . . from so simple a beginning endless forms most beautiful and most wonderful have been, and are being, evolved" through the mechanism of "migration . . . together with subsequent modification and the multiplication of new forms" (1968:459–460, 393). Darwin also explained why the qualitative differentiation of species to which dispersion leads is so essential to the quantitative proliferation of organisms: "more living beings can be supported on the same area the more they diverge in structure, habits, and constitution . . . [and] the more diversified [living things] become, the better will be their chances of

succeeding in the battle [for the survival of life as a whole]" (1968:170, see also Durkheim 1984:208–210).

The dispersion-differentiation hypothesis is so well supported empirically that Ridley concludes "The evolution of a new species happens when one population of interbreeding organisms splits into two separately breeding populations. . . . At least in vertebrates, the majority of new species probably evolve . . . in subpopulations geographically isolated from the ancestral population" (1993:444). Here are some examples: Australia, together with Antarctica, broke away from the primeval continent Pangaea during the dominance of marsupials (like the platypus) and the evolution of species on now-isolated Australia stopped with marsupials. Similarly, Madagascar broke away from Gondwanaland at the time when prosimians (lemurs) were dominant there, and the evolution of species on Madagascar stopped with prosimians; no monkeys are indigenous to Madagascar (see McEvedy 1980:8–10). One also notes that the same dispersion-differentiation pattern is attributed to the evolution of human languages from a single original language (see Wardhaugh 1993:148–155).

3. Regarding early Homo sapiens, Molnar remarks that because they "were likely dark skinned," in their new, more northerly, environments they "suffered the detrimental effects common to deeply pigmented peoples living in regions of low ultraviolet radiation." Therefore, "two things," Molnar argues, "made possible the continuous survival of Homo sapiens in the northern latitudes. The first is the steady decline in pigmentation throughout hundreds of generations. . . . The second is the increased use of fish in the diet during the past six thousand years—particularly herring, which is rich in vitamin D" (1992:232–233). Note that all the speciations just discussed were characterized by significant periods of overlap: Australopithecus continued to exist during the early part of *Homo habilis'* time; the latter two continued to exist during the early part of *Homo erectus'* time; and *Homo erectus* continued to exist during the early part of Homo sapiens' time (see Gamble 1993:71; Ayala 1995:1935; Swisher et al. 1996).

4. See Roberts 1984:45–46; Fagan 1989:153–154, 1990:66–73. For a model of climate-dependent changes in food supply, see Turner 1984:199; Fagan 1990:18–19; Gamble 1993:89. Someone (I have forgotten who) has referred to the Sahara Desert as a pump drawing in migrants from the south during wet times and expelling them northwrd during dry times. Gamble argues that "the extension of range, which occurred about a million years ago, was the product of selection on the social organization of these savannah groups not on their skulls and brains" (1993:116). Sowell applies the principle to much later migrations: "During the era of large-scale emigration from Sweden in the late nineteenth century . . . few Swedes left their homeland from the favorable situated flatlands and forested regions of the country, while most left from regions lacking these advantages. Similarly, migration from southern Italy began in remote mountain regions with the most backward agriculture" (1996:5).

5. Gamble is referring here to the dispersal of *Homo erectus*, which antedated the dispersal of Homo sapiens by the better part of a million years (but may have survived well into the latter's tenure—see Swisher, et al. 1996). Lamphear, writing speculatively about the migration of Bantu-speakers from central Africa into southern Africa that began about two thousand years ago, adds further insight into how the much

earlier migration northward out of Africa might have occurred: "First, these movements were, for the most part, carried out very slowly and over very short distances. . . . It was usually small kinship groups or small bands of associates that carried out a particular move. . . . In some cases a migration would be undertaken for economic reasons. Where shifting cultivation was the basis of subsistence, migration would often take the form of a move from one place, where perhaps population pressures had developed or the soil was being leeched of nutrients, to another site a mile or two away. . . . There were countless other reasons for a migration: family quarrels, disease, misfortunes thought to be caused by the supernatural, succession and inheritance disputes, famines, feuds, or even simply the love of adventure—each would be sufficient cause for setting a group in motion" (1977:89–91; compare Gamble 1993:96–116).

6. According to the most widely accepted hypothesis (called "rapid replacement"), *Homo erectus* migrated first (about 1.8 million years ago) into Eurasia, but was later (see note 3) succeeded by Homo sapiens after it, too, migrated out of Africa. The bulk of evidence now supports this hypothesis (see Klein 1989:356; Fagan, 1989:151–153; 1990:15–62; Gamble 1993:88–92, 149–157, 174–176, 181; Swisher, et al. 1996). By contrast, the second, "multiregional," hypothesis accepts as true the early *Homo erectus* migration mentioned above but rejects a single place of origin for Homo sapiens, arguing that *Homo erectus* "diversified into morphologically distinct regional populations [i.e., in Africa, Asia, and Europe], each of which then evolved progressively [and separately] toward modern *H. sapiens*" (Klein, 1989:255; see also Wolpoff, et al., 1984:464–467; Fagan, 1989:148–149; Barinaga, 1992:686–687). Ayala states the rapid replacement hypothesis as follows: "The weight of the molecular [genetic] evidence favors a recent African origin for modern humans. Ethnic differentiation between modern human populations would therefore be evolutionarily recent, a result of divergent evolution between geographically separated populations during the last 50,000 to 100,000 years" (1995:1936).

7. Actually, Schwartz says "consolidation" rather than "formalization" here, meaning not the integration of different groups but a single group's internal effort to, in his words, "formalize its social institutions and associations" (1985:238). In order to avoid confusion, I substitute "formalization" for his "consolidation" here.

8. Back-migration, too, contributes to consolidation, in the long run. Thus, Ahmed and Donnan note that "migrants return to their place of origin not only with novel versions of the world which challenge the views of those who never left . . . but also on occasion with fossilized and outmoded versions of what they left behind: ways of dressing, behaving, believing and so forth which have been developed and reshaped in their absence but which they have lovingly and carefully preserved intact while abroad. Either way, old certainties are challenged" (1994:6; see also Sowell 1996:20–27).

9. Espenshade reports an estimate that "the total foreign-born population in the United States is growing by about 700,000 each year. . . . In addition, total immigration accounts for about one third of US net annual population growth" (1995:201).

10. The study also found that members of the group that consistently lost in the competition developed hostility and aggression toward themselves as well as toward their competitors (see the discussion of mutually supporting cultural structural and social

structural strategies in the next chapter). "Probably the most effective event for [uniting the two groups of campers] was a camp-wide softball game in which a team of the best players from both in-groups elected by the boys from the entire camp competed on the camp grounds with a group coming from the neighboring town. In this game the boys participated as campers, not as in-group members. . . . The camp team easily won the game and there was considerable feeling of common pride following it" (Sherif and Sherif 1953:285–286).

11. See Dawkins, 1987:237–239, and Diamond, 1992:120–121, for the essentially Darwinian claims implied here.

12. It should go without saying that the social, ethnic, and gene pool differentiations that emerged following the first Homo sapiens dispersion out of eastern Africa are not at all the same as those we see around us today. Those earlier differentiations have long since disappeared (each through its own evolution and through contact and consolidation with other groups). The present differentiations are only their very distant, and very mixed, descendants (see, for example, Diamond's sketch of the differentiation, starting around 5000 BC, of the so-called "Indo-European" languages, 1992:249–275). As Molnar says, "There is no reason to assume there is now, or ever has been, a *fixed number* of races" (1992:184), and this is certainly true for ethnic groups as well.

13. Wilson argues that "life in a local site struck down by a passing storm springs back quickly because enough [biological] diversity still exists. Opportunistic species evolved for just such an occasion rush in to fill the spaces. They entrain the succession that circles back to something resembling the . . . state of the environment [before the storm]. . . . This is the assembly of life that took a billion years to evolve. . . . It holds the world steady" (1992:15). Instead of maintaining an actual sociocultural diversity that recapitulates virtually all of human history (paralleling the biological diversity to which Wilson refers), several social science disciplines—including cultural anthropology, archaeology, and history—have taken on responsibility for maintaining their blueprints, so to speak, through the written interpretations these disciplines make of dying and dead human societies the world over. On the role of urbanization-related diseases in this die-off, see McNeill 1978.

14. Lipset and Raab refer to "tribal" (rather than "ethnic") groups, saying they are "cohesive ancestral group[s] with particular customs, traditions, and values" (1995:7)—implicitly taking for granted the objectivity of the ancestry in question. Barth, on the other hand, adopts Weber's emphasis on "*subjective* belief" and on "*presumed* identity" as the criterion of ethnicity when he gives "primary emphasis to the fact that ethnic groups are categories of ascription and identification by the actors themselves" (1981:199; see also 15), and Smith shares Weber's claim that such ascription and identification must focus on "common descent" insofar as he defines an ethnic group as "one that emphasizes myths of descent [etc.]" (1991:20). Van den Berghe, however, claims "ethnicity is common descent, *either* real or putative" (1987:16, italics added), giving primacy to objectively true ("real") descent. But here (remembering, again, the geese who were imprinted on humans) one must ask how can anyone know that some line of descent to which s/he is claimed to belong is "*real*"? Van den Berghe does not

address this question, but it is fairly well known that every mechanism so far employed by humans (or, for that matter, by nonhuman organisms) to establish "real" descent can err or be deliberately manipulated. When such error or manipulation is the case, the evidence is that it usually goes undiscovered by the individuals involved (see Lorenz 1970; Wilson 1971:especially 272–277).

15. According to this definition, the Hitlerian view of race, insofar as it "fastened on psychosocial rather than physiological hereditary features" (and note, again, that both types of features were presumed, not known, to be hereditary), was not racist but ethnocentrist. Indeed, the Nazis resorted to identification by artificial substitutes for distinctive anatomical features, namely, "compulsory emblems like the wearing of a yellow star" (Schermerhorn 1978:77, 76).

16. Weber says "the belief in ethnic affinity has at all times been affected by outward differences in clothes, in the style of housing, food and eating habits, the division of labor between the sexes and between the free and the unfree" (1978:391). Blalock, however, makes such differences as these central to ethnicity (see 1982:4), omitting reference to the subjective beliefs in common ancestry that Weber makes central.

17. The distinction between genetically objective race identification (assuming there is such a thing) and subjectively presumed race identification is what Weber has in mind when, on the one hand, he says race may refer to "common inherited and inheritable traits that *actually* derive from common descent," but then adds that "of course, race creates a 'group' only when it is *subjectively perceived* as a common trait" (1978:385, italics added). See also Molnar's distinction between "biological [and] social definitions of race" (1992:290; see also 291).

18. According to von Fritz, "the concept of race goes back at least to the 5th century BCE. and the regional consolidation attempted by the Persians which ended in their defeat at the battles of Salamis and Plataeae" (and here one recalls Weber's idea that *contact* evokes a sense of "blood disaffinity"). "It was then that the race theory first raised its head . . . [as a theory] in which racial differences are derived from climatic differences" (1973, II:500; see also Barker 1952:296). Then, during the first century BCE., a Stoic philosopher, Posidonius, extended this theory to the claim that "every tribe or nation had its racial characteristics which were the product of hereditary factors, climate, diet, training, and traditions. Because of the interaction of these factors there was also a correlation between their bodily constitutions, their temperaments, and their habits" (von Fritz 1973, II:509–510).

19. Note Griffin's (1977) first-person account of a self-identified White man who, with the anatomy-faking aid of skin-darkening chemicals and shaved head and hands—voluntarily passed as Black, among Blacks as well as Whites, for six weeks in 1959, in the southern United States.

20. Obviously, we must say "after" some particular date because, as already indicated here, *all* living humans share the same objectively African ancestry if we look back the 8,000 to 16,000 generations mentioned earlier.

21. Williamson cites an estimated number of Blacks passing as Whites as "between 2,500 and 2,750 a year, with some 110,000 living on the white side of the line

[in 1946]. Probably the great age of passing began around 1880 and was over, practically, by 1925" (1980:103). Williamson also notes that "frequently mulattoes passed only part-time. Sometimes they passed to have comfortable accommodations while traveling. . . . [or] to attend the theater, a musical performance, or a lecture from which they might otherwise be excluded. Sometimes they passed for simple revenge—to trick the whites. Walter White, a blue-eyed, blond-haired Negro from Atlanta . . . passed for the purpose of investigating lynchings in the South. . . . Sometimes the passer lived in the North as a white during part of the year and lived at home in the South as a Negro during the remainder" (1980:101).

22. "Degler (1971) claims the existence of an intermediate, mulatto, category in Brazil, more than anything, accounts for the diminished hostility between blacks and whites. . . . 'The presence of the mulatto,' explains Degler, 'not only spreads people of color throughout the society, but it literally blurs and thereby softens the line between black and white'" (Marger 1991:414). Compare, however, Segal's view of Brazilian racial relations, in which he claims the dominance of "essentially racist policies of a whitening Brazil" (1995:347, see also 344, 345), policies with which (according to Segal's description) Brazilians of all skin colors are agreed. Segal seems to hold the view that only a status quo, *no-change,* policy with respect to skin color merits the judgment of being non-racist (assuming that a policy of a *blackening* Brazil would be deemed equally racist). My own view is that only a public policy of *no-policy* on this issue—permitting private, individual, policies (preferences) to fall where they may—serves global species consolidation.

23. Weber attributes the special power of ethnicity in uniting large numbers of individuals to the breadth of its applicability: "The idea of a chosen people derives its popularity from the fact that it can be claimed to an equal degree by any and every member of the [group]" (1978:391)—regardless of their different family, kinship group, age, gender, class, and/or other statuses.

24. Note the exchange (between a people-chosen god and a god-chosen people) implied in "And Moses went up unto God, and the LORD called unto him out of the mountain, saying, Thus shalt thou say to the house of Jacob, and tell the children of Israel. . . . Now therefore, *if ye will obey my voice indeed, and keep my covenant, then ye shall be a peculiar treasure unto me above all people*" (Exodus, 19:3, 5, italics added).

25. "[T]he monopolistic closure . . . of political, status or other groups and . . . the monopolization of marriage opportunities. . . . produced a high incidence of inbreeding. The 'endogamy' of a group . . . [may be defined] as a process of social action in which only endogamous children [i.e., children of endogamous sexual unions] are accepted as full members" (Weber 1978:386).

26. This suggests that *prior* to any remembered contact with any other group each isolated group should be thought of as having an attitude that we might call "ethno-onlyism" which becomes "ethnocentrism" only *after* the comparison that contact enables is made (insofar as a "center" is by definition a relative position).

27. Similarly, Decalo, et al., say, "South of the Sahara, where most Africans live, blacks form the great majority of the population. But they are divided into over 800 ethnic groups, each with its own language, religion, and way of life. The large number of

ethnic groups . . . has helped make it difficult for many African countries to develop into unified, modern nations" (1993:98–99). Leakey and Lewin note that "some five thousand languages [have been] documented in recent historical times. . . . each rooted through complex evolutionary relationship to an original mother tongue" (1992:274–275).

28. This seems clearly implied in Smith's view that nations "require *ethnic cores* if they are to survive . . . despite the fact that they often had significant *ethnic minorities*" (1986:212, italics added). However, although a nation may start its life under domination by a single racial and ethnic core (and perhaps also one kinship group and one family group); its survival over the long haul is likely to depend much more on its ability to consolidate different in-migrating groups than on its ability to sustain perm-anently the domination of that original group (compare Smith 1986:214–217; and see my comments on Tocqueville and Alexander in note 7 of chapter 1). Although Huntington admits that "almost all countries are heterogeneous in that they include two or more ethnic, racial, and religious groups" (1996:137), this does not stop him from asking his readers to look upon "civilizations" (each of which, he says, can include *many* "countries"—see 1996:46) as being themselves ethnic groups and, as such, homogeneous in (presumed) descent. Thus, "civilizations are the ultimate human tribes, and the clash of civilizations is tribal conflict on a global scale"; "in civilizational conflicts, unlike ideological ones, kin stand by their kin"; "what counts for people are blood [sic] and belief, faith and family. People rally to those with similar ancestry, religion, language, values and institutions and distance themselves from those with different ones" (1996:207, 217, 126). For reasons that he leaves mysteriously unspecified (considering his emphasis on common "blood," and "ancestry"), however, Huntington makes race an exception: "A significant correspondence exists between the division of people . . . into civilizations and their division by physical characteristics into races. Yet . . . people of the same race can be deeply divided by civilization; people of different races may be united by civilization" (1996:42). On the question of whether "clash" is a permanent mode of interaction among "civilizations," Huntington takes both sides. On the one hand, he tells us that "the fundamental cultural gap between Asian and American societies precludes their joining together in a common home" (1996:307; compare this with Naisbitt's view, quoted in chapter 1. But on the other hand, Huntington also claims that "Resolution of the economic issues between Japan and the United States depends on fundamental changes in . . . the society and culture of one or both countries. Such changes are not impossible. Societies and cultures do change" (1996:226).

29. Said also says "No one can deny the persisting continuities of long traditions, sustained habitations, national languages, and cultural geographies, but there seems no reason except fear and prejudice to keep insisting on their separation and distinctiveness, as if that were all human life was about" (1993:336).

30. Tilly asks "why do people sacrifice, die, hate, and kill on behalf of the nations with which they identify?" and the first part of his answer notes that "the institutionalized form of nationhood builds on and reinforces non-national social rela-tions and identities in which people invest trust, resources, solidarity, and hopes for the *future*" (1994:18, italics added; compare Arnold 1991:7). Bauman also echoes Weber on this point: "National states . . . are engaged in incessant propaganda of shared attitudes.

. . . They preach the sense of common *mission*, common *fate*, common *destiny*" (1990:154, italics added).

31. Arnold, however, does not include an imagined common destiny (his focus is on imagined common fraternity, fostered by "the development of print-as-commodity" and "reading coalitions") in his definition of a nation (see 1991:6–7, 36, 80). Gellner offers definitions of a nation that differ, both from each other and from the definition adopted here. First, a definition based on objective criteria: "Two men are of the same nation if and only if they share the same culture, where culture in turn means a system of ideas and signs and associations and ways of behaving and communicating" (Gellner 1983:7). Second, a definition based on subjective criteria: "Two men are of the same nation if and only if they *recognize* each other as belonging to the same nation" (Gellner 1983:7; a third definition combines the two just cited—see 1983:55). But two men may think they share the same culture without doing so objectively (i.e., in the eyes of some third, "scientific," person), and their respective spheres of life-activity may be so widely separated in space and/or time that the men do not even know of each other's existence, even though they may share the same culture objectively. In order to avoid problems like these, it seems better to say simply that a person has a given nationality according to whatever criteria may be laid down by the political institution of the nation in question. Such criteria need have nothing whatever to do with sharing a culture or displaying mutual recognition between individuals, but may be confined to strictly territorial considerations like parents' place of birth, own place of birth, own current place of residence and employment, and so on. This allows every nation's state apparatus to be free to incorporate, quite opportunistically, whomever it wishes in constructing a nationality that may wholly include, or cut across, some given set of pre-existing ethnic, racial, and nationality groups. This, in turn, allows different nation-states to agree, or disagree, about a given person's nationality—which is sometimes the case at present.

32. Note that even the purely defensive power to resist encroachments from other communities curtails the freedom of those other communities in this respect and is, therefore, a kind of power *over* them.

33. Weber also says "The great power structures . . . [are] held to have a responsibility of their own for the way in which power and prestige are distributed between their own and foreign polities. It goes without saying that all those groups who hold the power to steer common conduct within a polity will most strongly instill themselves with this idealist fervor of power prestige. They remain the specific and most reliable bearers of the idea of the state as an imperialist power structure demanding unqualified devotion" (1978:921–922).

34. Smith says, "To this day, the serried monuments to the fallen, the ceaseless ritual of remembrance, the fervent celebration of heroes and symbols across the globe testify to the same impulse to collective immortality, the same concern for the judgment and solace of posterity" (1990:183).

35. To this, Weber adds that "war does something to the warrior which . . . is unique: it makes him experience a consecrated meaning of death which is characteristic only of death in war. The community of the army standing in the field today feels itself . . . to be a community unto death, and the greatest of its kind. . . . Death on the field of

battle differs from merely unavoidable dying, in that in war, and in this massiveness *only* in war, the individual can *believe* that he knows he is dying "for" something. . . . This location of death within a series of meaningful and consecrated events ultimately lies at the base of all endeavors to support the autonomous dignity of the polity resting on force" (1946:335).

36. For example, Braudel claims that "the strenuous effort on both land and sea [of militarily defending and pushing outward the frontiers of France] was in itself an instrument of unity: in some sense, it penetrated and mobilized the whole country, not merely the frontier regions. . . . Under the *ancien régime* . . . recruitment to the army mingled Frenchmen of different origins, creating a melting pot, obliging men who did not speak the same language to live together and sever their provincial ties. Alongside the crown administration then, the army became the most active instrument in the unification of France" (1988:373–375). Finally, we have McNeill's view of the impact of "learning to move in unison and keep formation": "All modern armies depend upon being able to generate an entirely subrational comradeship among new recruits simply by marching about on a parade ground. . . . Drill, and the psychological residue it left behind, was indeed the principal secret of [the Greek, Macedonian, and Roman armies'] imperial success" (1985:47–48).

37. Huntington has in mind some of these inter-nation coalitions when he refers to "civilizations" (1996) and to this limited extent, he too acknowledges, albeit reluctantly, the increasingly inclusive extent of human coalitions as they move toward globality.

38. Ridley summarizes the larger evolutionary process of which the human Grand Cycle is an instance: "One species could split into two [populations] if a physical barrier divided its geographical range. . . . If the barrier is large enough, gene flow between the two groups would cease and each would evolve independently. Over time, different alleles would be fixed in each, whether because of the hazards of mutation and drift, or because selection favored different characters in the two. Whether two full species would evolve depends on whether the populations persist long enough. . . . The two might . . . meet again, either because the barrier between them disappeared or because of migration. If they had diverged enough, they might not recognize each other as members of the same species and would not interbreed: they would have speciated. . . . Alternatively, the two populations might meet up again before they had diverged as far as separate species. They might recognize each other as conspecifics, interbreed, and their offspring develop normally; the two populations would soon merge back into one" (1993:412–413).

3

HUMAN HISTORY AND ITS INTERNAL ENGINES

This chapter addresses two very big questions within a very small space: First, what do the last ten thousand years of history look like when viewed as humanity's finally turning toward global consolidation after some ninety thousand years of dispersion and differentiation? Put differently: Do the broad facts of history offer any evidence that such a turning actually occurred and had the consequences here claimed for it? Second, given the first chapter's soap bubble analogy and its proposition that certain "engines" inside human societies have been major factors in bringing about this turn, just what are these engines?

THE NEOLITHIC REVOLUTION AND ITS AFTERMATH

Gamble (see 1993:116, 187) argues strongly for the overlap, even in prehistoric times, of dispersion and differentiation with local consolidation among humans. The first really big drive toward eventual global consolidation, however, seems to have begun with the unique kick that farming, and then, perhaps four thousand years into the Neolithic Revolution (that is, five or six thousand years ago), large-scale agriculture gave to the technologies of food production, metallurgy, transportation, and communication. This, in turn, soon led to more rapid population growth and greater spatial extension and complexity of human society than ever before. Thus, McNeill says "About 8000 BC, [the initial dispersion of humankind out of eastern Africa] began to reach inelastic limits. This led many different human communities to intensify their search for food [which] . . . soon provoked the invention of agriculture in several different parts of the earth. . . . The result was the emergence of cities and civilization by about 3000 BC" (1978:4). Lamphear continues:

The impact of food-production on the development of any society is tremendous. A food-producing population, especially one engaged in agriculture, has to become more sedentary than a food-gathering population, so that farmers can remain close to their fields. As agricultural technology develops and production intensifies, farmers often begin to produce more food than their own families can consume. This surplus not only brings about . . . population explosions, but also enables some of the population to become involved in non-food-producing activities. Such people can devote their energies exclusively to religious, political, or military activities, or they can become full-time artisans, craftsmen, or traders. Such specialization and the expansion of population ultimately leads to a clustering together of sedentary agricultural communities (1977: 86–87).

Indeed, during the roughly five thousand years of the Neolithic Age, the world human population is believed to have increased forty-fold over what it was during the preceding four million years of the Paleolithic Age (see Campbell 1985:397; Desmond 1975:21–23; 1992:237; Molnar 1992:295–299), despite the death rate increases brought about by diseases preying on the newly crowded urban populations (see McNeill 1976, 1978). In addition, Leakey and Lewin tell us, "There is no evidence of frequent violence or warfare in human prehistory until after about ten thousand years ago, when humans began to practice food production—the leading edge of agriculture" (1992:xviii, see also 233).[1]

In short, "with the domestication of plants and animals. . . . [there began] a radically new phase of human history. . . . [in which the] grain-centered agriculture of the Middle East provided the basis for the first civilized societies" (McNeill 1963:10, 11; see also Molnar 1992:295–296; Curtin, et al. 1978:7).[2]

As this reference to "the Middle East" suggests, however, grain-centered agriculture did not originate everywhere at exactly the same moment or develop everywhere with the same speed or to the same extent. Some populations forged significantly ahead of others in these respects.

THE LUCK OF THE TERRITORIAL DRAW

Why was this the case? "Why," Diamond asks, "was the ancient rate of technological and political development fastest in Eurasia, slower in the Americas (and in Africa south of the Sahara), and slowest in Australia?" His answer is that the development differences stemmed "ultimately from continental differences in geography" (1992:235, 237; see also Sowell 1996:9–19). In other words, the differences were due to simple, dumb, territorial *luck*—the luck of the territorial draw. I refer to differences in the climate, terrain, water supply, mineral deposits, domesticable and nondomesticable flora and fauna—in short, the natural ecology, both above and below ground—of the territories in which different human groups were lucky or unlucky enough to settle as they dispersed from their common point of origin in eastern Africa.

To grasp the basic idea, one has only to think of the territorial luck that ruled out any possibility that the peoples (now called collectively "Eskimos" although they, too, have become differentiated into distinct ethnic groups) whose migrating ancestors settled near the Arctic Circle would invent large scale agriculture and experience its historic consequences—except by later contact with peoples whose ancestors had much better territorial luck.

The details of geography are second only to the solar system location, spherical shape, and basic chemical constituents of Earth among the compelling external forces to which the first chapter's pond-and-streams analogy alluded. The sheer luck (good or bad) of various dispersing human populations in settling on territories that happened to have (or not have) readily exploitable combinations of these forces was a crucial determinant of their subsequent histories. Such combinations were, in largest part, invisible and unknown (indeed, they were unknowable, given the state of science at the time) to those who made the first settlement. What Neanderthal settler in the neighboring areas that we know as the French Lorraine and the German Ruhr Valley could have foreseen the underground presence of iron and coal there, and the world's currently heavy reliance on the steel that they have been made to produce?

Territorially uneven access to raw materials that were exploitable with the tools then available meant that human groups lucky enough to settle in territories that combined bountifulness with just the right kind and amount of challenge would grow more rapidly in economic wealth, political power, empirical knowledge, and honor in its own and other groups' eyes. Then, the fact that we humans are a land-dwelling species living on a planet only thirty percent of whose surface is land meant that sooner or later the more rapidly growing populations would impinge on the others. In the ensuing competition and conflict, the more powerful would probably win out over the others. Diamond's conclusion is very clear:

Continental differences in level of civilization arose from geography's effect on the development of our cultural hallmarks, not from human genetics. Continents differed in the resources on which civilization depended—especially in the wild animal and plant species that proved useful for domestication. Continents also differed in the ease with which domesticated species could spread from one area to another. . . . [Such factors] determined who colonized and conquered whom (1992:236, 237).[3]

For example, Wilford reports on climatic conditions surrounding the spread of agriculture from the Middle East to Europe as follows:

Beginning 12,000 years ago . . . Europe and parts of Asia underwent a 1,000–year interval of especially arid conditions. The level of the Black Sea plummeted, but still its fertile shore must have been an inviting oasis. People who already lived there or flocked there . . . could have developed an early farming culture [as did people nearby in Anatolia]. . . . Fleeing the sudden flood [of the Black Sea] 7,500 years ago, these people must have taken their skills somewhere else. Archaeologists have established that within the next 200 years, farming settlements began to appear for the first time in the river valleys and plains of Central Europe. The displacement of people in that direction could be explained [by the Black Sea flood] (1996).

Munson adds that

viewing the Old World as a whole, the Middle East occupies a 'crossroads' position; movement of ideas or techniques between eastern Asia, western Europe, and the African continent would very likely pass through this area. Given this and the fact that most of what is called invention or innovation is simply the combining of two or more preceding ideas or techniques, the peoples of the Middle East occupied a unique position. They were most likely to obtain the greatest number of new ideas and techniques before other areas (1977:72).

Settling in what later turned out to be an intercontinetal crossroads position, then, was a case of *good* territorial luck. But let us compare it with a case of what turned out to be *bad* luck; in fact, the most consequential case of bad territorial luck so far known. Chapter 2 has suggested that in the climate-initiated competition among early Homo sapiens groups in eastern Africa, the winners may have driven the losers out of their originally shared homeland. That that loss may have been the best thing that ever happened to them; it may have propelled them into far better territorial luck than they could possibly have imagined at the time, and left the winners holding the territorial bad luck bag. (For an account of the much earlier *good* territorial luck in eastern Africa that seems to have contributed to the origin of our species, see Gamble 1993:79–91.)

Africa

Consider the following recent facts (from Population Reference Bureau 1996) that sum up the lingering traces of this reversal of fortune:
• Sub-Saharan Africans generally live shorter lives than do people who live elsewhere: Life expectancy at birth is about fifty-two years in sub-Saharan Africa today, but sixty-four years in Northern Africa, sixty-five years in Asia; sixty-nine years in Latin America and the Caribbean; seventy-six years in North America; seventy-three years in Europe; and seventy-three years in Oceania.
• Sub-Saharan Africans live less comfortable lives than do people who live elsewhere: Per capita GNP in 1994 was $550 in sub-Saharan Africa, but $1,100 in Northern Africa, $2,150 in Asia, $3,290 in Latin America and the Caribbean, $25,220 in North America, $12,310 in Europe, and $13,770 in Oceania.
• Sub-Saharan African youths receive less formal education than youths elsewhere: The percent of age-eligible youths enrolled in secondary school there today is twenty-six for males and twenty-one for females, but in Northern Africa the comparable figures are sixty-one and fifty-two; in Asia they are fifty-seven and forty-five; in North America they are ninety-nine and ninety-

eight; in Europe they are eighty-nine and ninety-four; and in Oceania they are seventy and seventy-one (figures are not available for Latin America and the Caribbean).

The roots of such differences between sub-Saharan Africa and the rest of the world are not recent. Indeed, they go back all the way to the Neolithic turning point that we have already identified here.

Prior to 10,000 BC, sub-Saharan Africa had been a major center of cultural innovations [including a succession of manufacturing techniques for stone axes, knives, hoes, picks, and projectile points], "exporting" these innovations, in a sense, to the remainder of the inhabited world. After 10,000 BC, however, many of the major cultural developments that occurred in man's prehistoric past appeared earliest in areas outside of Africa [i.e., in the Middle East]. Foremost among these developments are food production and metallurgy (Munson 1977:72).

And, giving us our first glimpse of the smoking gun here, Munson also tells us that "much of sub-Saharan Africa, again like much of western Europe and quite unlike much of the Middle East, was an area with a great wealth of game and edible wild plants. Man in Africa had been adapting and perfecting methods to exploit these abundant wild resources and had developed a very efficient and satisfying hunting and gathering subsistence pattern. There was therefore little initial pressure to change these well-tried methods and patterns" (1977:73). To this, we must add Lewis and Berry's detailed geographical observations:

The overall landform patterns of Africa present disadvantages to economic development. First, coastal zones are narrow (averaging about 32 km in width), a particularly important factor when it is remembered that about 70 percent of the world's population live on lowlands within 80 km of the sea. Usually, the African coastal zones are backed by steep scarps dividing the coast from the uplands. . . . Because of this, African rivers are marked by rapids close to the coast and are difficult transportation routes to the interior. . . . Partly as a result of the topography in Africa, road and railroad construction costs are generally quite high. Africa also has the shortest coastline in relation to area of any continent. The generally straight coasts present few natural harbors, and where these exist navigation is often handicapped by offshore bars, shallow water, and shifting channels. Finally, the tropical location of Africa meant that it was not directly affected by recent glaciation, except in a few mountain areas. Thus most of its soils are generally old and not rich in soluble minerals. . . . There are proportionately fewer young, rich alluvial soils than on any other continent (1988:10–12; see also McNulty 1977:36–40).[4]

There is more: "A major part of the landmass of Africa . . . has either short-term or long-term water deficiencies. This one fact may be the single most important thing to remember about Africa; for the most part, it is a dry continent" (Lewis and Berry 1988:1). In addition, Africa is a continent of highly seasonal rainfall: "The city of Chicago has slightly less rainfall *annually* than does the West

African city of Kano, but the Chicago rainfall is distributed relatively evenly throughout the year while the Kano rainfall occurs in only six months. . . . The contrast is remarkable: Kano looks like near-desert in comparison to Chicago . . . [consequently,] Northern Illinois has much more productive farm land than does northern Nigeria" (Vaughan 1977: 13).

As if all this were not enough, "the diseases of the African environment are legendary; they range from exotic new discoveries like Lassa and green monkey fevers to one of the world's great killers, malaria. . . . It is not unusual even today to find societies in which 50 percent of the children born never reach adulthood" (Vaughan 1977:15–16).

In such a profoundly inhospitable natural ecology, the sub-Saharan African population could grow only slowly over the millennia of prehistory and early history (see Vaughan 1977:22) and the emergence of ethnicity-consolidating nations was long delayed. It was not until the fifth century AD that the first sub-Saharan African empire, Ghana, was formed—some four thousand years after the Sumerian and Egyptian empires flourished (see Lamphear 1977:88).

Even today "The total number of named African societies is very high, probably in excess of two thousand, although . . . many of them differ only slightly. . . . [and] considering differences such as those between English and German, there are perhaps as many as a thousand African languages" (Vaughan 1977:9).

In addition, the whole continent of Africa, despite its crow-flight's nearness to the Eurasian territories in which large-scale agriculture, the wheel, and writing, were first invented, has long (that is, since the breakup of Gondwanaland some 100 million years ago) been physically cut off from those territories by the Mediterranean Sea, the Red Sea (except for the isthmus of Suez), the Atlantic Ocean, and the Indian Ocean, and, undoubtedly for the territorial reasons just discussed, sub-Saharan cultures never developed large-scale agriculture, or the wheel, or writing on their own. To these primordial water barriers a formidable land barrier was then added—one that divided North Africa from sub-Saharan Africa: Starting about four thousand years ago, the Sahara changed from a region that received enough rainfall to sustain "huge, shallow lakes . . . particularly in the southern half, and lush grassland-scrub vegetation" (Munson 1977:74) into what is now the world's largest desert—a long, broad, tough continental divide.

All these factors, combined, meant that "the post-Neolithic development of human society in Africa, especially in what is now predominantly Black Africa south of the Sahara, [was] essentially an internal phenomenon free from external influences except, to some extent, along its east coast fronting the Indian Ocean. North of the Sahara, however, Africa was part of the Mediterranean world, and also in close contact with major developments in nearer Asia" (Fage 1995:32).

With the introduction, from Asia, of the camel to North Africa in the third century AD (see Lamphear 1977:87–88), a web of north-south trade routes was woven across the Sahara (see Phillips 1985:116–117), and it was on this long-distance trade that the first sub-Saharan African empires (Ghana, Mali, Songhai, Kanem-Bornu) were built. But consider the material components of this trade and the story they tell about the different levels of development of its southern and northern terminals: "In return for slaves and gold, and perhaps ivory, [from sub-Saharan Africa] the towns of [North Africa] dispatched south across the Sahara camel-loads of textiles, metal bars and rods, steel weapons, knives, ceramics, and other manufactured goods derived from Muslim countries, or occasionally from Europe" (Martin 1977:100; see also 102, 104, 108).

In short, as a direct result of their bad luck of the territorial draw, sub-Saharan African societies became (to the extent that they had any contact at all with the emerging world economy) suppliers of certain raw materials used in the overseas production of luxury goods, and suppliers of huge numbers of slaves used in the overseas production of basic as well as luxury goods and services.

Both sorts of supplies went, first and for more than a thousand years, to Eurasia and only later to the New World. Thus, Goody says, "already in the second century AD, slaves were coming across the Western Sahara; the Eastern route to Egypt was used much earlier" (1980:29; see also Martin 1977:107); but "The discovery [sic] of America and the subsequent European expansion into it inaugurated a new stage in the history of slavery. . . . due to the creation of the New World plantation system, which initially produced sugar [in a globally] expanding market economy" (Phillips 1985:4, 171; see 67 regarding the history of Western sugar production and its roots in the Crusades).

The ubiquity of slavery in the ancient world is worth emphasizing, as is the fact that slavery appears to have had almost as long a history among sub-Saharan Africans as anywhere else. Thus, Patterson tells us that "in both the pagan and Islamic regions of precolonial Africa advanced political and cultural developments were usually . . . associated with high levels of dependence on slavery. Medieval Ghana, Songhay, and Mali all relied heavily on slave labor" (1982:viii; see also Goody 1980:30).[5] Indeed, for many centuries the intercontinental trade in African slaves differed little from the intracontinental trades then common inside Africa or inside Europe. What changed matters dramatically was the European development of regular transoceanic voyages between Europe, sub-Saharan Africa, and the New World. New World sugar, tobacco, and cotton plantation agriculture became part of an emerging world trade and African slaves became central to that agriculture: "Not only were Africans plentiful. They were also skilled in tropical farming and mining. . . . As the years went by, they became so valuable . . . that the Portuguese from Brazil were even bringing gold to the Gold Coast . . . in order to purchase with it slaves who could not otherwise be had" (Davidson 1992:211).[6]

Of course, the supplier status of sub-Saharan Africa became far more deeply entrenched by European colonial exploitation,[7] but the fact that Europe could, and did, colonize sub-Saharan Africa rather than the other way around rested on long-standing differences between the societies inhabiting the two continents, and these differences, in turn, rested (and still rest) on even longer-standing differences between the geographies of the continents themselves. The smoking gun of sub-Saharan Africa's depressed past and present history, then, is simply Africa—*the territory*—and no other population of Homo sapiens could have done any better with it.[8]

Fortunately (and not a moment too soon), the energy, agriculture, manufacturing, transportation, literacy, numeracy, communications, health, and other technologies that have been developed by peoples with better territorial luck are now being globalized and that globalization is rendering territorial luck increasingly irrelevant to the distribution of wealth, power, knowledge, and honor. This is what Waters means when he tells us globalization is "a social process in which *the constraints of geography on social and cultural arrangements recede* and in which people become increasingly aware that they are receding" (1995:3, italics added; see also 62–64).

So no matter what its past and present may be, sub-Saharan Africa's long-run future looks not a bit different from that of any other part of the world. Note, however, that by "the long-run future" I do not mean next month or next year, nor do I believe it is something for which the world can simply look up at the ceiling and wait. But these are issues reserved for chapter 6.

WAR AND CONQUEST

Although its influence on human history as a whole has been declining ever since the Neolithic Revolution, territorial luck continues to operate, from influencing which societies continue to develop most rapidly in wealth, in power, in knowledge, and in honor, to influencing whether your basement or your neighbors' basement will be flooded in the spring.

The playing out of such luck and its sociocultural consequences has, for ten thousand years, propelled wars and conquests in relationships between ethnic, racial, and nationality groups. Herbert Spencer argued strongly (surely too strongly) that "By force alone were small nomadic hordes welded into large tribes; by force alone were large tribes welded into small nations; by force alone have small nations been welded into large nations" (1961:176). Carneiro explains: "As population density increases, and arable land comes into short supply, fighting over land ensues. Villages vanquished in war, having nowhere to flee, are forced to remain in place and to be subjugated by the victors" (1981:64). Accordingly, "Sumerian and Egyptian civilizations, the earliest on record, both began with conquest" (McNeill 1985:7–8; see also Childe, 1942:88, 141–143, 154–155).

The result was that "by the time they enter the historical record, perhaps half a million inhabitants of southern Mesopotamia were part of a single civilization. . . . They may have spoken the same language. Their few professional scribes wrote in a common script" (Mann 1986:90; see also Adams 1966:153). Similarly,

China's size and ecological diversity initially spawned many separate local cultures. In the fourth millennium BC those local cultures expanded geographically and began to interact, compete with each other, and coalesce. . . . [F]ierce competitions between warring chiefdoms drove the formation of ever larger and more centralized states. . . . China's political unification [came] under the Chin dynasty in 221 BC. China's cultural unification accelerated during that same period (Diamond 1996:3–84; see chapter 5, below, for further discussion of how fierce competition produces cooperative coalitions).

And regarding the Roman Empire, Robertson quotes Polybius' strikingly con-solidation-conscious remark that "formerly the things which happened in the world had no connection among themselves. . . . But [now] all events are united in a common bundle" (1992:54), although Polybius' second century BC "world" was a very much smaller, regional, affair compared with the completely global world we see emerging today.

Although the idea of highly localized consolidations of various kinds seems almost sure to be prehistoric in origin, and the idea of regional consol-idations has its roots in early ancient times, the idea of *universal* inclusiveness (i.e., of all people in all societies, everywhere) is a concept invented after widespread interethnic and interracial contact had become more commonplace. "The stoics," Palmer says, "drawing on Greek science, reached a conception of cosmic law . . . embodying a universal reason, of which all men, slave and free, possessed some spark. By this spark of reason all men resembled each other." Then the Apostle Paul "launched with a new force the message of universalism. . . . [writing] to the Galatian Christians . . . 'There is neither Jew nor Greek, there is neither bond nor free, there is neither male nor female: for ye are all one in Christ Jesus'" (1973:140).

Palmer attributes the rise of such radically universalistic ideas to the rise of an extensive regionwide coalition—an empire that consolidated many different local communities:

The failures of the Greek city-state, as much as the growth of science and mathematics, turned men either to skepticism or to monotheism and universal law. It became impossible to believe in inherited myth, local deities, or merely civic religion. . . . Populations became very mixed, especially in the great cities; men also became more mobile. Both Stoicism and Christianity reflected the growth of the Roman Empire, in the universality of their doctrines and in the geographical extension of their adherents (1973:140).

Robertson argues that "Much of world history can be fruitfully considered as sequences of 'miniglobalization,' in the sense that, for example, historic empire formation involved the unification of previously sequestered territories and social entities" (1992:54)—a remark to which the next section is but an extended footnote.

ANCIENT REGIONAL CONSOLIDATIONS GAINED AND LOST

By the first century AD, "a chain of civilized empires . . . extended all across Eurasia, from the Atlantic to the Pacific" (McNeill 1963:316)—including China (see Michael 1986)—and similar empires had flourished, were flourishing, or would soon flourish in sub-Saharan Africa (see the discussions of the empires of Kush, Ethiopia, Ghana, Mali, and Songhay in Davidson 1992), and in Mesoamerica and South America (see the discussions of the Olmec, Maya, Aztec, Chavin, and Inca empires in Willey and Sabloff 1980). Within each of these empires, there occurred an unprecedented consolidation of different ethnic and racial identities—for example, such that "altars dedicated to the Egyptian Isis and the Iranian Mithra have been dug up even in remote [Roman] frontier posts in Scotland and Germany" (Childe 1942:267–268). Slavery, too, played a major consolidating role as it "brought to the great international mart on Delos victims from Britain and Ethiopia, South Russia and Morocco, Iran and Spain, Greeks, Jews, Armenians, Germans, Negroes, Arabs, to be redistributed to Seleucia, Antioch, Alexandria, Carthage, Rome, Athens or Pergamon (Childe 1942:239; see also Daniels 1990:12).

All the ancient empires, however, proved technologically and administratively incapable of the rapid, reliable, and inexpensive mass transportation and communication required to maintain their militarily enforced consolidations—consolidations that called for the rapid deployment and sustained close coordination, across great distances, of police and military forces.

So, typically after not more than a few centuries, these empires disintegrated. For example, by AD 150, "the whole [Eurasian] system began to contract. Each province tended to become an economic unit that supplied its own needs. . . . [This] resulted from the deficiencies of the transport system. . . . Not even the splendid Roman roads had made the carriage of bulky goods by land really cheap" (Childe 1942:273–274).[9]

The "barbarians" had long "supplied slaves, amber, furs and other materials. In return they acquired wines, pottery . . . metal-ware, glass vessels and coins" (Childe 1942:264), but this exchange was not destined to be stable and lasting, for "throughout its length [the] Eurasian civilized belt confronted steppe nomads whose raids and migrations continued, like ocean waves, to break from time to time upon the fringes of civilized, sedentary societies" (McNeill 1963:316).[10] Such raids and migrations eventually fragmented the "Eurasian civilized belt": "The balance of forces across [the nomad] frontier changed decisively in the late fourth century. . . . In the Far West, barbarian war bands and migrating hordes broke into the Roman empire; and similar, though less numerous groups invaded North China" (McNeill 1963:362).[11]

REGIONAL CONSOLIDATIONS RESURGENT

The drive toward global species consolidation, however, hardly missed a beat. For one thing, as soon as the ancient Atlantic-to-Pacific, Eurasian belt of societies was broken up, shorter belts began to grow again on this great landmass. Not only did "the invaders set up a series of short-lived states and gradually acquired some of the culture of their subjects," but "by the sixth century, the initial impetus of these invasions had spent itself; and in China a restoration of imperial unity proved possible" (McNeill 1963:362).

In addition, a new, Islamic consolidation took hold: "In the eastern and western Mediterranean basins, and in Western Asia almost as far as the Chinese frontiers, the spread of Islam was nearly complete by 750 AD . . . With its new-found political stability under Islam, commerce in North Africa, throughout the Mediterranean basin, in the Indian Ocean region with later extensions to Russia and China and Southeast Asia, was now linked together" (Martin 1977:98–99). One result was the opening of "opportunities for Europeans to rediscover ancient Greek philosophy and to partake of the subsequent advances in science and mathematics made in the Islamic world (Fage 1995:215–216). The latter advances included, among many other things, the compass and the astrolabe, both of which would become crucial to European sea voyages around Africa, to Australia, and to the New World.

Meanwhile, "the outpouring of Turkish, Mongolian, and Tungusic peoples from the Eurasian steppe, reaching a climax in the thirteenth century with the conquests of Genghis Khan and his successors" (McNeill 1963:484) ended in what Morgan calls "the largest continuous land empire that has so far existed. At its greatest extent it stretched from Korea to Hungary, including, except for India and the southeast of the continent, most of Asia, as well as a good deal of Eastern Europe" (1987:5).

Then, starting in the fifteenth century, western Europe, with the support of its now rapidly developing transportation, communication, social organization, and finance technologies (see Waters 1995:145–146), "turned out to be the agent that . . . brought the Americas, southern Africa, and Australia into the circle of Old World civilization" (McNeill, 1963:485–486). As a result, "a new dimension [was] added to world history. An ocean frontier, where European seamen and soldiers, merchants, missionaries, and settlers came into contact with the various peoples of the world . . . began to challenge the ancient pre-eminence of the Eurasian land frontier" (McNeill 1963:578; see also Daniels 1990:13–15).

THE ROCKY RECENT ROAD TO GLOBAL CONSOLIDATION

Now although most aspects of the new technologies mentioned, above, by Waters as facilitating communication, especially including the mechanization of movable type printing (see Gaur 1992:194–205; Gouldner 1976:39–44, 96–117), worked in global consolidation's favor, other aspects favored localization. For example, printing resulted not only in the wide diffusion and critical appreciation of given ideas but in the rapid development of literatures and literacies in ethnically different languages. This constituted a major supplement to face-to-face talk in the maintenance of those languages and the particularistically ethnic traditions they supported (see Arnold 1991:33–80).

As a result, it became possible for the concept of nations that were (or rather, claimed to be) ethnically homogeneous rather than heterogeneous to gain wide appeal.

Local Ethnic Homogeneity and Heterogeneity

This gain became more fully manifest with the French Revolution and its aftermath (see McNeill 1985:34; Birch 1989:221) raising the slogan *Liberté, Egalité, Fraternité*—that is, liberty and equality among *brothers* (and sisters), which is to say, among people sharing a particular presumed common descent. The upshot was that

between 1792 and 1815 the power attained by the French nation dazzled all of Europe, and made adaptation of the political practice that sustained such power a matter of urgency for other European governments. . . . Shared national identity, on the French model, seemed the key. Greatness awaited peoples who could act together as brothers in harmony with one another and with their government . . . [for] the myth of national brotherhood and ethnic unity . . . justified sacrifice in war; it sustained public peace at home; it strengthened the hand of government in everyday affairs (McNeill 1985:50–51, 56).

All Europe, then, seems to have pursued the ideal of territorially self-segregated and ethnically homogeneous nation-states down to the first World War.[12] Thus, "the nineteenth century . . . saw the birth of a series of movements of national awakening, liberation, and consolidation resulting in the formation of modern Italy and Germany" (Wirth 1945:366). In addition, "lesser ethnic groups which were involuntarily enveloped by the nascent nations were frustrated and retarded in realizing their national aspirations. There were thus kindled seething movements of unrest. . . . Minorities, especially those of the secessionist and militant variety, are in large part by-products of the ideology of nationalism, whose fundamental tenet it was that every people ought to have its own state" (Wirth 1945:366; see also Schermerhorn 1978:134–152; Weiner 1995:46–47).[13]

The United States of America. Shortly before the French Revolution, there emerged among the British colonies of the eastern middle section of North America a new nation—one separated from Eurasia by thousands of miles of ocean on both sides (more luck of the territorial draw) and composed of invaders from several northwestern European nations who formed coalitions to drive the original Asian discoverers of America off the land by force and fraud (see Steinberg 1989:13–21).[14]

In addition, starting in the early seventeenth century and continuing for some 200 years, a total of some 670 thousand sub-Saharan Africans were imported to the United States as slaves (perhaps fifteeen to twenty millions were landed in all parts of the Americas [see Taeuber and Taeuber 1966:100, 9], and Segal surmises that "at least as many people died in Africa itself as a direct result of the Atlantic trade as were carried away from Africa" [1995:4]). Then, during the ninety years following 1840, came the huge voluntary immigration to the United States of some thirty-two million new European settlers, many of whom were members of southern and eastern European ethnic and nationality groups that were until then nearly absent from North America (see Steinberg 1989:32–35; Lieberson and Waters, 1988:28–33).

In consolidating a new nation out of this ethnic, racial, and nationality heterogenity, two mechanisms proved especially important. One was the language-and-knowledge-consolidating public school system.[15] The second was a series of wars (of 1775–1783, 1812–1815, 1846–1848, 1861–1865, 1898, and culminating in the two "world" wars of 1914–1917, and 1939–1945).

World Wars I and II. World War I, however, had mixed impact on global consolidation. On the one hand, Woodrow Wilson's Fourteen Points supported localism by assuming that "nationality and self-determination meant the same thing and that, if a man had the objective distinguishing marks of a Pole or a Southern Slav, he wanted to be a citizen of a Polish or Southern Slav state" (E. H. Carr, quoted in Wirth 1945:367). But on the other hand, the same Fourteen Points called for the formation of "a general association of nations," and this association—the League of Nations—was the first great twentieth century effort that moved toward consolidating the state apparatuses of all the world's nations into a single global political institution.

The United States, however, refused to join the League at all; the Soviet Union did not join until 1934; Germany and Japan withdrew in 1933, and Italy withdrew in 1937.[16] Weakened in these many ways, the League was powerless to prevent predatory attacks by powerful nation-states—as in Italy's 1935–1936 invasion of Ethiopia, Japan's invasion of Manchuria in 1931, and Germany's 1936 reoccupation of the Rhineland and its 1938 invasion of Austria.

Largely as a result of the League's many weaknesses, a second world war broke out in Europe in 1939. Remarkably, in view of the recency of the League's failure (but indicative of how nearly irresistible is the tendency toward eventual global species consolidation), the American and British allies immediately undertook a second effort in that direction, and its most significant fruit has been the United Nations. World War II had apparently driven home a lesson of World War I that had not been well enough learned during the twenty years of the League of Nations' slow expiration[17]—namely, that every violent local conflict can quickly blow up into a global one and that the best defense is, therefore, a permanent, global coalition of all nations against local as well as global wars.

One of the truly revolutionary principles of the United Nations is that all nations—regardless of their ethnic and racial composition, wealth, power, knowledge, or religious beliefs—have equal sovereignty (see McNeely 1995: 158).[18] This is revolutionary because throughout all previous history it was assumed that some nations, because of their size and military strength and their ethnic and/or racial compositions, had the moral right—indeed, the obligation, "the white man's burden"—to disregard others' sovereignty.

But there is more to this revolution: To the principle that all *nations* have equal rights there has been added the still more emphatically globalizing principle that all *individual persons*, regardless of their geographical location and their status there, have equal rights. Thus, the Charter of the United Nations (signed in 1945) declares a determination "to reaffirm faith in fundamental human rights, in the dignity and worth of the human person, in the equal rights of men and women and of nations large and small" (Vincent 1976:191); and the Universal Declaration of Human Rights, adopted by the UN General Assembly in 1948, asserts that "recognition of the inherent dignity and of the equal and inalienable rights of all members of the human family is the foundation of freedom, justice and peace in the world," and that "All human beings are born free and equal in dignity and rights. . . . and should act towards one another in a spirit of brotherhood" (United Nations 1994:1, 2).[19]

Contrast this with the far more long-standing principle of sovereignty —that every nation-state possesses, inalienably, the right to deal with its own citizens in its own way, without outside interference. It is in this context that the Nuremburg trials of Nazi war criminals were of such signal importance, for they unambiguously put the rights and obligations of the human individual above those of the nation-state. In these trials, "'following orders' by the German state proved to be no defence against an accusation of crimes against humanity. Indeed, the judicial tribunal went so far as to specify that, where state laws are in conflict with international norms specifying human rights, individuals must . . . transgress the state laws" (Waters 1995:102).

Zolberg draws the obvious conclusion: "Globalization . . . has fostered the dissemination of liberal norms regarding persons, expressed in the remarkable emergence of a widely shared notion of universal human rights, as well as of an unprecedented sense of *'species' consciousness in the face of common dangers*" (1995:37, italics added). Chapter 6 will return to this latter idea, which we have already encountered in Robertson's claim that "through historical time it is the world, or 'humanity,' as a whole which becomes the dominant survival unit" (see chapter 1).

Now, against the background of that swift survey of our species' ten thousand year-long drive toward eventual global species consolidation, let us turn to the second topic of this chapter—namely the engines inside human societies that, together with the outside geographical forces first mentioned in chapter 1, help account for that drive.

THE PRINCIPAL INSTITUTIONS OF EVERY SOCIETY AND THEIR PRODUCTS

A human society may be thought of as a throughput system, that is to say, a system whose constituent elements pass into, and through, it.[20] Such a conceptualization (see Wallace 1994:47–72, 257–261) draws attention to the bedrock facts that the living organisms composing every society are born in time and in time die, and that during their lifetimes they are able to move about from place to place and from society to society.

It follows that every human society will possess institutions for taking in participants, institutions for organizing the activities of these participants while they remain in the society, and institutions for letting out participants.[21] Thus, first, there is always a set of institutions for birthing, capturing, purchasing, or otherwise admitting new members, and for socializing, educating, and training them for roles in the second set of institutions. In the latter set, trained participants are put to work generating, distributing, and consuming the products—namely, wealth, power, knowledge, and honor—that sustain and "run" the whole system and its participants. (This set of institutions comprises what I refer to as the internal "engines" of the society and of human history in general.) Finally, there is a set of institutions specialized for temporarily or permanently discharging disaffected, unwanted, disabled, or dead participants (including hospitalization and incarceration, forcible expulsion, monitored voluntary emigration, and corpse-disposal).

The extrardinary extent to which the second set of institutions—the engines—have developed is responsible for the almost six billion-strong population of Homo sapiens alive today. These institutions vary widely in their degree of separation from one another, organization, effectiveness, and efficiency, but they are all present, in some form, in every known human society.[22] They are called the economic, the political, the scientific-educational-technological, and the religious institutions, and each has its specialized primary product, as follows.

• The economic institution is specialized for the production and distribution of material *wealth*. This includes the physical goods and services that sustain the society's individual participants as living, functioning, organisms.

• The political institution is specialized for the production and distribution of decison-making *power*. This includes the legislative, judicial, executive and administrative controls (backed by physical force) over what the society's participants do and do not do, think and do not think, do and do not experience emotionally.

• The scientific-educational-technological institution is specialized for the production and distribution of *knowledge*. This includes interpersonally confirmed, sense-based information about the universe and everything in it (including ourselves), plus practical skills for its manipulation.

• The religious institution is specialized for the production and distribution of *honor*. This includes the emotional feelings of prestige, esteem, dignity, and self-respect that the society bestows on its participants and their behaviors, and on itself, thereby generating high levels of group morale and personal self-confidence. The religious institution is increasingly assisted in the production of honor by secular honoric organizations.[23]

All four engines form a single integrated system because they share the same set of individual participants (that is, every member of a society participates, simultaneously but via different roles, in all of that society's internal engines), and because they exchange and thrive on each other's products—products that also serve as the primary rewards, and the primary resources, of social life. The latter point means that (1) wealth, power, knowledge, and honor are all *produced* by individuals acting together in societies; (2) the distribution of this socially-produced wealth, power, knowledge, and honor *rewards* successful competition among these individuals, and (3) the wealth, power, knowledge, and honor that these individuals possess then become *resources* with which they enter the next round of production and competition. It also follows, from the mutual exchangeability of these products-rewards-resources, that wealth can buy power, knowledge, and honor; power can determine how wealth, knowledge, and honor are produced and distributed; knowledge can show how to get and keep power, wealth, and honor; honor can lay claim to disproportionate shares of wealth, power, and knowledge.

Therefore, a group's successful competition for any one of the indicated rewards gives it an edge in the competitions for all the others as well, and similarly, a group's defeat in any one competition sets it up for more defeats in other competitions. In short, and as everybody knows, unless there are inhibiting factors (see chapter 6), the rich get richer and the poor get poorer—in more ways than one.

Now let us consider, from the standpoint of their contributions to global species consolidation, the engines themselves—that is, the economic, political, scientific-educational-technological, and religious institutions that operate in every society.

The Economic Institution

Weber claims the economic market is typically a place of intergroup contact and consolidation: "The market is a relationship which transcends the boundaries of neighborhood, kinship group, or tribe. Originally, it is indeed the only peaceful relationship of such kind" (1978:637). Leakey and Lewin point out the complex role of economic trade in generating and sustaining intergroup political alliances—the latter sometimes manifested in local and regional consolidations: "In most small-scale societies, [trade] operates as a vehicle of social obligations . . . [which are] bonds capable of tying together different social groups. . . . [Such alliances] between modern hunter-gatherer bands are maintained and strengthened during occasional aggregations of the bands" (1992:324; see also 232; see also Durkheim 1965:245–246). To this, McNeill adds the following consolidation effects of the early market-centered cities' constant recruitment of fresh labor forces—a recruitment driven by the prevalence of high disease and death rates inside those cities (see 1978):

Figure 3.1
Institutional Systems of Human Societies

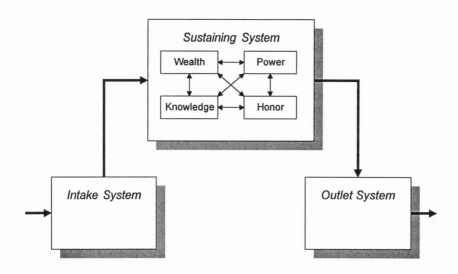

In many instances, when spontaneous immigration from the nearby countryside proved insufficient, resort to enslavement supplied the shortfall, moving across cultural boundaries and greater distances to bring an unfree labor force into action. The result . . . was ethnic mixture and pluralism on a grand scale in major centers of imperial government (1985:14–15; see also Bonacich, 1972).[24]

Referring to somewhat more recent economic developments, Marx and Engels make the explicitly global consolidation claims that "big industry . . . produced world history for the first time, in so far as it made all civilized nations and every individual member of them dependent for the satisfaction of their wants on the whole world, thus destroying the former natural exclusiveness of separated nations. . . . [In addition,] big industry created a [bourgeois] class, which in all nations has the same interest and with which nationality is already dead" (1947:56–57); "stripped [the proletariat] of every trace of national character" (1969, I:118); and "created everywhere the same relations between the classes of society, and thus destroyed the peculiar individuality of the various nationalities" (1947:57). And more recently, Leontiades tells us that "today virtually all major firms have a significant and growing presence in business outside their country of origin." Thus, although at one time, "the U.S. market comprised the bulk of the total world demand for telephones, automobiles, petroleum, radios, and various household appliances . . . [this] is no longer the case. . . . Industrialization, which at one time was confined almost exclusively to Western Europe and North America, has spread to include a host of additional countries" (1985:3; see also Clarke 1985:1–16; Kotabe 1992:1).

By way of illustrating this spread, Sider points out that in the Ford Escort (which he calls "the first real 'world car'") "every single component . . . is manufactured in at least two different countries" (1992:237). Consider the consequently international movement of goods: Using the value of exports and imports in 1980 as criterion, the value of the former rose 138 percent and the value of the latter rose 145 percent, between 1975 and 1993. These figures include export increases of 127 percent and 145 percent in the developed, and the developing countries, respectively, and import increases of 130 percent and 186 percent in these two groups of countries (see United Nations 1993:26–27). Appadurai notes, also, the movement of money, that now nearly universal mediator of the exchange of goods and services: "Currency markets, national stock exchanges, and commodity speculations move mega-monies through national turnstiles at blinding speed, with vast absolute implications for small differences in percentage points and time units" (1990:298).

Reich's conclusion is specific to one nation but easily generalized to others as well: "There is coming to be no such thing as an American corporation or an American industry. The American economy is but a region of the global economy" (1992:243; see also 6–9, 172; and Kennedy, 1993:54).

The Political Institution

As the discussion of war and conquest in the first part of this chapter has suggested, the political institution has worked powerfully toward the consolidation of local ethnic and/or racial groups. The feature of this institution that has been most influential in this respect, of course, is that action which Weber claims is "peculiar to [the state], as to every political association, namely, the use of *physical force*" (1946:77–78, italics changed). This includes military force applied to offense and defense against external powers that it would swallow or that would swallow it, and police force applied to internal secessionists and other dissenters that would break it up.

Largely through the use of such force, a new and explicitly consolidationist entity—namely, the nationality group—emerged as both a product and a sustaining influence of the invention of large-scale agriculture. A nationality group was defined in the preceding chapter as a primarily destiny-oriented coalition of two or more descent-oriented ethnic and/or racial groups. Though not universal (Africa is the continent on which it is most clearly still struggling), and never unchallenged by its constituent groups (witness the former Soviet Union and the former Yugoslavia), the nationality group has been the not-yet-global pinnacle of species consolidation so far.

Over the last century or so, however, more global coalitional inventions (international and supranational political organizations of many kinds), some relying on physical force but increasingly not, have arisen as political fore-runners of an even higher pinnacle still to be scaled. More on this in chapter 6.

The Scientific-Educational-Technological Institution

Among the earliest protoscientific and technological contributions to global consolidation were the pure knowledge and the practical skills associated with the stone hand axe and controlled fire; pottery and metallurgy; the plough, sledge, wheel, loom, kiln, forge, ship, and sail; the spear, spear-thrower, bow and arrow; the domestication of grain plants and certain herbivores plus the dog; the domesticated horse and its reins, bit, collar, saddle, stirrups, chariot, travois, and cart; the astronomical prediction of seasonal changes; bureaucratically organized work, war, police, religious, and scientific-educational-technological forces; and perhaps most important of all, the technical skills of computation and literacy. Gaur elucidates the impact of the latter on consolidation:

a common script is a strong tool for unification. Neither China nor Mesopotamia would have survived and prospered without it. Mesopotamia has always been . . . an area of conflict where the centre of power fluctuated between ethnically and linguistically unrelated groups. But the economic survival of Mesopotamia, linked with irrigation, depended on a continuously effective system of administration. . . . Continuity and stability were largely provided by the scribe-administrators who, for over 3,000 years, irrespective of political changes, used the cuneiform script first created by the early Sumerians (1992:183).

Sowell notes that "the change from wind-driven ships to steam-powered ships caused a drastic change in the origins of immigrants to America. . . . In the era of wind-driven ships, an ocean voyage on a passenger vessel was beyond the financial means of most immigrants. They could reach America only in the hold of a cargo vessel from its deliveries in Europe. This meant," Sowell says, "that mass immigration was possible only from areas with large-scale trade with the United States—northern and western Europe, but not eastern or south-ern Europe." But when steamships came on the scene, all this changed: "The time of the voyage shrank from a variable thirty to ninety days to a dependable ten days, and it now became economically feasible for working-class people to travel on ships specializing in passengers rather than cargo. No longer were immigration patterns tied to trade patterns." And, more recently, there has been a further change: "The great migrations of Puerto Ricans began after World War II, when the cost of air travel came down within the reach of working people" (1981:11–13, 231; see also 1996:38–44). In connection with the consolidation effects of changes in transportation technology, Molnar tells us that one researcher,

after studying census records, noted that in rural England during the nineteenth century, a man used to find his mate within six hundred yards of his residence. But, after the bicycle was invented, the average distance between prenuptial households jumped to sixteen hundred yards. . . . As modern transportation has increased mobility further still, a broader exchange of genes is to be expected. Whereas formerly, small breeding units were restricted by economics, politics, or geography to a village community, today, mating circles have expanded and the gene pool is much broader (1992:195; see chapter 6 on intermarriage).

We should also note that "mortality reduction throughout the world has been more rapid in the twentieth century than in any previous period. The expansion in longevity ranks among the great social achievements of our time. Life expectancy at birth in the United States has increased from 47.3 years in 1900 to 75.7 years in 1994. . . . Among the causes are a better understanding of disease etiology and the translation of this understanding into preventive health practices; improvements in nutrition, housing, and general living standards; and the deployment of new therapeutic interventions" (White and Preston 1996:415). Indeed, according to White and Preston's calculations, "half of the [American] population [now alive] owes its existence to twentieth-century mortality improvements" (1996:428).

Regarding education, it seems clear that in a complex and globalizing society, every individual's knowledge of that society would be confined to a rapidly shrinking proportion of the whole were it not for mass education and mass communication. This highlights the consolidation significance of the fact that the total number of television receivers, and radio receivers, in the world increased by 128 percent and 104 percent, respectively, between 1975 and 1992—including 866 percent and 396 percent increases in Africa; 303 percent and 310 percent increases in Asia; 214 percent and 174 percent increases in South America (see United Nations 1993:124–131). Similarly, "35 percent of American families and 50 percent of American teenagers have home computers. Worldwide, two to three million computers provide hookup to the Internet for an estimated thirty million users, a population that grows monthly by ten percent" (Yom 1996:735).[25] Broad quotes one consolidation-oriented scientist as saying, "One wants a unifying fabric for the human race. The Internet is pointing in that direction. It promotes a very egalitarian culture" (1993; see also Negroponte 1995:5; Rheingold 1993:79–81; Waters 1995: 150).[26]

The Religious Institution

I have referred to the specialization of the religious institution for the production and distribution of honor. The following line of thought underlies this claim.

The primary status distinction that is drawn by all religions is between people (worshipful believers) who have the honor of being acceptable to the god or gods of the religion and people who do not have this honor (nonworshipful believers, nonbelievers, and disbelievers). Weber says, "When fully developed, [the god] was altogether exclusive with respect to outsiders, and in principle he accepted offerings and prayers only from the members of his group, or at least he was expected to act in this fashion" (1978:413). In addition, believers draw honorific distinctions among themselves (for example, among prophets, priests, and laypersons—and sometimes different castes of each), and Wuthnow notes that "most religious organizations orchestrate rituals in such a way as to prevent the full benefits of the organization from being distributed to persons who are not actively contributing members" (1987:172). To this, one should add that believers draw honorific distinctions among nonbelievers as well (e.g., among devotees of gods thought to be friendly to the believers, devotees of gods thought to be unfriendly, and devotees of no gods at all).

Group morale and personal self-confidence come with the conviction that one's own ethnic, racial, and/or nationality group—and therefore oneself, personally—has been specially "chosen" by supernatural forces (and if the choice is mutual, a coalition or "covenant" is said to exist). Consequently, expansionist "crusading," "evangelist," or "missionary" tendencies in the religious institution have often gone hand-in-glove with similar ("imperialist") tendencies in the political institution. Accordingly, as chapter 2 indicated, Weber claims that in classical times, "every permanent political association had a special god who guaranteed the success of the political action of the group" (1978:413) and who guaranteed the divine rightness of its cause.

With increasing separation of church and state, however, religions have grown more and more free to make their own independent impacts upon global consolidation:

The gods of locality, tribe, and polity were only concerned with the interests of their respective associations. They had to fight other gods like themselves, just as their communities fought, and they had to prove themselves in this very struggle. [Eventually, however,] these barriers of locality, tribe, and polity were shattered by universalist religions, by a religion with a unified God of the entire world (Weber 1946:333).

Such religions, of course, prominently include Christianity—a successful evangelistic sect of non-evangelistic Judaism—and Islam, an almost equally successful evangelistic religion that combines Judaic and Christian beliefs.

In conclusion, this chapter has suggested that the case for the progressively global consolidation of all ethnic, racial, and national populations of the human species rests on two kinds of evidence: First, that the broad facts of ten thousand or more years of human history since the start of the Neolithic Age may be usefully understood in its light. Second, that certain types of institutions inside every human society have been driving human history in that direction. These include the economic institution (producing and distributing wealth), the political institution (producing and distributing power), the scientific-educational-technological institution (producing and distributing knowledge), and the religious institution (producing and distributing honor).[27]

The next chapter considers what happens when different societies, after having gone largely their own separate ways for some 90 thousand years (!) and each possessing its own full complement of the institutional engines just discussed—but operating at levels of development that vary according to sociocultural founder effect and drift (see chapter 2), and according to the luck of the territorial draw—come, at last, into contact with one another.

NOTES

1. War and conquest seem to have played these roles largely for two reasons: (1) for the first time there were large stores of harvested food, as well as large expanses of arable land and large aggregates of laborers, to be conquered and enslaved, and (2) the domestication of the horse, the smelting of metals that could be forged into efficient military weapons, and the development of sea-going ships and navigational methods made such war and conquest feasible at some distance from home (see Diamond, 1992:240; Leakey and Lewin, 1992:234).

2. A few years ago, Diamond took the radically negative view that "the adoption of agriculture . . . was in many ways a *catastrophe* from which we have never recovered. With agriculture came the gross social and sexual inequality, the disease and despotism, that curse our existence" (1987:64, italics added). Fortunately, however, Diamond has tempered this view by claiming that "the introduction of agriculture [was] a mixed *blessing*" (rather than an unmitigated, or even mixed, "catastrophe") and that "agriculture inextricably combines causes of our *rise* and fall" (rather than only or mainly our fall, our curse) (1992:138, 139, both italics added; see also 180–191). The point I would emphasize, however, is not that agriculture brought a better life for individuals (although it seems clear that it did so for a larger absolute number of individuals, even when it did not always do so for a larger proportion of the world's population) than did the hunting and gathering economies that preceded it. What agriculture did was to make possible a more populous life, an occupationally more complex and technically more competent life, and a territorially more widespread life for human societies. This combination of societal features that has tended strongly toward the survival, and the eventual global consolidation, of our species.

3. Diamond also notes that "China's long west-east rivers (the Yellow River in the North, the Yangtze in the south) allowed crops and technology to spread quickly between inland and coast, while their diffusion north and south was made easy by the broad, relatively gentle terrain north of the Yangtze, which eventually permitted the two river systems to be joined by canals. All these geographical factors contributed to the early cultural and political unification of China. In contrast, western Europe . . . fragmented by mountains such as the Alps, and with a highly indented coastline and no such rivers, has never been unified politically" (1996:84). Blaut applies the same ideas to the European conquest of the Americas when he claims that (1) the fact that "America was vastly more accessible from Iberian ports than from any extra-European mercantile-maritime centers that had the capacity for long-distance sea voyages" (1993:182) helps explain why it was Europeans, rather than Africans or Asians, who sailed to America in 1492; and (2) "the massive depopulation caused by the pandemics of Eastern hemisphere

[i.e., European-African-Asian] diseases that were introduced to America by Europeans" (1993:184) helps explain why Europeans so readily conquered the Americas.

4. Indeed, Fage points out that "the Blacks were the only people to be confined to a large land mass which (except for its remote southern tip) lay wholly within the tropics. This immediately posed problems for the agriculture they possessed before the growth of the desert confined them to the Sudan and to the lands south of it" (1995:17; see also McNulty 1977:40–48).

5. See also Phillips 1985:114–127. Fage, however, argues that "Africa . . . evolved systems of dependence which were not all that different [from European feudal serfdom], but for which the word 'slavery' is commonly used" (1995:268).

6. Brooks says "Clearly, one of the crucial factors [that explain African societies' participation in the slave trade] was the independence of action afforded African traders, who could engage in commercial activities detrimental to their own societies. A second and closely related factor was the self-serving collusion of political elites. Rulers and elites were so often attracted to foreign luxuries, especially spirits, that they were induced to wage war on neighboring societies to obtain captives and, in some instance, even sold their own people as slaves. Sometimes military elites became uncontrollable and subsisted off slave-raiding of agricultural and pastoral groups" (1977:120–121; compare Fage 1995:268–270).

7. As McNulty says, "Urban centers and transportation systems [in sub-Saharan Africa] were . . . designed for the purpose of colonial administration and economic exploitation. As part of an export-oriented, primary producing economy, they connected coastal areas and ports to important sources of raw materials and agricultural production but afforded little opportunity for internal circulation of goods or people" (1977:48).

8. It follows that had the territories of the world been as well known then as they are now, the reversals of fortune described earlier between peoples inside, and outside, sub-Saharan Africa could have been reliably predicted prior to the first migration out of Africa. Needless to say, such long term increases in predictability would seem to contradict those who insist that human history remains unpredictable in principle.

9. Mann attacks "conventional notions concerning the supposed technological stagnation of Rome," but he also claims that "*routine* [movement of military supplies over long distances by the then available technological means of transportation] would eat up the profits of empire—and eventually did so" (1986:297, 279; see also 274–275, 310–317).

10. "The mass migrations into Europe chiefly took three routes: across the narrow straits at either end of the Mediterranean . . . and, most important, westward across the eastern European plain. Successive migrations of whole peoples . . . were sometimes set off by repeated incursions into eastern Asia and Europe itself by armies of mounted horsemen from the grasslands of central Asia" (Daniels, 1990:12).

11. Similarly, Mann assigns "the precipitating role in [the decline and fall of the Roman Empire] to the military pressure of the barbarians," and adds that "different levels of outside pressure probably account for the continued survival of the eastern empire . . . for another thousand years" (1986:293).

12. "[T]he disruptive force of nationalism within a polyethnic context...was less apparent in India and China," and in "Latin America . . . nationalism had both divisive and unifying impact" (McNeill 1985:52, 53–54).

13. At the same time, however, a very different consolidationist trend manifested itself in "the rapid development of modern empires and the crystallization of such movements as Pan-Slavism and Pan-Germanism" (Wirth 1945:366).

14. Turner says "the frontier promoted the formation of a composite nationality for the American people. The coast was preponderantly English, but the later tides of continental immigration flowed across to the free [sic] lands. . . . In the crucible of the frontier the immigrants were Americanized, liberated, and fused into a mixed race, English in neither nationality nor characteristics" (1920:22–23; see also Gordon 1964:118–119).

15. Steinberg says "Ethnicity in the United States would be an altogether different phenomenon had Germans, Irish, Italians, Poles, Jews, Latins, Asians, [Africans,] and others been permitted to use tax revenues to develop their own schools. . . . [T]he common school served the nation in its determination to minimize ethnic division and mold a unified and harmonious people" (1989:54–55).

16. Of the world powers, only Great Britain and France stayed with the League until it disbanded, superceded by the United Nations, in 1946.

17. McNeill argues persuasively, however, that the swiftness with which World War II followed World War I was fortunate for the species insofar as it provided an effective mechanism for remembering some of these lessons: "in all belligerent lands veterans of the first conflict were still in positions of authority from which they swiftly reconstituted and then expanded the transnational administrative structures needed to fight efficiently"—although, no less fortunately, "The Japanese and Germans were notably less successful in concerting transnational mobilization" (1985:65, 66).

18. Of course, the word "principle" should be underscored here, because in practice the notion of equality among nations was contravened by "The Yalta and Potsdam conferences . . . [which divided] the world into spheres of interest and [assigned] them to the victors: Eastern and Central Europe to the Soviet Union; Western Europe to Britain, France and the USA; the Middle East, Africa, South and South and South-East Asia to Britain and France; the Asia-Pacific region and Latin America to the USA" (Waters 1995:115).

19. See also the International Convention on the Elimination of All Forms of Racial Discrimination, and the Covenant on Civil and Political Rights, adopted in 1965, and 1966, respectively.

20. Nicolis and Prigogine call such a throughput system a "dissipative structure" and argue that such structures "can be maintained in far-from-equilibrium conditions only through a sufficient flow of energy and matter. An appropriate illustration would be a town that can only survive as long as it is a center of inflow of food, fuel, and other commodities and sends out products and wastes" (1977:4). Needless to say, a social scientist must first point to the inflow and sendout of the living humans (the "townspeople") that are the town's most essential components.

21. An *institution* of society may be defined as a relatively stable set of product-defined working physical relationships plus a relatively stable set of supporting mental relationships among the individual participants in a society.

22. In addition, there is important variation in the extent to which given resources are actually put to present use rather than stored for future use (or allowed to deteriorate beyond any human use at all). Thus, Blalock identifies resource "mobilization" as "the proportion of the total resources that are actually utilized or expended to achieve a given objective. . . . Obviously, the more the total resources the less the degree of mobilization needed to carry out a given objective," and, Blalock continues, "resources may be mobilized not only in different degrees but also with varying efficiency" (1967:126). So a society (or a group within a society) that possesses a high level of resources but mobilizes them poorly may well lose out in competition with a group that possesses a lower level of resources but mobilizes that at a high level.

23. Durkheim says "Before all, [religion] is a system of ideas with which the individuals represent to themselves the society of which they are members. . . . This is its primary function; and though metaphorical and symbolic, this representation is not unfaithful" (1965:257). Such a view might lead one to argue that the wealth of a society and its members is symbolized by Paradise; the power of a society and its members is symbolized by an omnipotent God; the knowledge of a society is symbolized by an omniscient God; and the honor of a society is symbolized by an infinitely glorious God.

24. McNeill also cites another economic mechanism of consolidation: "long-distance trade . . . gave birth to permanent communities of aliens in major urban centers" (1985:16; see also Bonacich, 1973). The same recruitment of fresh labor forces, through both "spontaneous immigration" and "enslavement," characterized the ethnic mixing and pluralization of the New World.

25. Naisbitt says "There are now more than 50 million individuals on the Internet. And that number could reach one billion by the year 2000" (1996:22).

26. Wriston adds that "The current attack on the power of [national] sovereigns is the proliferation of knowledge that used to be confined to small groups of leaders but is now popping up on [TV] screens all over the world. When a monopoly of information is broken, the power structure is in danger" (1992:136).

27. Even Huntington—who insists (almost unbelievably) that "A multicultural America is impossible because a non-Western America is not American" (1996:318) while asserting, at the same time, that a multicultural *world* is not only possible but the only viable possibility ("The world will be ordered on the basis of civilizations or not at all" 1996:156])—cannot help expressing some support for eventual global species consolidation: "peoples in all civilizations," he says, "should search for and attempt to expand the values, institutions, and practices they have in common with peoples of other civilizations," for, he says, "the world's great civilizations . . . [will] hang together or hang separately" (1996:321)—a view chapter 1 has already extended beyond the "great civilizations" to the entire human species.

4

CONTACT

Almost needless to say, all human groups (indeed, all human individuals) have *always* been in "contact" with one another in the sense that we all live on the same tiny dust-mote, whirling around the same life-giving (and eventually life-taking) ball of fire; we all breathe the same air and drink the same water, with what chaos theorists call the "butterfly effect" result that whatever any one of us does, anywhere on Earth, always exerts some influence, however small, round-about, and delayed, over things that all the others, everywhere, do.

But it is essential to add that—owing to the near-exclusivity, in the past, of *face-to-face* (that is, spatiotemporally proximal) communication rather than *tele*communication—every ethnic, racial, and nationality group so far has come into being as an entity claiming cultural and social structural jurisdiction over some particular *territory* of the Earth. As a result, two individuals living a thousand kilometers apart but inside the same territorial border have generally been in much closer sociocultural contact with each other than individuals who may live a mere half kilometer apart but on different sides of that border.

It follows that when people (migrants) who grew up on one side of an ethnic, racial, and/or nationality border move across that border, their contact with individuals on the other side (hosts) increases suddenly rather than gradually.[1] This suddenness is almost sure to cause painful shocks, hostility, and resentment, with an alarmed (aliens! aliens!) awakening of ethnocentrism on both sides. For example, one essayist on race relations tells us that

I grew up in the apartheid South. . . . [W]e did not constantly think about white suprem-acy and its impact on our social status. We lived a large part of our lives not thinking about white folks. . . . [But when] I first left the apartheid South, to attend a predom-inantly white institution of higher education . . . I remember my first feelings of political rage against racism. . . . It changed my relationship with home—with the South—made it so I could not return there. . . . I felt like an exile. . . . During that time in my life when racial apartheid [forbade] possibilities of intimacy and closeness with whites, I was most able to forget about the pain of racism. The intimacy I share with white people [now] . . . is the cultural setting that provokes rage (hooks 1995:13, 17; see also Nagel and Olzak 1982).

On the other side of this American racial divide but quite similarly, Rieder reports one White respondent's nostalgia: "'I used to walk Flatbush Avenue when I was dating my wife. It was all white then. I remember joyful occasions. . . . It was one big happy Flatbush family,'" and another's comment after Blacks began moving into Flatbush in large numbers and the occasions for Black-White contact quickly escalated: "'I bag all the niggers together. . . . They have different traits from us. I don't want to mingle with them'" (1985:93, 81).

The thing to remember, however, is that without contact of *some* sort, whether it be painful or pleasureful to those immediately involved, the development of each separate group is necessarily limited to only its own paltry stock of resources. Seen in this light, the mutual shocks of stranger-contact are simply the price our species as a whole pays for combining these stocks and thereby guaranteeing faster and more survival-insuring development. Locke and Stern tell us "Cul-tures may develop complexity through certain internal development and variation, but by far the main source of cultural growth and development seems always to have been through the forces of external contact. . . . Civilization is largely the accumulative product and residue of this ever-widening process of culture contact, interchange and fusion" (1946:7); Kallen agrees: "Creation comes from the impact of diversities. . . . Cultural values arise upon the confrontation, impact, and consequent disintegration and readjustment of different orders, with the emergence therefrom of new harmonies carrying unprecedented things in their heart" (quoted in Gordon 1964:147),[2] as does McNeill: "Intercivilizational exchange and stimulus provided a major—perhaps *the* major—stimulus to change within civilized communities" (1978:12).

Let us, therefore, focus our attention next on the primary process whereby contact among different ethnic, racial, and nationality groups has been achieved —namely, migration, in its several forms.

MIGRATION

Migration is a pattern of human sociocultural behavior that reaches back through recorded history, back beyond the earliest farming settlements, back, indeed, to prehistoric and perhaps prehominid times. Thus, Pan notes that

A thousand years ago there were no Irishmen in Australia; no Thais in Bangkok; no white, nor black, Americans in America. Migration is the great travel saga of all time. People have always moved to find land and work; and to flee from war, famine and oppression. They have also, at times, been forcibly relocated; for several centuries people were transported into slavery from one part of the world to another by Europe's imperial powers, and when the slaves were freed a substitute was found in Indian and Chinese indentured labour. The . . . population relocations flowing from voluntary movement, mass transportation or expulsion have been immense (1994:375).

Moreover,

the earliest civilization known to archaeologists seems to have arisen as a result of sea-borne migration of the people we know as Sumerians into Mesopotamia from somewhere south, presumably along the shores of the Persian Gulf. The newcomers established themselves as rulers of whoever may have lived in the marshy estuaries of the Tigris-Euphrates before they got there, and soon began to develop new skills and techniques for exploiting the agricultural as well as the fishing and fowling possibilities of that exceptional environment. The result was the emergence of cities and civilization by about 3000 BC (McNeill 1978:3).

In modern times, Weiner claims there have been five distinct "waves of migration" (see also Daniels 1990:11–16). In the first wave, which lasted from the seventeenth to the nineteenth centuries, Western European nations invaded and established colonies in the Americas and then in Asia, Africa, Australia, New Zealand.[3] The second wave, during the same period, saw European traders transporting sub-Saharan Africans as slaves to the New World (see Brooks 1977:120–124; Fage 1995:244–291) and, after slavery was outlawed, this wave saw indentured workers transported from South Asia and China to eastern Africa, Southeast Asia, and the Caribbean (see Pan 1994:43–83). The third wave, after World War I, consisted largely of refugees forced to move by the breakup of the Hapsburg and Ottoman empires and the formation of new nations that "sought to create [ethnically] homogeneous populations through forced emigration," the Russian Revolution and civil war, and the rise of the Nazis to power in Germany. The fourth wave followed World War II and the worldwide breakup of colonial empires and the founding of new independent nations in Asia, the Middle East, and Africa that sought to create ethnically homogeneous, or at least rigidly hierarchical, social systems. A fifth wave took place during the 1950s and 1960s when labor was imported into Western Europe (from Turkey, North Africa, and Yugoslavia), into the United States (from Mexico and the Caribbean), and into the Middle East (from Egypt, Yemen, and South and Southeast Asia) (see Weiner 1995: 21–25).

The current upshot is that "according to the United Nations Population Fund, in 1993 there were over 100 million migrants worldwide—including 15.5 million migrants in Western Europe; 20 million in the United States; 8 million in Australia and Canada; and several million in the Gulf states . . . and 19 million refugees. These figures do not include . . . an estimated 280,000 [illegal migrants] in Japan in 1992, a million . . . [in Malaysia, several million in India], over 3 million in the United States, and significant numbers in Spain, Portugal, and Italy" (Weiner 1995:2).[4]

Add to these figures an estimated 18.9 million refugees worldwide in 1993, up from 2.8 million in 1976 (see Weiner 1995:2, 5, 23), and it seems clear that the global ethnic, racial, and nationality melting pot continues to be powerfully stirred by migration. Thus,

in Germany, Turkish foreign residents numbered 1,675,000 in 1990, with Yugoslavia, Italy, and Greece providing the next largest contingents. . . . By the mid-1990s, approximately 4 million Muslims lived in France and up to 13 million in Western Europe overall. In the 1950s two-thirds of the immigrants to the United States came from Europe and Canada; in the 1980s roughly 35 percent of the much larger number of immigrants came from Asia, 45 percent from Latin America, and less than 15 percent from Europe and Canada (Huntington 1996:199–200).[5]

The expanded geographic scope of migration is partly a consequence of political changes and changes in emigration and immigration laws, but it also results from changes in transportation technologies and economics (see Huntington 1996:198–199; Weiner 1995:11, 25, 212). For all these reasons, migrations "now function on larger scales, as men and women from villages in India think not just of moving to Poona or Madras, but of moving to Dubai and Houston, and refugees from Sri Lanka find themselves in South India as well as in Canada, just as the Hmong are driven to London as well as to Philadelphia" (Appadurai 1990:297). As a result, Rudolph reports that

over the last 20 years or so Oklahoma City has acquired five mosques, four Hindu temples, one Sikh gurudwara, and three Buddhist temples. . . . There may be as many as 70 mosques in the Chicago metropolitan area and 50 temples in the Midwest Buddhist Association. Muslims outnumber Episcopalians in the United States by two to one, and are likely to outnumber Jews in the near future (1996:26).

Naisbitt warns that "many people in the world, especially Americans, associate Islam with the Iranian hostage crisis, fighting in the Middle East and terrorism. These incidents have created stereotyped images of Islam, which are a gross distortion of the mainstream religion" while, at the same time, "the American Muslim community is the U.S.'s fastest growing religious minority" (1996:252). Indeed, Ahmed and Donnan tell us that "Muslim society . . . totals something like one billion people living in about 50 countries with significantly some ten to fifteen million living in the USA and Europe," and that "the bulk of Muslim migrant labor has settled abroad on a permanent basis. . . . Muslim doctors and engineers live as American or British citizens. Their children have no intention of going back to their place of origin" (1994:2, 5).

Other "diasporas" seem to be waiting in the wings—including a voluntary one, this time, from sub-Saharan Africa, and a very different one in terms of its social class composition, from Asia to the rest of the world. Regarding the latter, Naisbitt tells us that "from 1945 to 1995 . . . Asia went from rags to riches. It reduced the incidence of poverty from 400 million to 180 million, while its population grew by 400 million during the same period . . . [and] as we move toward the year 2000, Asia will become the dominant region of the world: economically, politically and culturally." "The old Asia," he says, "was divided by culture, language, political ideology, religious philosophies and geography. The new Asia, forged by economic integration, technology, especially telecommunications, travel and mobility of people, will increasingly look like one coherent region" (Naisbitt 1996:10, 11).

Regarding the world as a whole, then, Weiner's conclusion makes complete sense: "There is every reason to expect that . . . more and more people will want to leave their home country. . . . More than ever before, individuals have become aware of the opportunities for employment and income [and, I would add, for what they regard as improvements in their political, knowledge, and honor statuses, as well] in other countries. . . . The declining cost of travel, moreover, is making it easier for migrants and refugees to go longer distances" (1995:221). And note Portes' observation that "Migration . . . develops an increasingly dense web of contacts between places of origin and destination. Once established, such networks allow the migration process to become self-sustaining and impervious to short-term changes in economic incentives" (1995: 22). And regarding the United States' current place in all this global species consolidation, Pan tells us that

America is not just the fount of a culture whose marks are adopted, if only superficially, worldwide; it is also the world's ultimate immigration destination. At a time when most Western countries are slamming their doors on foreigners from poorer countries, the United States is experiencing the highest tide of immigration since the early decades of this century, taking in more newcomers than the rest of the world combined (1994:275).

So let us consider the principal types of migrants and the types of resources they are likely to bring with them when they cross the border into a given hostland. After that, chapter 5 will address the very next question: What types of *strategies* do such in-contact migrants and hosts use when competing for wealth, power, knowledge, and honor?

Types of Migrants

Figure 4.1 classifies migrants into four basic types according to their predominant attitude toward leaving their homeland and their hosts' predominant attitude toward receiving them.[6] Thus:

• *Immigrants* are defined as migrants who leave their homeland voluntarily and are also voluntarily received by their hosts. Immigrants include persons planning to settle permanently in the hostland, and persons planning only a temporary stay in the hostland—migrant workers, guest workers, sojourners, as well as exiles, expatriates, diplomats, students, merchants, and tourists.[7] This category also includes indentured servants—to the extent that they voluntarily accept their indentures.

Figure 4.1
Types of Migrants

| | **Migrants Received by Hostland** | |
Migrants Leave Homeland	Voluntarily	Involuntarily
Voluntarily	Immigrants	Invaders
Involuntarily	Slaves	Refugees

• *Invaders* are migrants who leave their homeland voluntarily but are involuntarily received by their hosts. They are likely to use arms to overcome host resistance. They include colonizers (who settle in parts of the hostland), raiders (who hit and run), conquerors (who subjugate the hostland), as well as sundry other types (illegal immigrants, escaping criminals, spies, saboteurs, terrorists) that choose to leave their homeland and enter a hostland against the will of their hosts.

• *Slaves* are migrants who leave their homeland involuntarily but are voluntarily received by their hosts, for whose benefit they are then compelled, by force of arms, to generate wealth, power, knowledge, and honor. Included here are persons involuntarily taken prisoner in their homeland by invaders, as well as persons captured and sold by their fellow-homelanders to middleman merchants who then transport them to some hostland for resale there as legally owned property.

• *Refugees* are migrants who leave their homeland involuntarily and are typically received involuntarily by their hosts.[8] They are less likely than invaders to use political force to overcome their hosts' resistance owing to the circumstances under which they leave their homeland and are more likely to be dependent on other, often honorific (that is, publicly moral), considerations to do so.

Note that although immigrants, invaders, slaves, and refugees have all played important roles in local, regional, and global consolidation processes so far, their proportions have varied widely from time to time and place to place. Indeed, apart from short-term shifts in such proportions as have been associated with wars, famines, plagues, genocides, and slave trades, it seems reasonable to hope that a permanent shift may now be afoot. In a word, the old predominance of invaders, slaves, and refugees may be giving way to a new predominance of immigrants. That is to say, the thousands of years during which slavery was a widespread, almost completely taken-for-granted, social phenomenon had nearly come to an end by 1900, and military invasions (and their massive contribution to the flow of refugees) seem likely to come to a permanent end in the next hundred years or so.

The persistently high number of refugees, however, is certainly cause for serious concern: "The world's refugee population . . . has [now] risen to 23 million people living outside their countries of origin. In 1989, the figure was 15 million. And as recently as the mid-seventies, only about 2.5 million people could claim refugee status—about the same number as in the fifties and sixties" (Kane 1995:133). If we are able to make the changes that will be discussed in chapter 6, however, this flood seems likely to dwindle down to only those persons displaced by whatever natural catastrophes remain beyond human ability to control.

Resources of Intergroup Competition

In any case, however, every group of migrants—whether invaders, slaves, refugees, or immigrants—brings some wealth, some power, some knowledge, and some honor with it to the hostland, and the quality, quantity, mobilization, and efficiency of these resources will go a long way toward determining the outcomes of the migrants' competitions with their hosts and with other migrants in that hostland. Such resources will vary with the success of the migrants' homeland in its prior competition with other homelands (including the migrants' hostland), and they will also vary according to the migrants' prior competitive success in their homeland.

This implies that what matters in hostland as well as homeland is not a group's absolute level of resources but its level relative to those of its competitors—and whether its resources fill empty slots in the hostland's (or the homeland's) society. Inbar and Adler cite two factors influencing the experiences of immigrants in a hostland: "One is the fit between the expectations that the newcomers harbor toward the host society, and the reality that they in fact encounter. The second is the fit between the educational-vocational background of the immigrants and the labor-market conditions that they actually experience in the new country" (1977: 128). Related to this question of "fit," migrants may move in response to their possession of one resource which they think will be adequate to assure success in the hostland but find that what they really need there is quite another resource. Thus, Blalock says "the migrant [often] moves to a city that contains relatives or close friends who can provide him with temporary aid and emotional security. . . . [but s/he may be] virtually unemployable owing to [her/his] poor education and lack of experience in urban occupations" (1967:182).

Wealth

With the exception of slaves, migrants of all types are likely to have moved at least partly to gain more material wealth than they expected to accumulate in their homelands. As a consequence, "the evolution of production, distribution and exchange over the last five centuries—with a tendency toward ever-greater integration of the world economy—has clearly been a major determinant of migrations" (Castles and Miller 1993:22, 23).

In the emerging world economy to which Castles and Miller refer, however, homelands are likely to vary widely in the kinds and amounts of their wealth and in the distribution thereof among their citizens. Bonacich suggests that "in general, the poorer the [home] economy of the [migrants], the less the [other] inducement needed for them to [migrate to] the new labor market. Crushing poverty may drive them to sell their labor relatively cheaply" (1972:549). Needless to say, such discounted sale can hardly fail to generate animosity among hostland workers whose livelihoods are thereby undercut.[9]

Note that population size is an important wealth, and power, resource that both hosts and migrants bring into play—as indicated by the twin adages that "Many hands make light work," and that "There is safety in numbers." So whenever it is claimed that a large group of migrants may "overrun" a hostland (or that it is at least difficult for the hostland to "assimilate" them), it is the aggregate wealth and power of such a group that is being referred to, even though its per capita wealth and power may be small. For example, the Haitian slave rebellion that began in 1791 succeeded largely because the African slaves initially outnumbered the French colonialists on the island eight-to-one and because a yellow fever epidemic further reduced the number of French soldiers stationed there.

Power

It almost goes without saying that the political resources (i.e., decision making, and decision enforcing, power) of migrants and hosts, and of nonmigrants still in the homeland, play important roles in determining the course of a migration and its subsequent migrant-host competition when the migrants are invaders, slaves, or refugees—and, for the most part, I shall not address these cases. The same importance, however, holds for political resources when the migrants are immigrants and this is the case on which the following discussion will focus.

We consider the hostland's political power, the homeland's political power, and finally the immigrants' own political power in the hostland.

Hostland Political Power. Castles and Miller claim "the [hostland] state almost invariably plays a major role in initiating, shaping and controlling [migration] movements. . . . Immigration as part of nation building has played a major role in new world countries such as the USA, Canada, Argentina, Brazil and Australia. State policies on refugees and asylum-seekers are major determinants of contemporary population movements," and then they note that "racism and discrimination are also to be found in all countries. . . . The main differences are to be found in state policies on immigration, settlement, citizenship and cultural pluralism" (1993:21–22, 196).[10]

Hostland governmental policies are powerful influences on immigrants' competitive success of failure: "In countries where permanent immigration is accepted and the settlers are granted secure residence status and most civil rights . . . immigrants are able to plan and build a future for themselves and their families, as part of the receiving society. Where the myth of short-term sojourn is maintained . . . the result is [immigrant] isolation, separatism and emphasis on difference" (Castles and Miller 1993:199, 201).

Homeland Political Power. "[A] strong homeland government can protect and help organize its emigrants. . . . Japan kept close watch over the fate of her nationals who migrated to Hawaii and the [U.S.] Pacific coast; and the British colonial government in India tried to guard against abuses [by other countries] of the indenture system" (Bonacich 1972:550). Thus, when hostility against Japanese immigrant agricultural competitors developed strength in California and that state led the drive to stop Japanese immigration, "because Japan was emerging as a major world power around the turn of the century— having defeated China in war in 1895 and Russia in 1905—the ending of Japanese immigration . . . could not be done in the same abrupt, unilateral, and contemptuous manner in which Chinese immigration had been stopped a generation earlier." Moreover, "the rising role of Japan on the world scene made it easy for [that nation's emigrants] to maintain their pride in being Japanese" (Sowell 1981:163, 164).

Homeland attitudes toward emigrants, however, vary: Pan says "When the Dutch sent the Manchu Emperor an apology for their massacre of Chinese in Batavia in 1740 . . . he is reported to have replied that he was 'little solicitous for the fate of unworthy subjects who, in the pursuit of lucre, had quitted their country and abandoned the tombs of their ancestors.'" (1994:22). Local sub-Saharan African chiefs were, with some exceptions, deeply complicit in the capture and sale into slavery of members of neighboring societies—and sometimes of their own societies (see Fage 1995:265–266)—and so were not at all disposed to protect those members once they had been sold. Even if those governments had become interested in such protection, however, they were insufficiently strong either economically, politically, scientifically-educationally-technologically, or honorifically to make much of a difference in this respect.

Immigrant Political Power in Their Hostland and in Their Homeland. Castles and Miller argue that "immigrants have fostered transnational politics linking homeland and host society political systems in fundamental ways. . . . As migratory movements mature. . . . [their concerns shift from] homeland politics to mobilisation around the interests of ethnic groups in the immigration country. If political participation is denied through refusal of citizenship and failure to provide channels of representation, immigrant politics is likely to take on militant forms" (1993:258–259).

No hostland has been impervious to such political influence. For example, though post-World War II German government policies tried to cling to the concept of temporary "guestworker," it proved impossible to maintain this limitation. "Competition with other labour-importing countries for labour led to relaxation of restrictions on entry of dependents in the 1960s. Families became established and children were born." In the end, "the guestworkers and their families could not be excluded from Western European democracies without grievous damage to the fabric of democracy" (Castles and Miller 1993:70, 252). As a result, "since the 1970s, immigrants have increasingly articulated [their] political concerns, participated in politics and sought representation. . . . Immigrant protest movements became part of the tapestry of Western European politics and frequently affected policies towards immigrants" (Castles and Miller 1993:237, 235).

In addition to their political influence in their hostland, immigrants can also have significant influence in their homeland. Thus, during the 1970s, the "principal political concern [of many immigrants to Western Europe] continued to be politics in their homelands. . . . Immigrant communities in Western Europe became the object of competition—occasionally violent—between pro-status quo and anti-status quo homeland political forces" (Castles and Miller 1993: 232–233).

It seems clear that both these political influences of immigrants—on their hostlands and on their homelands—are powerful forces tending toward the global political consolidation of our species.

Knowledge

In "knowledge" we have to consider the effects of migrants' and hosts' "pure" knowledge of the world at large, as well as their command of the "applied" or "practical" (including vocational) skills needed to manipulate that world, and we have also to recognize the interdependence in which the pure and the practical are bound together (see Wallace 1983:355–457; 1988: 23–28).

Although migrants (especially invaders) may possess greater general knowledge, hosts are almost certain to possess more knowledge of the hostland itself. Schermerhorn quotes Thompson regarding the role of American Indians' knowledge of their own territory: "'The planter [in the West Indies] resorted to the importation of outside [African] laborers not only because the native [Indian] population was numerically insufficient but . . . because it was difficult or even impossible to obtain a satisfactory degree of control over people who were at home in the local environment'" (1978:108–109).

Partly for the same reason and partly because the local chiefs would not permit it, European and Arab slave traders almost never traveled deeply into Africa to capture slaves on their own. Instead, they waited for native African slave-catchers to bring native African captives to holding pens on the trading coasts for wholesale purchase there (see Curtin et al. 1978:244–248; Davidson 1992:212–216; French 1994; Fage 1995:265–266). The same idea suggests that earlier immigrants from a given homeland to a given hostland are apt to "know their way around" in that hostland better than later immigrants from the same homeland, and this difference will feed oldtimer-versus-newcomer schisms within the group.

Perhaps the most far-reaching of all differences in knowledge is that between societies in which literacy and numeracy are well-developed and those in which they are substantially absent, because these two practical skills have so greatly increased pure knowledge of the world at large, and the latter, in turn, has revealed the possibility and potential usefulness of developing still more advanced literacy and mathematical, as well as other, practical skills—and so on, pure and practical, each now supporting, now leapfrogging, the other.

It seems especially significant, therefore, that the sub-Saharan Africans who were forcibly brought to the New World as slaves came mostly from homeland cultures in which literacy and sophisticated numeracy were—for reasons traceable to the territorial luck of the draw (discussed in chapter 3)—absent. Such migrants, then, came not only with personal illiteracy but cultural nonliteracy (the latter entailing unfamiliarity with the sometimes mystifying ways of literate people) to a hostland well-versed in skills of these kinds (see Schermerhorn 1978: 153). Jones, indeed, goes so far as to say "peoples . . . whose languages, and therefore whose cultural and traditional histories, are not written, are the *antithesis* of Western [i.e., European] man and his highly industrialized civilization" (1963:6, italics added; see also Stinchcombe 1965: 150; Ong 1982; Gaur 1992). And Mizrui says "There is a good case for the argument that Africa's crisis of documentary deficit [sic] had a good deal to do with the origins of racism. . . . Indeed, why did Europeans pick on Africans to enslave? . . . It was partly because most of Black Africa [had no] written records" (1986:77).

So it may be argued that their homeland cultures' widespread nonliteracy (despite the Arabic literacy that had been imported after the eighth century AD into some areas directly connected to the trans-Saharan trade—including Timbuktu and Mali generally) was the chief component of the "cultural reasons" that Jordan leaves unspecified when he says "for cultural reasons Negroes were relatively helpless in the face of European aggressiveness and technology" (1968:91). The same factors should come first in any reasonable answer to Jordan's question of "what was it about Indians and Negroes which set them apart, which rendered them different from Englishmen, which made them special candidates for degradation [by the latter]?" (1968:91).[11]

Of one thing we may be sure, however: If the luck of the territorial draw (discussed in chapter 3) had favored the Indians' and Negroes' (rather than the Englishmen's) rapid development of mathematics, scientific knowledge, technological expertise, literature, and the high degree of self-confidence and aggressiveness that almost always accompanies such development, then Englishmen would have been the ones set apart as special candidates for degradation by Indians and Negroes, rather than the other way around. In other words, the *actors* would have changed their roles but the *play* would have remained the same, and the play would have *gone on* no matter which actors filled its roles.

The general point I would make is this: Whatever any large population of Homo sapiens has done in its struggle to survive—whether one regards it as morally good or bad—any other similarly large population would almost surely have done, given a similar amount of time occupying a similar geographical territory. That interchangeability, indeed, is the heart of what it means to be a single species.

Honor

Individuals who share a common ethnicity, race, or nationality share, by definition, the same high estimation of each other's honor and the honor of their way of life relative to that of other communities. Weber emphasizes that "The sense of ethnic honor is . . . accessible to *anybody* who belongs to the subjectively believed community of descent" (1978:391, italics added)—which is to say, regardless of the other, personal, characteristics they may have. For this reason, migrants who share one or more ethnic, racial, and nationality identifications with their hosts will almost always find it easier to form coalitions with these hosts than will other migrants: "The more closely [a migrant group] corresponds in ethnicity, nationality, culture, and class to the existing [host] society, the less severe the identity problem [between migrants and hosts] is likely to be" (Daniels 1990:8; see also Wirth 1945:353). Chapter 5 will have more to say about this.

Moreover, it seems that if hosts honor a particular *homeland* from which migrants come—even when hosts and migrants do not share that homeland in common—that honor is apt to spill over into honor for the *migrants* themselves. This spillover is probably most influential on the fate of first-generation migrants, but it is likely to persist for several generations. For example, there can be little doubt that the strength of the African-American civil rights movement during the 1960s was partly due to the rise of African nations from colonial status and the resulting increment in the esteem in which African Americans were held by themselves and by others (see Fanon 1968:79–80; Carmichael 1970:244). The same may be expected of the impact, on their emigrants' honor in all hostlands of the probably forthcoming ascent of virtually all the Asian nations, and of South Africa, to the status of "developed" nations (see Naisbitt 1996).

DOMESTIC MIGRATION

Migrants, of course, having arrived in a given hostland, may continue to migrate *inside* that hostland. For example, after arriving in the United States, European immigrants typically migrated to areas where their grapevines led them to believe the resources they brought with them could bring good competitive rewards. Thus, the concentration of some central and eastern European peoples in the industrial Midwest and Northeast reflects developments of heavy industry . . . coupled with the minimal skills that many possessed at the time of arrival. . . . Similarly, Germans migrated . . . at a time when they were able to take advantage of the agricultural opportunities opening in the upper Midwest. . . . The pronounced early concentration of various Asian groups on the West Coast [also] reflects the ports of entry and the location of economic opportunities for them (Lieberson and Waters 1988:52).

Such domestic dispersion of ethnic groups in the United States has had lasting effects:

Germans and Scandinavian groups (Swedes, Norwegians, Finns, and Danes) are still located disproportionately in the Midwest; eastern and central European groups (Poles, Russians, Czechs, Hungarians, Austrians, Slavs, and Ukrainians) remain overrepresented in the Mid Atlantic and Midwest divisions; Italians and Greeks maintain their largest numbers in the Mid Atlantic. The largest Asian groups (Filipino, Chinese, and Japanese) remain concentrated on the Pacific Coast. The Latino groups remain most numerous in their divisions of initial settlement—Mexican Americans in the Southwest, Puerto Ricans in the Northeast, and Cubans in the Mid Atlantic and South Atlantic. (Lieberson and Waters 1988:65–66, 57, 60).

Nevertheless, despite the tendency of migrants and their descendants to remain where they first put down roots in the hostland, "Geographic concentration declines over time, perhaps with dispersion occurring through the generations" (Lieberson and Waters 1988:68) such that at least 59 percent of the German group now lives outside the Midwest, 31 percent of the Polish group now lives outside the Mid Atlantic and Midwest, 56 percent of Italians now live outside the Mid Atlantic, 48 percent of Chinese now live outside the Pacific Coast, 67 percent of Mexicans now live outside the Southwest—and so on (see Lieberson and Waters 1988:58–59).

The single largest migration to date inside the United States of an ethnic, racial, or nationality group has been that of African Americans moving out of the rural areas of the states of the former Confederacy—states in which their ancestors were, until about 130 years ago, legally held as slaves.

Domestic Migration of African-American Slave Descendants

More than 100 years after the end (in 1808) of the involuntary migration of Africans to the United States, and about 50 years after the abolition of legal slavery in the United States, there began the first large migration of African Americans that could be called voluntary.[12]

Conditions for the mass migration to the North were set by the outbreak of World War I, which resulted in the virtual cessation of European immigration to the United States. . . . In 1914 alone, more than one million immigrants arrived. But the following year, the number . . . declined to about one-third that number, in 1916 to about one-fourth, and by 1918, there were only 110,000 new arrivals to the United States. At the same time, almost 100,000 emigrated from the United States to return to their European homeland (Johnson and Campbell 1981:71–72).

"In response," Massey and Denton say,

employers began a spirited recruitment of blacks from the rural south. [This] coincided with [the arrival] of the Mexican boll weevil, which had devastated Louisiana's cotton crops in 1906 before moving on to Mississippi in 1913 and Alabama in 1916. The collapse of southern agriculture was aggravated by a series of disastrous floods in 1915 and 1916 and low cotton prices up to 1914. . . . Thus the demand for black tenant farmers and day laborers fell just when the need for unskilled workers in northern cities skyrocketed (1993:29).

The result was that "between 1910 and 1920, some 525,000 African Americans left the south . . . and during the 1920s the outflow reached 877,000" (Massey and Denton 1993:29). In all, between 1860 and 1910 the percentage of African Americans living in the South declined only slightly, from 92 to 89 percent; but between 1910 and 1940 it dropped to 77 percent, and then to 53 percent in 1970 (see Taeuber and Taeuber 1966:106–107; Jaynes and Williams 1989:270). Moreover, in 1910 only one-fourth of African Americans lived in cities, but by 1940 that proportion had risen to almost half, and by 1970, it stood at slightly more than four-fifths (see Taeuber and Taeuber 1966:116; Jaynes and Williams 1989:270).

European Americans Hosts Versus African American Migrants

Northern manufacturing employers eagerly formed employment coalitions with Black refugees from the South when the wage and other terms of long-established employment coalitions with White workers were challenged by the labor union movement:

Blacks were repeatedly employed [as strikebreakers] in northern labor disputes between 1890 and 1930: black strikebreakers were used seven times in New York between 1895 and 1916, and were employed in Cleveland in 1896, in Detroit in 1919, in Milwaukee in 1922, and in Chicago in 1904 and 1905. Poor rural blacks with little understanding of industrial conditions and no experience with unions were recruited in the south and transported directly to northern factories, often on special trains arranged by factory owners (Massey and Denton 1993:28).[13]

This newly emancipated, newly Northern, newly urban, but largely illiterate and nonliterate, and naively strikebreaking Black migrant population—whom striking White host workers could hardly be expected to welcome with open arms (see Wilson 1978:147)—was subjected to a variety of discriminations (centering on residential and job segregation) leading to the formation of a persistent Black urban lower class. But partly because the segregation was never airtight, partly because of new access to formal education and literacy-numeracy, and partly due to industrial union policies and governmental affirmative action policies, some African Americans were able to cross some of these discriminatory barriers.

Then, with the coming of World War II, the heightened demand that it generated for labor, and the end this brought to the Great Depression, a second voluntary migration began among African Americans. This was the migration of middle-class and some working-class African Americans (a "Black flight" that accompanied "White flight") away from center-city neighborhoods that have since become lower class African American urban ghettos (see Wilson 1987:7–8; Massey and Eggers 1990:1170–1171).[14]

Wilson terms the African Americans who now live in these ghettos "truly disadvantaged"—that is, "individuals who lack training and skills and either experience long-term unemployment or are not members of the labor force, individuals who are engaged in street crime and other forms of aberrant behavior, and families that experience long-term spells of poverty and/or welfare dependency." He argues that "many of the problems plaguing the truly disadvantaged minorities in American society can be alleviated by a [government program]. . . . to promote both economic growth and sustained full employment" (1987:8, 121).[15] Wilson, therefore, looks to government as arbitrator between the disproportionately Black lower class and the disproportionately White middle and upper class—an arbitration that he predicts would provide an environment of such deeply shared common cause and such abundance of resources for all Americans, regardless of race, that interracial competition would be minimized.[16]

To Carmichael and Hamilton, however, the relationship between White and Black Americans deserves to be called "colonialism" (1967:5). They imply, therefore, that the struggle against this colonialism is a potentially, and legitimately, violent war of national liberation like those which occurred in post-World War II colonial Africa. Thus: "a 'non-violent' approach to civil rights is an approach black people cannot afford and a luxury white people do not deserve" (1967:53). And in advocating a racially separatist movement that they see not as permanent but as preparatory to eventual integration, they argue that "Before a group can enter the open society, it must first close ranks. By this we mean that group solidarity is necessary before a group can operate effectively from a bargaining position of strength in a pluralistic society" (1967:44; see also Malcolm X 1966:376). With the achievement of that solidarity, Carmichael says, "integration ceases to be a one-way street. Then integration doesn't mean draining skills and energies from the ghetto into white neighborhoods; then it can mean white people moving from Beverly Hills into Watts, white people joining the Lowndes County Freedom organization [Black Panther Party]" (1970:241–242).[17]

Moskos and Butler combine elements of Wilson's proposal of government intervention ("Our linchpin proposal is to extend to civilian service the educational and job training benefits principle of the GI Bill" [1996:125]) with Carmichael and Hamilton's proposal of preparatory separation ("an 'away from home' experience, as traditionally accompanies military service, coupled with generous GI Bill benefits, dramatically improves the life chances of the youths who were most disadvantaged prior to entering the Armed forces. . . . Residential programs away from the participants' home area seem to be the most effective way to resocialize young people toward productive goals" [1996:135, 138]).

The next chapter describes the basic strategies that all ethnic, racial, and nationality groups use—after establishing the contact discussed in the present chapter—in competing with each other (whether as hosts or as migrants) for what chapter 3 has indicated are simultaneously the resources, products, and rewards of human life: wealth, power, knowledge, and honor.

NOTES

1. "Hosts" are defined here simply as people who are already present in the hostland when the "migrants" arrive (compare Lieberson's requirement that hosts be "indigenous" to the hostland; see 1961:903) This definition permits us to call "hosts" all people who have moved at some earlier date from the same point of origin, or from a different point of origin, as migrants. Hosts from the same point of origin play basically the same role as hosts who came from other places of origin. Thus, "Mexican immigrants were . . . viewed with repugnance by many Mexican Americans descended from families that had been in the United States longer—especially when those families were more acculturated, had higher incomes, and were lighter in skin color" (Sowell 1981:252). Similarly, "Not only whites withdrew from contact with [the African Americans who migrated out of the south between 1940 and 1970]; the older and more stable, settled, and financially secure black middle-class families tended to separate themselves from the newer arrivals socially and to lead an expansion of the ghetto into the surrounding white community" (Sowell 1981:211). Finally, "the eastern European Jews [who began arriving in the United States in great numbers in the 1880s] were an acute embarassment to the German Jews in America. . . . The Jewish press, controlled by German Jews, was openly critical of the new immigrants, whom they described as representing 'Oriental antiquity,' speaking a 'piggish jargon,' and 'slovenly in dress, loud in manners, and vulgar in discourse'" (Sowell 1981:252, 211, 80).

2. The principle here—namely, that of progress through intimate contact between diversities—has a long and distinguished pedigree. Hegel argues for the "dialectical process" as the origin of each individual's knowledge (1967:142–145); Marx and Engels argue for a "dialectical materialism" wherein "The history of all hitherto existing society is the history of class struggles . . . that each time ended, either in a revolutionary re-constitution of society at large, or in the common ruin of the contending classes" (1969, I:108–109); Mannheim argues for the intellectualizing results of contact, within the same individual's mind, of "forms of thought and experience which had

hitherto developed [in different individuals' minds] (1955:9); and Kuhn discusses the progressively revolutionizing results of contact between an established natural science paradigm and anomalous findings (1962).

3. As a result, even on the eve of World War II, Dower tells us, "[Southern Asia was] a place where a half million British ruled 350 million Indians, and another few score thousands of Englishmen ruled 6 million Malayans; where two hundred thousand Dutchmen governed a native population of 60 million in the East Indies; where twenty thousand Frenchmen controlled 23 million Indochinese, and a few tens of thousands of Americans ruled over 13 million Filipinos. Eight hundred thousand whites, the tally went, controlled 450 million Asians" (1986:24). Using data pertaining to the same period, Du Bois notes that Britain, the United States, Belgium, France, Italy, the Netherlands, Portugal, and Spain controlled colonial populations totalling 725,614,000 (1945:30).

4. After duly noting that "It is axiomatic that states decide which people to admit, how many, and from where," Weiner adds that that decision is not always easy to carry out: "Advanced industrial countries can protect their borders from invading armies but not from hordes of individuals who slip into harbors, crawl under barbed-wire fences, and wade across rivers. . . . [In addition, the] smuggling of migrants across boundaries has become an organized international business" (1995:9).

5. Kane adds that "about 2.5 million Mexicans live in the United States. Some 400,000 South Africans and Middle Easterners were living in Kuwait before the fled the war in 1991, and some 1.2 million foreign workers were in Saudi Arabia at the same time" (1995:143). Ahmed and Donnan tell us that "Muslim society . . . totals something like one billion people living in about 50 countries with significantly some ten to fifteen million living in the USA and Europe," and that "the bulk of Muslim migrant labor has settled abroad on a permanent basis. . . . Muslim doctors and engineers live as American or British citizens. Their children have no intention of going back to their place of origin" (1994:2, 5).

6. See Sowell 1996:1–2 for mention of all four types shown here. For discussion of factors entering into forming those attitudes, see Borjas 1989:461; Castles and Miller 1993:21–22. Lieberson's (1961) typology of migrants only takes into account relations (specifically, dominance relations "in the political, social, and economic spheres") between "indigenous" and "migrant" groups in the hostland. This ignores relations between each of these two groups and the migrants' homeland groups (i.e., non-migrants)—relations here represented by the voluntary-involuntary distinction. Schermerhorn proposes five types of migrations, ranging from high to low "on a continuum of coercive control exercised by the receiving or host society": Slave transfers, movements of forced labor, contract labor transfers, reception of displaced persons, and admission of voluntary immigrants (see 1978:98). The typology offered in the present essay takes into account the control exercised by the homeland as well as that of the hostland. It also regards contract laborers as a variety of immigrants, insofar as they voluntarily agree to the contract, and forced laborers as a variety of slaves, insofar as they do not voluntarily choose to migrate from their homelands.

7. Daniels reports that "as many as one in six of of the seventeenth-century migrants [to America] may have returned to England, either permanently or temporarily. If this is so, it involved some 3,500 persons who might be styled sojourners rather than settlers" (1990:51). Regarding tourists, Waters tells us that "[I]nternational tourism, measured by arrival from another country, expanded seventeen-fold between 1950 and 1990" and that "[T]he extent of globalized tourism indicates the extent to which tourists themselves conceptualize the world as a single place which is without internal geographical boundaries" (1995:154, 156).

8. The exceptions are refugees who perform some specially valuable role for the host group, either within the host group itself or in its relations with other groups. For example, Sowell says "With the rise of Hitler and Nazis in Germany in the 1930s. . . . one of the largest transfers of intellectual talent from one nation to another in human history [began]. The transfer of Einstein alone was historic, for it made the United States the first nation to achieve nuclear power" (1981:67)—which is to say, Einstein brought an especially valuable addition to this nation's knowledge resources and for this, not for himself alone, he was welcomed with open arms. The term "refugees" here include "political refugees . . . who are forced to flee because they are being persecuted by those who control the governments in their own countries. . . . politico-economic refugees, [who are] victims of economic crises aggravated by political circumstances. . . . [and] refugees created as a direct result of an economic crisis" (Chonchol 1989:2; for discussion of the definition based solely on ethnic, racial, nationality, and political persecution established in 1951 by the United Nations Convention on Refugees, see Kane 1995: 133–134). Regarding Jewish refugees during the Holocaust, and Irish refugees during the potato famine, see Sowell 1981:21. Certainly, American Indians qualify as having been forced to flee their homelands by European American (aided by African American "Buffalo soldiers") attacks; and Rwanda presents a case of persons forced to flee their homeland by privately organized attacks on the ethnic groups to which they belong: "On April 29 [1994] more than a quarter of a million Rwandan refugees poured across the corpse-laden Kagera River into Tanzania during a twenty-five hour period, making it the largest short-term refugee migration in world history. Tens of thousands more made their way into Zaire, Uganda, and Burundi" (Garrett 1994:593). Joly and Cohen point out that whereas Europe had for many centuries been the world's largest refugee-producing center, for reasons too numerous to mention here (but in which all the industrialized nations of the world were in some way implicated) by the late 1960s "refugees were being engendered everywhere, not least in the third world" (1989:5). By the 1970s "a new phenomenon emerged. Refugees from the crisis areas of Africa, Asia and Latin America began to move in increasing numbers to the industrialized countries . . . the arrival of many refugees from geographically and culturally distant areas constituted an unprecedented challenge to the legal machinery and conscience of the receiving countries" (Independent Commission on International Humanitarian Issues; quoted in Joly and Cohen 1989:6). "The special character of post-1970 refugees has led to the expression 'new refugees', who are . . . 'culturally and ethnically different from their hosts; they come from less-developed countries, at a different stage of development from that of the host, and they are likely to lack kin and potential support groups in their

country of resettlement'" (Joly and Cohen 1989:6). Regarding the reluctant reception of Jewish refugees from Nazi Germany, Dippel says "immigration barriers . . . were hastily erected all over the world to keep unwanted refugees out. Jews who desperately wanted to leave had no place to go, no welcoming haven" (1996:xxii). And referring to refugees of later times, Joly and Cohen say "European governments are reluctant hosts, barely fulfilling their international obligations and barely recognizing the humanitarian values that purportedly underlie their own democratic institutions" (1989:11).

9. Many migrants, of course, move not only to increase their own personal wealth but that of (usually kin-related) non-migrants in their homelands. Indeed, "the foreign workers of the world]. . . . are believed to remit over $67 billion annually to their homelands. If accurate, this figure would place labour second only to oil in world trade" (Castles and Miller 1993:4–5; see also Kane 1995:143; Sowell 1996:21–22). Obviously, such remittances mean the migrants themselves have less wealth with which to continue their competition in the hostland.

10. See also Castles and Miller's discussions of "classical countries of immigration" (the USA, Canada, and Australia), "intermediate" countries (France, the Netherlands, Britain), and "countries which have tried to cling to rigid 'guestworker' models" (Germany and Switzerland) (1993:26, 196–199).

11. Jordan's own answer to this question is that "it was the Negro's blackness which proved his most important characteristic," adding that "If his appearance, his racial characteristics, meant nothing to the English settlers, it is difficult to see how slavery based on race ever emerged, how the concept of complexion as the mark of slavery ever entered the colonists' minds" (1968:257, 97). Carmichael expresses a similar view: "We are oppressed because we are *black*" (1970:243, italics added). In my view, Schermerhorn is very much closer to the mark: "European . . . dominants fastened on color as a *symbol* of both status and cultural difference" (1978:73, italics added), thereby implying that had the latter difference (especially its technological aspects) favored sub-Saharan Africans—as it would have, if the luck of the territorial draw had gone their way—then the "White Over Black" status symbolism would have been reversed to "Black Over White."

12. Jones identifies this volition as follows: "It was a *decision* Negroes made to leave the South, not an historical imperative. And this decision must have been preceded by some kind of psychological shift; a reinterpretation by the Negro of his role in this country" (1963:96)—i.e., a role that now included freedom of movement, something strictly denied to slaves.

13. Bonacich points out that sojourners, of whatever ethnicity, race, or nationality, are also liable to strikebreaking. They "are more willing [than permanent settlers] to put up with undesirable work conditions since these need not be endured forever," and they "avoid involvement in lengthy labor disputes. . . . They may be willing to undercut wage standards if need be to get a job, and are therefore ripe candidates for strikebreaking" (Bonacich 1972:550–551). Spence notes that "there were occasions when employers used the Chinese [immigants] as strikebreakers. Knowing little or no English, the Chinese were often ignorant of the social and economic battles into which they had been projected" (1990:213).

14. The income bifurcation implied here is growing larger—not only among Blacks, but Whites as well (for discussion of the different consequences, traceable to racial housing segregation, for the low-income Blacks and for their counterparts among Whites, see Massey and Denton 1993:150–153): In 1970, 26.7 percent of Black households had incomes under $10,000; in 1994, 26.3 percent remained in this category. In 1970, 2.0 percent of Black households had incomes of $75,000 or more; in 1994, 6.3 percent had such incomes. Comparable figures for White households are 13.3, 11.7, 7.4, and 14.7 (U. S. Bureau of the Census 1996:461).

15. Wilson argues that four changes are responsible for the plight of the truly disadvantaged, one of which is "the exodus of [Black] middle- and working-class families from many ghetto neighborhoods" (1987:56), and Crane's (1991) data suggest that the tipping point came when the percent professional and managerial workers living in those neighborhoods dropped below 4 percent. In addition, Nightingale (1993) argues that their "aberrant behavior" is not the independent creation of these non-migrants, but reflects many features of the general American culture as portrayed in the mass media to which they have ready access.

16. Axelrod says "one of the primary functions of government [is] to make sure that when individuals do not have private incentives to cooperate, they will be required to do the socially useful thing anyway. . . . No one wants to pay taxes because the benefits are so diffuse and the costs are so direct. . . . [But if] you avoid paying your taxes, you must face the possibility of being caught and sent to jail. This prospect makes [non-cooperation] less attractive" (1984:133).

17. Steele argues against the preparatory collective secession advocated by Carmichael and Hamilton. The truth, Steele says, is that "racial development will always be the [result of] *individuals* within the race bettering their own [individual] lives" (1990:158, italics added). Steele also tells us that "my middle-class identity involved a dissociation from images of lower-class black life. . . . Yet I ended the sixties in graduate school a little embarrassed by my class background and with an almost desperate need to be 'black'" (1990:98, 99). Grier and Cobbs (1968; see also Sowell 1981:120, 280; Blalock 1982:109) describe some of the feelings of guilt and divided loyalty that may accompany the class-selective out-migration to which Steele refers, and Goodman (1984) reports on similar guilt feelings on the part of American Jews—migrants who felt they did not do as much to save homeland non-migrant Jews from the Holocaust as they could have done.

5

COMPETITION STRATEGIES

Suppose, then, that one group of migrants, including any combination of the types shown in Figure 4.1, enters another group's homeland, thereby establishing contact between populations that were formerly separated. The question arises: What kinds of *strategies* are open to both hosts and migrants in their competition to win wealth, power, knowledge, and honor?[1]

The first point to be made here is that complete strategies are almost always extremely complex and changeful as each side constantly adjusts to changes in the general situation and to its opponent's most recent move. But the second point is that there seems to be a limited number of simple elements that go into composing those complete strategies (in the same way that only a few simple types of moves go into constructing complete chess strategies). This chapter will focus on these universal elements of competition strategies—even though I shall call them here simply "strategies."

It is also important to fix in mind that all the (elements of) strategies to be discussed here may be used by *both* sides in an intergroup competition, that is to say, by *both* migrants and hosts, in the same way that both white and black pieces in a chess game are limited to the identical set of basic moves. Here are three quick examples of this identity: First, although community segregation is usually thought of as a strategy used by hosts against migrants, Blalock points out that

for groups that have become minorities as a result of conquest, segregation is a means of self-preservation and a mechanism for maintaining a previously successful way of life. It also facilitates the socialization of younger generations and inhibits them from migrating to urban areas where their minority identification would become diluted. . . . Segregation also provides important psychic protections for members of both the dominant and minority groups (1982:91, 97; see also Steele 1990:48–55; Portes and Rumbaut 1996: 53–56; Sowell 1996:5–9).

Second, Dower notes that both sides in the Pacific theater of World War II used the same strategy of stereotyping: "An Imperial [Japanese] Army document from the summer of 1942 . . . divided the nationalities of Asia into 'master races,' 'friendly races,' and 'guest races,' reserving the position of undisputed leadership for the 'Yamato [Japanese] race'", while, for their part, "the Western Allies . . . persisted in their notion of the 'subhuman' nature of the Japanese, routinely turning to images of apes and vermin to convey this" (1986:8, 9). Third, Ogbu argues that the "oppositional" culture of high school students who are descendants of slaves makes "crossing cultural boundaries and engaging in cross-cultural learning . . . problematic" (1991:16; see also Steele 1990)[2] —and one could add that the matching oppositional culture of descendants of slave-masters makes crossing the boundaries problematic too.

　　　　Armed with this analytically simplifying symmetry between the strategies available to both hosts and migrants, we then find a further simplification: the strategies themselves fall into only three types:

　　● Strategies used by the ingroup (whether migrant or host) to influence the things its own, and the outgroups', members mentally think and feel. These will be called *cultural structural strategies.*[3]

　　● Strategies used by the ingroup to influence the things its own, and the outgroups', members physically do. These will be called *social structural strategies.*

　　● Strategies used by the ingroup to form, refuse, broker, or break up cultural structural and social structural alliances between itself and outgroups, and among the latter. These will be called *coalitional strategies.*

　　　　Note that migration itself exemplifies the complex character of what were referred to above as complete strategies. That is, migration can be counted on to change the things a group's members (and outgroup members) think and feel, and the things they physically do, and, especially, to change the coalitions in which groups in both the homeland and the hostland participate—and this holds whether the migration is voluntarily or involuntarily made.

　　　　The rest of this chapter examines the three types of strategies, in the order just given.

CULTURAL STRUCTURAL STRATEGIES

　　　　The core of any group's cultural structure is its norms, which are learned, shared, psychological states that (in the case of intergroup relations) constitute answers to the following questions: (1) Who *are* we and who are they? In other words, How should members of the ingroup, and members of the outgroup be *described*? (2) What moral, aesthetic, and practical *value* should be attached to members of the ingroup, and to members of the outgroup? (3) How should one *behave* toward members of the ingroup and toward members of the outgroup?[4] When the answers to these questions are crafted specifically as weapons for use by a particular group in its competition with one or more other groups, they are often called "stereotypes," "prejudices," and "discriminatory tendencies," respectively.

Stereotypes, Prejudices, and Dispositions to Discriminate

The descriptive weapons called "stereotypes" have at least two features that set them apart from scientific descriptions (the latter defined as descriptions made and collectively agreed-to by observers who are "disinterested," in the sense that they consciously strive to withhold their personal favor from either of the competing groups and let the chips, the data, fall where they may). First, stereotypes claim that the outgroup is more homogeneous than the ingroup ("They are all alike").[5] Second, stereotypes assign more weight to the role of internal, dispositional, factors (especially inborn internal factors—see Ross 1977:184; 193–196) in accounting for outgroup members' behavior than ingroup members' behavior ("They do the things they do because that is just the way they are; they can never change").[6] Both these characteristics of stereotypic descriptions encourage ingroup members to deal with outgroup members as faceless, featureless, "invisible," entities with whom they are forbidden to identify, while addressing ingroup members with sensitive awareness of their complexity as individual personalities just like themselves.[7]

In applying the evaluative weapons called "prejudices," the ingroup judges (prejudges) the outgroup as being of low moral, low instrumental, and low ethical and aesthetic value, and judges itself as being of high value in all these respects (see Dower 1986:28).[8] In this way, prejudices—which are readily extended beyond the natural attributes of the ingroup to presumptions that supernatural, divine, forces support it—automatically endow ingroup members with confidence in their personal deservedness of victory over all members of the outgroup.

Finally, the behavioral disposition weapon called a "discriminatory tendency" calls upon ingroup members to behave toward outgroup members in ways they would not apply to members of their own group under the same circumstances. For example, an ingroup member may become disposed to respond automatically with vigorous help on hearing cries of distress from fellow ingroup members but to respond, no less automatically, with deafened ears and turned back to cries of distress from outgroup members.

Note that stereotypes, prejudices, and discrimination-dispositions are not all-or-nothing propositions; a given ingroup norm may be more, or less, stereotypic in its descriptions; more, or less, prejudicial in its valuations; more, or less, discriminatory in its behavior dispositions. Moreover, each of these components is also subject to change—sometimes dramatically—as Ross and Nisbett indicate when reporting that as recently as 1840 a mayor of Boston claimed Irish Americans were "a race [sic] that will *never* be infused into our own, but on the contrary will *always* remain distinct and hostile"; and that

"Early observers of Japan concluded that the country would *never* have any wealth. . . . [because] the Japanese were too indolent and pleasure-loving ever to have a productive economy" (1991:193–194, 199; italics added).

The extent to which normative descriptions, valuations, and behavior dispositions change toward becoming less extremely stereotypic, prejudiced, and discriminatory between groups is therefore a good indicator of the extent to which the groups in question are consolidating into a single group. It will be important, then, to inquire into the circumstances in which such changes occur, and we shall do that shortly.

Ethnocentrism, Racism, and Nationalism

Before that, however, it is essential to note that one norm in particular —complete with automatically stereotypic descriptions, prejudiced valuations, and discriminatory behavior dispositions—arises almost instantly on both sides when ethnic, racial, and nationality groups make their first contact. This norm is, therefore, a condition with which migrants and hosts alike must cope; it is called *ethnocentrism* and its more specific manifestations in their respective spheres are *racism*, and *nationalism* (including Eurocentrism, Afrocentrism, and Asiacentrism—and including American and all other patriotisms). Stephan and Rosenfield tell us ethnocentrism is "universal among ethnic groups around the world" (1982:104); Castles and Miller say "racism and discrimination are . . . found in all countries" (1993:196); and in studies asking respondents to list minority groups in order of their preference it was found that "each minority rates itself at or near the top in terms of preferred contacts" (Blalock 1982:96; see also Bauman 1990:143–145).[9]

Ethnocentrism (again, including racism and nationalism) is the socially learned, shared, mental tendency to think, feel, and behave as though one's own ethnic, racial, and/or nationality group were the absolute center of the universe, while all others were, in varying degrees, peripheral and inferior. Note that, in referring to "The conviction of the excellence of one's own customs and the inferiority of alien ones, a conviction which sustains the sense of ethnic honor" (1978:391), Weber reminds us that ethnocentrism goes beyond mere xenophobia—that is, *fear* of the strange—to claim *superiority* over the strange.

Ethnocentric Descriptions and Their Transformation

Descriptions (variable, as previously indicated, in their degree of stereotypy) that contrast people in the ingroup with people in the outgroup attempt to draw sharp lines in the sand: We of the ingroup look, behave, and think like *this* and therefore we belong together; the others do not look, behave, and think like us and therefore they do not belong with us. Conversely, people who belong to a given outgroup are like *that*; we are *not* like that, therefore we do not belong with them.

Moreover, to the extent that such descriptions specify how ingroup and outgroup individuals not only *do* look, behave, and think, but how they *will* look, behave, and think, the descriptions serve as predictions (see Jones 1990:77–111; and Stephan and Rosenfield 1982:97) that give ingroup members time to prepare for future interactions with members of each group before they occur. But it should be clear that the ingroup's descriptions of the outgroup can confer this predictive advantage only to the extent that they are accurate, but they may *not* be accurate—partly because they may be based on faulty sampling or faulty observations, partly because they may be out of date, and partly because some descriptions of outgroups are *deliberately designed* to be inaccurate. The following discussion considers the latter case more closely.

The Two Audiences of Intergroup Descriptions. In any given competition, the ingroup's descriptions of a given outgroup are called upon to perform different functions depending on their intended audience. One audience is the outgroup about which the descriptions are made; the other audience is the ingroup that makes them. For consumption by the ingroup, accuracy is highly desirable (one wants to know one's enemy in order to anticipate the things that enemy will do, and prepare defenses and counterattacks in advance), but for outgroup consumption, accuracy is beside the point; here, the ingroup only wants its descriptions, of itself and of the outgroup, to so deeply undermine the outgroup's self-confidence that it simply gives up without a struggle.

The ingroup's descriptions of the outgroup, then, face the ingroup—where they are chiefly informational—and they also face the outgroup—where they are chiefly propagandistic.

As a result, the ingroup may try to beam one description of the outgroup to the outgroup audience as demoralizing propaganda and keep another description of the same outgroup strictly inside the ingroup as valuable information. However, with increasing intergroup contact, the proliferation of multilingual people, and the advent of modern mass communications, audience separation of this sort becomes difficult. The result is that, one way or the other, descriptions of a given outgroup tend to become *either* informational *or* propagandistic. The following are some important considerations in determining which way such descriptions go.

The obvious is often a good place to start: some competitors of a given individual in the ingroup belong to outgroups. But not all of an individual's competitors are members of outgroups; many, even most, of them belong to the individual's own ingroup. In fact, because the ingroup competitors employ basically the same resources and strategies as the individual her/himself, these competitors may be even more dangerous than outgroup competitors. Indeed, it was for this reason that Darwin argued that the struggle for survival is carried on chiefly between members of the *same* species (see 1968:127; see also Durkheim 1984:208–209), and modern sociologists have agreed with this principle: Blalock says, "One would expect the greatest perceived competition among *near-equals*. The greater the average gap between the dominant and minority groups, the less is the perceived threat to the former group" (1967:148, italics changed); Hannan and Freeman say, "Organizations will compete most intensely with *similar* size organizations" (1977:245, italics added); Gamson, in a coalition experiment in which members of college fraternities were subjects, found that "some players preferred to take their chances with a stranger rather than to bargain with a 'difficult' fraternity brother" (1961b:568).

From the standpoint of a given individual, then, the competitive success of his/her ingroup over other groups represents only a first cut in the field of competitors. That first cut, of course, can make a huge difference in the average levels of wealth, power, knowledge, and honor that the individual takes home (see Blalock 1982:49). But *after* that first cut, people in the ingroup turn toward competition with each other, and in this competition among members of the same ingroup, who are seeking the same positions and have access to the same resources and strategies, each individual strives to collect as much *accurate* information as possible. Accordingly, Jones tells us "people use [broadly generalizing] classifications when dealing with actions of an outgroup member, whereas they characterize ingroup members acting in the same way [as that outgroup member] with a more differentiated schema," and suggests that "the in-group label is not very salient when we are looking at other in-group members. Relatively speaking, other [more detailed] labels become salient and are remembered better" (1990:103).

So it seems fair to conclude that the more a given individual thinks of other individuals as being so far *beneath* her/himself in wealth, power, knowledge, and/or honor as to present no conceivable competitive threat, the less s/he will be concerned with collecting accurate information about those individuals and the more propagandistic her/his descriptions of them will be. Similarly: the more a given individual thinks of other individuals as being so far *above* her/himself as to be in a different league entirely, the less s/he will be concerned with collecting accurate information about them and the more propagandistic her/his descriptions of them will be.

Typically, only when an individual starts to look upon other individuals as neither gnats nor giants but as *equals*, which is to say, as presenting strong (but not too strong) competitive threats, will their descriptions take on an increasingly informational function and leave the propagandistic function behind. Not only that, but the increase in informational function is a forerunner of coalition-formation among the individuals concerned—a crucial point to which I shall return shortly.

Meantime, two further points: First, it is worth emphasizing that competitive threats between groups may be made not only with respect to wealth, power, and knowledge, but also with respect to *honor*. This is especially true in the post-Hitlerian, post-colonial, and post-South African democratization era, when every group's honor is judged by universalistically humanitarian criteria more than ever before, and when that judgment is determined in a more globally communicative and interactive arena than ever before. Thus, Jaynes and Williams argue that "it was black claims on the public conscience made visible by disruptive public activism that forced national attention on civil rights" (and note that "conscience" is activated when one's *honor*—in one's own eyes, in other people's eyes, or in the eyes of a believed-in divine awareness—is thought to be in danger). They then point out "a striking correlation between the degree of [civil rights] movement activity and Gallup Poll figures on the proportion of the public identifying civil rights as the 'most important problem facing the country.' Both [sets of data] reach their peaks during the most intense period of movement activity from 1963 to 1965, which coincided with the adoption of the Civil Rights Act (1964) and the Voting Rights Act (1965)" (1989:223).

The second and related point is that the threat of *violence* by an otherwise weak opponent, especially in a world that is gradually growing appreciative of non-violence and the concepts of universal human rights and democracy, can threaten a strong opponent that responds violently to that threat with dishonor and some consequent loss in that opponent's other resources as well. For this reason, Fanon argues that "the violence of the native is only hopeless when we compare it in the abstract to the military machine of the oppressor. On the other hand, if we situate that violence in the dynamics of the international situation, we see at once that it constitutes a terrible menace for the oppressor" (1968:79).

Valuations Constrain Descriptions and Behavior Dispositions

Now if the way the ingroup describes the outgroup depends on the degree to which they are equals, and if we ask why such equality should be a factor, the answer immediately implicates the ingroup's perceived self-interest—that is, the almost invariably high degree to which all groups value triumphing over other groups.[10] Merton asks "Did Lincoln work far into the night? This testifies that he was industrious, resolute, perseverant, and eager to realize his capacities to the full. Do the outgroup Jews or Japanese keep these same hours? This only bears witness to their sweatshop mentality, their ruthless undercutting of American standards, their unfair competitive practices" (1957:429, 428). What explains this difference? Not sheer meanness or perversity, for in zero-sum games (whatever one side wins, the other side loses; see Hannan and Freeman 1977:940), it makes complete sense for the ingroup to describe a given winning behavior in positive terms when it appears among its *own* members. But when the very same behavior appears among the *out-group* members, it makes sense for the ingroup to describe it in negative terms because it entails ingroup loss rather than gain.

Behavior dispositions, too, are heavily constrained by valuations. For example, Staub says, "devaluation makes mistreatment likely. In one experiment each participant was asked to be a teacher and administer shocks to a learner who made mistakes on a task. When teachers 'overheard' a conversation in which the learner was described as one of a rotten bunch of people, they administered much stronger electric shocks. Learners described positively received the weakest shocks" (1989:60–61).

Valuations, then, strongly influence (one says they *bias*) both descriptions and behavior dispositions. In particular, the high valuation that every group understandably assigns to its own triumph over other groups is what accounts for the ubiquity, on *all* sides, of ethnocentrism—including racism and nationalism.

At this point, it is essential to emphasize that the behavior dispositions discussed so far (as elements of cultural structural strategies of intergroup competition) are not the same as the actual behaviors to which such dispositions dispose. The dispositions are mental readinesses (technically, they are called conations) to act in a certain way toward something. For example, members of one group may be taught a disposition or readiness to shake hands when greeting someone; members of another group may be taught a disposition to bow when expressing the same greeting. The behaviors, however, are the physical acts toward that something—the actual hand-shaking or the actual bowing.[11]

This leads to an important point: The presence of a given mental disposition to behave in a particular way does not guarantee that the actual physical behavior itself will occur. Any number of other factors, acting on the individual from inside or outside, may deflect or prevent that occurrence: a prisoner may be mentally *disposed* to escape but prevented from *actually* escaping by the bars on the prison's doors and windows. Nor does the occurrence of a given physical behavior guarantee that a particular behavior disposition was responsible for it, because any given behavior may have several alternative causes including the possibility that it may have so many small causes as to be considered "accidental" (see the discussion of equifinality in note 10 of chapter 1).

It follows that, as Merton puts it, "attitudes and overt behavior *vary independently*. Prejudicial attitudes need not coincide with discriminatory behavior" (1976:192, italics changed)—and Merton might easily have added the converse, namely, that discriminatory behavior need not coincide with normative dispositions to behave in that way. The separation of physical behavior from mental norm is essential because, for example, one may discriminate in one's actual physical behavior *without intending to*—that is, without being racist, nationalistic, or ethnocentric in one's mind; and one may be racist, nationalistic, or ethnocentric in one's mind *without it coming out* in actual physical behavior (see Merton 1976:192–199; compare Carmichael and Hamilton 1967:4–5).[12]

Obviously, then, what we have to do next in this chapter (and as promised above) is consider strategies of intergroup competition that directly influence the things members of the groups involved *do, physically*—whether these behaviors are called for by mental behavior dispositions, or not.

SOCIAL STRUCTURAL STRATEGIES

Where migrants move into an area that is already occupied by other humans (hosts), they are sure to find some cultural structural and social structural conditions already well-established there. In particular, some hosts are likely to have already accumulated disproportionately large shares of wealth, power, knowledge, and/or honor, while others will have accumulated small shares of these resources.

In addition, and of great importance, various coalitions are likely to be already established both between and within these different groups of hosts. For example, there may be some well-established officer-and-soldier coalitions called "armies" and "police forces"; some employer-and-employee coalitions called "employment" and "businesses"; some employer-and-employer coalitions called "partnerships," "corporations," or "cartels"; some employee-and-employee coalitions called "labor unions"; some government officeholder-and-voter coalitions called "political parties"; some priest-and-worshipper coalitions called "churches," "mosques," "temples," "shrines"; some scientist-and-assistant and teacher-and-student coalitions called "schools" and "departments," "apprenticeships" and "laboratories."

Such pre-established hostland factors generate, for migrants, what Hannan and Freeman (following Stinchcombe 1965:148) call "the liability of newness"—when "new [migrants] attempt to enter niches that have already been filled by [hosts who] have amassed social, economic, and political resources that make them difficut to dislodge" (1977:959).[13]

Partly as a consequence of differences in the extent to which their respective positions in the hostland society are both satisfactory and well established, different host groups are likely to behave differently toward the migrants. Consider the likely behavior of host employers and host employees. In pursuing the formation of coalitions between themselves and "as cheap and docile a labor force as possible" when hostland "labor costs are too high (owing to such price determinants as unions), employers may turn to cheaper sources" (Bonacich 1972:553; see also Wilson 1978:7, 13; Castles and Miller 1982:173). Such sources may include slaves and immigrants from other countries that have lower levels of living than the host employees. When this happens, the host employees have two basic types of social structural strategies for defending themsleves against an imminent loss in their levels of living.[14]

Both types of strategies are exclusionist. One type *totally* excludes the outgroup from the ingroup's wealth, power, knowledge, and honor markets; the other type *partially* excludes them.

Total Exclusion

Total exclusion involves militarily exterminating invaders, or setting up and enforcing legal barriers to outlaw a slave trade, or to bar refugees or immigrants.[15] These are examples of the total exclusion of migrants by hosts, but the total exclusion of hosts by migrants is not uncommon. For example, Gordon says "Probably the German migration to the American Midwest and to Texas in the 1830s, 40s, and 50s . . . was possessed of the greatest degree of national self-consciousness, and some of [its] leaders surely looked forward to the creation of an all-German state within the union . . . [or] to the eventual formation of a separate German nation." Similarly, "in the urban centers of the Northeast, the Irish, segregated in the slums and cut off occupationally and culturally from their Anglo-Saxon neighbors, developed a distinct group consciousness and a separate institutional life" (1964:132, 134–135).

Genocide. The most permanent, and the most ancient, of all total exclusion strategies is, of course, to exterminate the outgroup. The United Nations Genocide Convention (signed December 9, 1948) defines genocide as "'acts committed with intent to destroy in whole or in part, a national, ethnical, racial or religious group by killing members of the group, causing them serious bodily or mental harm, creating conditions calculated to bring about their physical destruction, preventing births, or forcibly transferring children to another group'" (Staub 1989:8).

Although it has been much in the news of Rwanda and the former Yugoslavia in recent years, genocide is a practice that almost certainly originated in prehistoric times. For one not prehistoric but nevertheless ancient example, Mazian cites Deut. 3:1–7, as follows: "'Og the King of Bashan came against us, he and all his people . . . and we smote him until none was left to him remaining. And we took all his cities at that time . . . and we utterly destroyed them . . . with the women and the little ones. But all the cattle, and the spoil of the cities, we took for a prey unto ourselves'" (1990:xi). Indeed, whenever the perpetrating group has sought not more human population but more land or some other nonhuman form of wealth, exterminating the people currently in possession of that wealth has been the strategy of choice.

Groups that have practiced genocide in modern times have been many: "[In] a short span of seventy-three years the British successfully eliminated the native population [of Tasmania]"; "the Dutch, upon settling the Cape of Good Hope, were bent upon exterminating the native Blacks. Bushmen and wild animals were considered 'dangerous vermin' to be shot on sight"; "the Portuguese in Brazil were determined to exterminate those Indians who resisted Portuguese settlement, frequently planting clothes taken from people who had recently died from smallpox in Indian villages"; "in American history, the 'Trail of Tears' depicts the ravaging effects of [deportation as a] method of extermination upon the Cherokee, Choctaw, Seminole, and others" (Mazian 1990:xi–xii). Dower says of the conflict between Japan and the Anglo-American powers that "war words and race words came together in a manner which . . . [reinforced] the impression of a . . . struggle between completely incompatible antagonists. The natural response to such a vision was an obsession with extermination on both sides" (1986:11). And Staub notes that "the word [Holocaust] refers to the extermination of about six million Jews by Nazi Germany from June 1941 to 1945."

However, Staub also tells us *five million non-Jews* were killed in the same extermination, including, he says, "political opponents; mentally ill, retarded, and other 'genetically inferior' Germans, Poles, and Russians. Gypsies, like Jews, were to be eliminated; more than 200,000 were killed, probably many more" (1989:9). These facts point up, first, the Holocaust's direct bearing on *many* ethnic, racial, and nationality groups—*non*-Jews as well as Jews (the Nazis intended it to bear, ultimately, on *all* "non-Aryan" groups)—*everywhere* in the world. Second, they therefore mark any limiting of the term "Holocaust" to its significance for only one such group (as Staub himself does; see also Jick 1993) as an instance of the competitive strategy to which we turn next.

Partial Exclusion

This less radical subtype of exclusionist strategy aims at partitioning one or more of the markets in the host society (for wealth, power, knowledge, and honor) into two or more differentially advantaged submarkets—and excluding the outgroup (whether migrants or hosts) from the more advantaged submarkets.

Again, host initiation of such partitioning is probably the more familiar phenomenon, but Nagel and Olzak point out that "organized [migrant] ethnic groups themselves can attempt to corner job or commodity markets for purposes of economic advancement" (1982:130), and Sowell says "The Chinese reaction to pervasive discrimination was withdrawal and inconspicuousness, much like the European Jews in the ghetto or the Pale. Chinatowns developed their own community organizations and leaders to conduct their own internal affairs with an absolute minimum of recourse to the institutions of the larger society around them" (1981:139).

Market-Segmenting. Markets may be partitioned in two directions: vertical and horizontal. When the partitioning is vertical, with the different parts stacked on top of one another from low rank to high rank, we have a "segmented" or segregated market, and we refer to "glass ceilings" (and "glass floors") if people in one segment can see and compare their lot with people in other parts. The essence of a segmented labor market is that members of the migrant and host groups are prohibited from doing the same kinds of work. As a result, migrants and hosts who participate in such a market have access to different opportunities to generate given kinds and amounts of wealth, power, knowledge, and honor.[16]

For example, Davidson says "In 1584 the king of Spain passed to his vice-regal council in Mexico an order that 'the Indians, a weak people, be left to their own business, and that the labor of the mines, construction, fields and mills be undertaken by mulattoes, negroes, and mestizos'. And so it was" (1980:120). Castles and Miller report a more recent "pattern of immigrant labour market segmentation [in Australia]," such that

(1) men born in Australia or in English-speaking background countries and other male immigrants from Northern Europe . . . were disproportionately found in white-collar, highly skilled or supervisory jobs; (2) men from non-English speaking background countries . . . were highly concentrated in manual manufacturing jobs; (3) Australian and English speaking background women, disproportionately in sales and services; and (4) non-English speaking background women . . . tended to get the worst jobs with the poorest conditions (1982:177–178; see also 188).[17]

Alba and Moore's study of data, collected in 1971–1972, on "ethnically different paths into the [American] elite" describes another instance of market segmenting: "White Protestants numerically dominate the important business and Congressional sectors . . . [while there is a] concentration of Irish Catholics in the labor sector, where their presence is nearly ten times as common as in the U.S. population. Another is the large proportion of Jews in the mass media sector, where one in four persons is Jewish. . . . Most other groups are also more likely to be found in certain sectors than in others" (1982:378).

As one might expect, whenever migrant (or host) groups succeed in breaking out of their assigned segment of a given market and penetrate a different segment, the typical first response is hostility by the outgroup. Thus, when "the Japanese in California moved up from the ranks of agricultural laborers to tenant farmers or (more rarely) landowners, the hostility against them as competitors. . . . was enough to launch a wave of anti-Japanese legislation and practices that continued for decades in California" (Sowell 1981:162).

Market-Splitting. Whereas in the vertical, "segmented," partitioning discussed above, members of different groups are not permitted to engage in the same *activity*, in the horizontal partitioning they are not permitted to receive the same *reward* (whether in terms of wealth, power, knowledge, and/or honor) for the same activity. In the latter case, we speak of a "split"[18] market and of "discrimination" rather than a "segmented" market and "segregation. " By way of extending the glass ceilings metaphor commonly used with reference to vertical partitioning, we may speak of "glass walls" if people on either side of the split can see and compare themselves with those on the other side.

"To be split," Bonacich says, "a labor market must contain at least two groups of workers whose price of labor differs for the same work" (1972:549). For example, Chinese immigrants to the United States, many of whom were sojourners, "were feared as competitors whose harder work and longer hours for cheap pay would drive down the standard of living of American labor. Labor unions were in the forefront of decades-long efforts to *exclude* Chinese immigrants and to *expel* Chinese residents from the United States" (Sowell 1981:137, italics added; see also Weiner 1995:66).[19] "Cheaper labor may be used to create a new industry having substantially lower labor costs than the rest of the labor market. . . . Or they may be used as strikebreakers or replacements to undercut a labor force trying to improve its bargaining position with business. If cheap labor is unavailable, business may turn to mechanization, or try to relocate firms in areas of the world where the price of labor is lower" (Bonacich 1972:553).[20]

Segmenting and Splitting Consumer Markets

The segmenting and splitting of markets devoted to various aspects of the *production* of wealth, power, knowledge, and honor are only half of the story.[21] The other half pertains to the segmenting and splitting of markets devoted to various aspects of the *consumption* of these products.

Thus, complementing the idea of a partition between high-ranking and low-ranking producers of wealth, Gans (1972; see also Caplovitz 1963) focuses on the partition between the affluent and the poor—that is, high and low consumers of wealth—and points out the many benefits (positive functions), for the affluent, of having poor people in their society (similar to Blalock's discussion of the benefits of segregation noted earlier in this chapter). Not surprisingly, these benefits are often tied to market segmenting and market splitting in economic production (as is implied by the differential reward that defines the latter): "The existence of poverty makes sure that 'dirty work' is done . . . the poor subsidize, directly and indirectly, many activities that benefit the affluent . . . for example, domestics subsidize the upper middle and upper classes, making life easier for their employers and freeing affluent women for a variety of professional, cultural, civic, or social activities . . . [and] by being denied educational opportunities or being stereotyped as stupid or unteachable, the poor . . . enable others to obtain the better jobs." Other benefits are more directly related to consumption: "the poor buy goods which others do not want and thus prolong their economic usefulness, such as . . . second-hand clothes and deteriorating automobiles and buildings" (Gans 1972:278–279, 281).

Gans also touches on the *negative* functions, or costs, of poverty to the "more affluent"—as well as to the poor themselves—and mentions among these, "crime" (1972:284). In a related analysis, Blau and Blau find that "the relative deprivation produced by much inequality rather than the absolute deprivation produced by much poverty provides the most fertile soil for criminal violence" (1982:122). Thus, they point to the costs in high rates of violent crime of having economic poverty and affluence (and, by my extension, political disfranchisement and enfranchisement, dishonor and honor, minimal knowledge and maximal knowledge)—located near enough to each other for people on the low side to actually *see* how people on the high side live. The mass media undoubtedly play prominent roles in generating and manipulating this visibility; see Nightingale 1993.

The imposition of partial exclusion from production and consumption markets within the same society, whether by segmenting or splitting—and especially when these two strategies are combined, and when wealth, power, knowledge, and honor markets are all covered—is what is generally referred to in the broad term "oppression." On this, Castles and Miller say:

Certain groups have been excluded from the mainstream of [advanced societies]. They are economically marginalised through low-status, insecure work and frequent unemployment; socially marginalised through poor education and exposure to crime, addiction, and family breakdown; and politically marginalised through lack of power to influence decision making at any level of government. All these factors join to produce a physical marginalisation, that is a concentration in urban and suburban ghettoes, where minorities of various kinds are thrown together—virtually cut off from and forgotten by the rest of society (1993:194).

When such cutting-off is more or less mutually agreed-upon between groups within the same society, it involves "defensive structuring" and the development of ethnic and/or racial "enclaves." Thus, Coleman says "hostility between Catholics and Protestants had remained strong from the seventeenth century and had been institutionalised by a process of 'pillarisation', involving the creation of parallel institutions—political parties, trades unions, newspapers divided on sectarian lines" (1992:213). Thus, too, when Portes and Rumbaut assert that "The presence of a number of immigrants skilled in . . . 'the art of buying and selling' can usually overcome other obstacles to entrepreneurship [in ethnic enclaves such as 'Koreatowns' and 'little Havanas']" (1996:21; see also Portes 1995:27–29), some degree of mutual agreement between the immigrant entrepreneurs in question and their hosts seems implied, for without it, obstacles too great for such overcoming could be, and have been, constructed.

Slavery

As genocide is both the oldest and the most extreme case of total exclusion from markets (see above), so slavery is the oldest and most extreme case of partial exclusion from those markets and, therefore, of oppression. Patterson says slavery "has existed from before the dawn of human history right down to the twentieth century. . . . There has been no region on earth that has not at some time harbored the institution. Probably there is no group of people whose ancestors were not at one time slaves or slaveholders" (1982:vii). Pinney tells us that in the ancient world,

in carefully inscribed records, the Sumerians acknowledged a slave population large enough to require special laws governing their treatment. Believed to date from around six thousand years ago, this stone document is the oldest remaining legal code in the history of man. And it is the beginning of the history of slavery in the civilized world. . . . Even before the Eighteenth Dynasty in Egypt, around 1580 BC, when ancient Egypt reached her height, the slave as legally defined as a commodity; and the same concept prevailed in Babylonia, Assyria, Rome, Greece, China, India, and parts of medieval Europe (1972:13, 15; see also Goody 1980:18; Hellie 1991:286–288).[22]

Typically, members of one ethnic group have enslaved members of a different ethnic, racial, or nationality group, not members of their own group.

Consequently, Finley says "The slave is an outsider; that alone permits not only his uprooting but his reduction from a person to a thing which can be owned" (1968:308; see also Watson 1980:5–13; Goody 1980:24; Phillips 1985:6; Davis 1984:16). Pinney tells us "the Sumerian ideograph for slave means 'male of a *foreign* land'" (1972:13, italics added), and Patterson notes "the reluctance of peoples to enslave those with whom they shared a common culture and felt a sense of ethnic identity" Patterson finds, among the "fifty-seven . . . slavehold- ing societies in the [*Ethnographic Atlas* sample of world cultures[23] on which data were available, that in] 75.4 percent slaves and masters were of different ethnic or tribal groups; in 15.8 percent the two were of the same ethnic group; and in 8.8 percent some slaves were from the same group as their masters, while others were from other ethnic groups" (1982:178, 179).[24]

It is also worth emphasizing, especially in view of the 250 years of European-American enslavement of sub-Saharan Africans (preceded by a brief period during which Native Americans were enslaved) that the line between enslaver and enslaved was, for most of the past ten thousand years, drawn between people belonging to different ethnic groups of the *same* race rather than different races. The reason is geographical: interracial contact of any kind has generally required intercontinental travel, while interethnic contact required only local or regional travel. One notes, for example, that Joseph, an Israelite, is said to have been sold as a slave (by locally neighboring but ethnically distinct Midianites) to a caravan of Ishmaelites (another neighboring ethnic group) on their way to Egypt (Gen. 37; see also Pinney 1972:23–27). And, using more current data, Patterson finds that of the "fifty-five societies in the [*Ethnographic Atlas*] world sample on which adequate data were available . . . 75 percent had populations in which both slaves and masters were of the same mutually perceived racial group, 21 percent had populations in which masters and slaves were of different racial groups, and 4 percent had populations in which some slaves were of the same racial group as their masters while others were not" (1982:176).

Phillips recites an imposing list of historically known enslavements between different-ethnicity, same-race, groups:

The Anglo-Saxons enslaved some of the conquered Celts in Britain. Because they each considered the other to be heretics, Arian Christians used Catholics as slaves, and vice- versa. When the Catholic Franks conquered soutern Gaul from the Arian Visigoths, huge numbers of captives entered the slave markets. Pagans and Jews could be made slaves by Christians of every persuasion, and slave traders always brought slaves from distant lands. Captured Slavs . . . were brought through western Europe to be sold in the Medi- terranean lands, and pagan slaves from North Africa reached France and Spain in the mid-sixth century (1985:47).[25]

Indeed, the word "slave" itself was "derived from [the name of] the most numerous ethnic group in the medieval [European] slave trade, the Slavs" (Phillips 1985:57).[26]

Slavery, however, extended its grasp toward globality as more and more neighboring ethnic groups became incorporated into the ancient empires and, by this incorporation, rendered less enslavable. For example, "After the Romans subdued Italy and began their overseas expansion, an increase in slavery kept pace with the rise of Rome as a great power. In the third, second, and first centuries BC, Roman generals sent back thousands of slaves drawn from the ranks of defeated armies and from the citizens of conquered towns and cities. . . . [V]ast numbers of captives who were enslaved . . . took the place of [Italian peasants who were dispossessed from their lands by the Roman elite]" (Phillips 1985:17; see also Pinney 1972:37–45).

Then, following the Roman Empire's direction of slaves mainly into Europe, the flow reversed direction twice, and with the second reversal came a racial change: "During the early Middle Ages the flow of slaves [went] from Europe to the Muslim states of the Near East and Egypt in exchange for the finished goods of those then more advanced regions; later, with Europe growing more developed, the flow was reversed and went from Africa to Europe" (Davidson 1992:210–211; also see the discussion of Africa in chapter 3).

Now let us consider what makes slavery slavery. To start with, it always entails a sharp segmenting and splitting of all wealth, power, knowledge, and honor markets. Slaves and their masters are almost always prohibited from performing the same work in the production of these reseources, and also almost always prohibited from receiving and consuming the same reward—whether in terms of wealth, power, knowledge, and/or honor.

However, one of these markets—the political—is pivotal in slavery insofar as the latter's defining mark is that the *decisions* regarding which work and how much work in any market of the society is to be performed by the slave, and the *decisions* regarding which compensation and how much compensation is to be received and consumed by the slave, rest exclusively with the master: "What separates the slave from [other laborers] including the serf or peon, is the totality of his powerlessness in principle" (Finley 1968:307; see also Phillips 1985:5–7), and what Finley means here is not physical powerlessness—after all, masters valued slaves for their power—but powerlessness to make *decisions* regarding how anyone's (including his/her own) power is to be used.

Slavery, then strips slaves of their will—i.e., their decison-making capability—and transfers it to the master: "whether the slave was degraded to the status of chattel property or elevated to that of governor of Egypt, he could be thought of as the *extension of his owner's will*" (Davis 1984:17, italics added). In this killing of another's will, slavery *domesticated* the slave in the same sense that "broken" and "trained" horses, cattle, and dogs are said to be "domesticated." Thus, the master-and-slave pair is parallel to the master-and-ox, or master-and-dog, pair except that the master and the slave belong to the same species (certain species of ants are the only other slavemaking animals that I know of, and ants also domesticate animals of other species; see Hölldobler and Wilson 1990:414–415; Wilson 1971:419–425).

How was this domestication invented? Childe says, "war helped to a great discovery—that men as well as animals can be domesticated. Instead of killing a defeated enemy, he might be enslaved; in return for his life he could be made to work. This discovery has been compared in importance to that of the taming of animals" (1951:109; Childe also calls slaves "human cattle" in 1942:239). Similarly, Davis refers to the "universal acceptance of the concept of the slave as a human being who is legally owned, used, sold, or otherwise disposed of as if he or she were a domestic animal. This parallel persisted in the similarity of naming, branding, and even pricing slaves according to their equivalent in cows, horses, camels, pigs, and chickens" (1984:13; see also 18).[27]

It is the absolute centrality of totalitarian decision-making to slavery that makes it—like all politics (even the democratic sort)—dependent on physical violence to enforce whatever decisions are made (see chapter 3; see also Wallace 1994:67–68, 259–260). Accordingly, "There is no known slave-holding society where the whip was not considered an indispensable instrument. . . . Naked force was the ultimate and essential sanction" (Patterson 1982:4, 207; see also 13, 303).

To put all this another way, insofar as the slave was *property*—and Phillips claims that "Because slaves were property, a master could do with them as he wished" (1985:5)—sooner or later it was physical force that supported it. The reason is quite general and straightforward: No one can do what they wish with a thing, whether the thing is animate or inanimate, unless they can muster sufficient force to carry out that wish against the inertia, friction, contrary motion, and other intransigence associated with the thing itself, and also against the force mustered by other persons who may have quite different plans for it. In short, whereas goods, services, and commodities are economic concepts, *property* is ultimately a political concept (it is property that puts the politics into political economy), and politics ultimately resorts to force and violence. So when Phillips says "the property relationship . . . was a necessary component of the master's dominance" (1985:7), he has it right—but backwards.[28]

Now add to this the fact that there seem to have been two broad types of slaveowners (although, unfortunately, the literature with which I am familiar does not seem to view the distinction as counting for much): the state—a political institution—and individual persons. Exemplifying the first type, Phillips tells us "the Roman Republic owned slaves and used them in public works projects and other governmental activities. The practice continued during the Roman Empire, when the emperor owned and directed a vast force of bureaucrats and public workers who staffed and maintained a number of essential services within the empire" (1985:9); and before that, during the Periclean Age in Greece, Caldwell says, "The state owned slaves who worked on the roads, in the dockyards, in the mint, and on public buildings. The Scythian archers who formed the police of Athens, the executioner and his staff, the inspectors of weights and measures, and many of the heralds and clerks were the property of the demos" (1949:226).

In the second type, chattel slavery—familiar from the recent history of the New World—the slave is the personal property ("chattel") of some particular individual. Chattel slavery appears to have coexisted with state slavery (which seems to have been confined to ancient civilizations—except for Nazi Germany) but outlasted it by two thousand years, probably because of the efficiencies of decentralized control that went with chattel slavery.

It appears that the defining social relationship in state slavery would have been largely between *categories* of people, in the sense that any and all members of the superordinate category (the "demos") could, at least in principle, command any and all members of the subordinate category equally—although such command was most often formally delegated to overseers. Chattel slavery, by contrast, is always a relationship between *individuals* by virtue of the slave's being personal property. As a result, although some category domination, and some delegation of command, may well be present, the master of a chattel slave exercises his/her maximum and most direct authority not over *all* slaves but only over his/her *own* slaves. By the same token, a chattel slave is most fully subject not to all masters but only to his/her *own* master.[29] This ultimately personal rather than categorical relationship is what made for "a constant struggle between master and slave in the effort of the former to gain as much as possible for himself with the least possible loss . . . and the effort of the latter to minimize the burden of his exploitation and enhance the regularity and predictability of his existence" (Patterson 1982:50, 207; see also 1982:334–342).

Finally, it seems clear that slavery (of chattel as well as state types)—like genocide, and war—although not yet dead today, is on its last legs after some ten thousand years of rampage: "There can be no doubt . . . that the prevalence of chattel slavery declined dramatically in the 1960s. . . . [and that] the absolute ownership of one person by another has become . . . rare" (Davis 1984:319, 320). At the same time, however, the unanticipated and unintended pro-consolidation legacy of slavery (as of genocide and war) should not be overlooked. Freedom, "an ideal cherished in the West beyond all others emerged as a necessary consequence of the degradation of slavery and the effort to negate it" (Patterson 1982:341–342; see also Malcolm X 1966:379); and Manning agrees: "The contrast of slavery and freedom came to be reinforced in the minds of people in every corner of this global system. . . . and the notion of human rights grew to be specified in contrast to the status of slavery" (1996:xvi; see also Patterson 1982:341–342).

Partial Exclusion Strategies Between Nations

To all this, we must now add that markets may be segmented and/or split between nations, as well as between persons. That, indeed, is the very meaning of a "sovereign" nation: such a nation always comprises a set of markets for the production, distribution, and consumption of wealth, power, knowledge, and honor that have been formally segmented off and split off from all other sets of such markets, and bound together (as indicated in chapter 2) by its participants' beliefs that they share a common destiny of superiority over those other sets.[30]

We have already noted here that market segmenting and market splitting differences between nations (as between the "developed" and "under-developed") often motivate workers to migrate to host nations that pay more for the same work than do their homelands, and also motivate employers to move their businesses in just the opposite direction—to nations where less is paid for the same work than in the employers' homelands. Note that the two moves together (see Weiner 1995:28) imply an altogether welcome globalizing trend toward equal pay for equal work no matter where the work is done or who does it. Moreover, both moves would seem to call for global organizations of employees (rather than the current national organizations) to help assure that the global level of that equal pay is equitable, relative to the profits of employers.

To this we have to add that the positive functions, for affluent people, of having poor people (poor in wealth, power, knowledge, and/or honor) in their country are matched by positive functions, for affluent nations, of having poor nations (Wallerstein calls the two "core" and "peripheral" countries—see 1979) in their world. Similarly, just as there are costs of various kinds of inequality within a nation, there are costs of inequality between nations: "unequal access [among different nations] to resources combines with population growth to produce environmental damage. This phenomenon can contribute to economic deprivation that spurs insurgency and rebellion" (Homer-Dixon et al. 1993:42, 45).

Finally, in this discussion of partial exclusion strategies, note that segmenting and splitting may serve as cultural structural strategies as well as social structural strategies. For example, Sears and Kinder claim that "beliefs, such as that Negroes are too pushy, that they get preferential treatment from government, or that they really do not need welfare money. . . . have almost no conceivable personal relevance to the individual [White person], but have to do with his moral code or his sense of how society should be organized" (1971:66). But this interpretation seems to overlook the possibility that individuals may feel no less personally threatened by migrants whom they regard as splitting the *morality* (i.e., honor) market than by migrants whom they regard as splitting the *wages* (wealth) market. Any outgroup perceived as seeking competitive gain— whether in wealth, power, knowledge, or honor—by following some moral code (especially an easier or less risky one) other than the ingroup's will be regarded as pocketing "ill-gotten gains," "cutting corners," and "getting away with murder"—in short, as cheapening the honor market.[31] Moreover, moral codes may not only be split; they may also be segmented: Ingroup members may (indeed, are apt to) apply a different code to each other from the code they apply to members of the outgroup.

MUTUALLY SUPPORTING CULTURAL STRUCTURAL AND SOCIAL STRUCTURAL STRATEGIES

All the cultural structural strategies and all the social structural strategies discussed above pursue the same goal: gaining the greatest possible share of wealth, power, knowledge, and honor for the ingroup at the expense of one or more outgroups. Fundamentally, what is involved in this pursuit are ingroup efforts to generate, on the one hand, collective actions (social structures) that generate collective thoughts and emotions (cultural structures) that, in turn, legitimate these actions, and on the other hand, to generate collective thoughts and feelings that generate collective actions which, in turn, express and fulfill these thoughts and feelings. When these strategies mesh successfully, actions that legitimate themselves and thoughts that fulfill themselves powerfully enhance a given group's chances for success over other groups—in the following way.

Self-Fulfilling Thoughts and Self-Legitimating Actions

Merton says "The self-fulfilling prophecy is, in the beginning, a *false* definition of the situation evoking a new behavior which makes the originally false conception come *true*."[32] For example, he says, "Consider the case of examination neurosis. Convinced that he is destined to fail, the anxious student devotes more time to worry than to study and then turns in a poor examination" (Merton 1957:423; see also Blalock 1982:59). But by the same token, a *positive* prophecy (i.e., the student's confidence that s/he will succeed—when the student deliberately generates such confidence, we say s/he is "psyched up") will help the student turn in a *good* examination. So there are two implications of the self-fulfilling prophecy: (1) the action-weakening power of negative thoughts, and (2) the action-strengthening power of positive thoughts. In both cases, thoughts are generating actions that correspond to them.

Now consider the student who (for some reason beyond his/her control) does poorly on a particular examination and then starts to believe s/he will never write good examinations. Alternatively, consider a student who (also for some reason beyond his/her control) does well on the examination and starts to believe s/he will write good examinations all the time. Here we also have two implications: (1) the thought-weakening power of negative action, and (2) the thought-strengthening power of positive action. In both these cases, actions are generating thoughts that correspond to them.

When this mutually positive feedback loop between cultural structural and social structural competitive strategies is unbroken, it is self-amplifying: Shared positive thoughts lead to shared strong actions, which lead to more positive shared thoughts, which lead to still stronger shared actions, and so on. By helping its own members to board this glory train, and by packing outgroup members on the gory train headed in the opposite direction (where negative thoughts lead to weak actions, which lead to more negative thoughts, and so on),

every ethnic, racial, and nationality group tries to work itself into a winning position and does its best to stay there.

No strategy, however, is invulnerable, and the one just described is apt to be vulnerable in both its social structural and its cultural structural components. Describing an example of such vulnerability, Shimahara points out that the recent upward social mobility of a Japanese outcast group ("Burakumin") "was not so much a function of relaxation of the ascribed cultural constraints imposed upon the group as a function of political and economic [social structural] factors. . . . Indeed, the occupational and social mobility that Burakumin have gained has itself contributed, in my view, to . . . some erosion of the traditional prejudice." In addition, "When [Burakumin] gained more access to economic opportunities, [their self-stereotypes as being dependent people] diminished. Burakumin students' enrolments in high school and college rose dramatically" (1984:350, 351).

COALITIONAL STRATEGIES

As the globalization of all competitive arenas for wealth, power, knowledge, and honor has picked up speed over the last ten thousand years, every individual and every group on Earth has found that, for all the differences that separate them, going-it-alone is becoming less and less feasible. Everybody needs more and more *allies* to stay in the competition at all. This is one major reason why ethnic, racial, and nationality separatisms almost never advocate total and permanent separation from other groups.

This brings us to the set of strategies that involve cooperative alliances or coalitions between groups that would otherwise be mercilessly competing with each other.[33] Needless to say, such strategies are vital to global species consolidation.

To begin with, it should be clear that in pursuing any or all of the above strategies, a group (or an individual), in principle, has the option of going-it-*alone* (without allies among other competitors), or going-it-*together* (with one or more allies among other competitors). Let us call going-it-together the coalitional strategy, and recognize that a given group's coalitions may vary (1) in the arenas of competition for wealth, power, knowledge, and honor in which the coalitions participate; and (2) in the number and strength of the competitors, at the group's own hierarchic level (see Figure 2.4) that the coalitions include as members.

In all such cases, however, a coalition may be said to exist to the extent that there is an agreement (for whatever reason on each side, whether tacit or explicit, voluntary or coerced, and including cooptation[34]) among two or more participants to pool their resources in pursuit of some common goal.[35] By contrast, "individualism" is the ultimate go-it-alone strategy. When choosing this strategy, individuals compete *by* themselves and *for* themselves alone.

Note, then, that whenever the terms "ingroup" and "outgroup" have been used here, they have referred to *coalitions* (whether of individuals, or of groups of individuals)—and this includes the families, kinship groups, ethnic groups, racial groups, and nationality groups shown in Figure 2.4. In all these coalitions, individuals compete not alone but arm-in-arm with other members of their coalition and for their mutual (though not necessarily, and not usually, equal) benefit. This means the choice between going-it-alone and going-it-together shows up at each level of this hierarchy: Individuals may choose either to go-it-alone or to go-it-together with other individuals in (or outside of) their own families; families may choose either to go-it-alone or to go-it-together with other families—thereby forming a kinship group. Then kinship groups may choose either to go-it-alone or to form coalitions with each other (forming ethnic groups), and so on.

Of course, a given ingroup may form a coalition with one or more outgroups; it may broker, or try to prevent, or try to break up coalitions among other outgroups; or it may remain aloof from (or be denied entry to) all coalitions. And it may, of course, switch (or be switched by) its coalition partners—as in the changing coalitions among the Zulus, British, Boers, and Swazi discussed by Schermerhorn (1978:54), and the back and forth "tilts" of third world countries between the United States and the Soviet Union during the Cold War, discussed by Waters (1995:116).

In specific connection with the denial, and the switching, of coalitions, Walters' report is well worth close and careful attention:

A proposal which profoundly shook the harmony of the drafters of the Covenant [of the League of Nations] was put forward by the Japanese, who asked for a sentence in the Preamble stating that the Members of the League endorsed the principle of the equality of nations and the just treatment of their nationals. . . . [However,] amongst the delegations to the Conference were the representatives of at least three countries—the United States, Australia, and New Zealand—which had enacted special laws limiting emigration [sic] from East Asia. . . . The British and Americans, therefore, met the Japanese request with a negative which they did their best to make friendly but which they refused to withdraw. The rejection of her request, which all the rest of the Committee would have been prepared to grant, was deeply wounding to Japan; and there was even for a time a fear lest she might in consequence refuse to be a member of the League. . . . [In addition,] a clause [favored by Woodrow Wilson, and] known as the religious liberty clause held its place for some time, but was eliminated just before the first draft of the Covenant was published on February 14th, 1919. . . . The clause might well have passed if the Japanese delegation had not taken the occasion to suggest adding to it their own proposal about the equality of nations. It was right, said [the Japanese delegate] to proclaim that no man should suffer on account of his religion; it was equally right to proclaim that no man should suffer on account of his race or nationality. The Japanese argument combined disconcertingly, from the British and American point of view, the qualities of being unanswerable and unacceptable. The course, therefore, was to abandon both suggestions (1952:63–64).

It seems not unreasonable to think that this British and American refusal of coalition with Japan was directly related to Japan's later switch to an alternative coalition with Germany and Italy, and related, thus, to Pearl Harbor. Indeed, Du Bois makes exactly this point: "Japan, after demanding racial equality in the League of Nations, and after being rather peremptorily denied even theoretical confirmation by Great Britain and the United States, gradually turned and began to work toward . . . the domination of the major part of mankind by an Asiatic imperialism. When this imperialism made common cause with dictatorship in Germany and Italy, world war became inevitable" (1945:6).

Advantages and Disadvantages

The main advantages of going-it-alone, in any competitive arena and at any level, are (1) not having to consult anybody about goals and strategies, and (2) not having to share winnings. Going-it-alone pays off best when the individual or group in question is far and away the dominant one (see Caplow 1968) either because there are no others in the vicinity or because it is superior in resources and mobilization to all possible coalitions that its competitors could form. The disadvantages of going-it-alone are equally clear: A group's chances of losing are very high when confronted with stronger adversaries, and if the group does lose, it has to foot the bill all alone.

The main advantage of going-it-together is, obviously, the additional strength it gives to each participant's resources.[36] Backed by the pooled strength of its partners, each ally in a coalition increases its chances of winning and sharing in the pot, while the costs to each partner of competing—and of losing, if that should happen—tend to be reduced. These considerations are why groups work so hard to prevent the formation of coalitions among their competitors ("divide and rule"), as Wirth points out: "Where there are several distinct minorities in a country the dominant group can [treat] some of them generously and can at the same time . . . secure its own dominance by playing one minority against another" (1945:353).

The ingroup's search for coalition partners, however, can only increase as time goes on (for reasons discussed below) and that search has both immediate and long-run consequences pointing toward eventual global species consolidation. In the Caribbean, for example, after master-and-slave coalitions were terminated by Emancipation, plantation and estate owners tried to form new, wage-based, coalitions with the freed slaves. However, "where there were virgin lands for the former slaves to occupy and develop as petty farmers, the rewards for remaining on the plantation were not sufficient and the consequent dearth of estate labor led to the importation of East Indians to fill the gap. 'This led to the characteristic multiracialism of places like Trinidad, Surinam and British Guiana'" (Schermerhorn 1978:111). Similarly imported coalition partners were crucial in southern Africa, where "contract laborers were imported as indentures from India into Natal . . . [to work] on sugar plantations, railways, dockyards, coal mines, municipal services and domestic labor in lieu of the Zulu who were unwilling to serve in such confining occupations. At the close of their period of indenture, the great majority of Indians remained in South Africa, in spite of government inducements to leave" (Schermerhorn 1978:112).

A major disadvantage of forming a coalition (in addition to having to consult about strategies and tactics and having to share winnings with the other parties to the coalition) is the extra calculation—more things to think about—that such a coalition brings with it. Obviously, every coalition has constantly to assess the advantages and disadvantages of competition versus those of coalition with coalitions *outside* it. But at the same time it must also assess the same considerations regarding coalitions *inside* it. For example, every nation strives to make sure its citizens' nationality-loyalties outweigh their loyalties to the familial, kinship, ethnic, racial, and foreign-nationality groups inside (and outside) it to which these citizens also belong. Each of the latter groups does the same, and strives to make sure its members' loyalties to itself outweigh their immediate self-interests. Dippel describes such competitions as they manifested themselves among Jewish citizens of Germany during the 1930s:

Despite everything, Germany was still their home. And, despite almost everything, they were prepared to stay there. Jews had lived in Germany for over sixteen centuries and had been emancipated during the Enlightenment. . . . Unlike Jews in many other countries . . . they experienced no unsettling ambivalence about either their identity or their loyalty to the state in which they resided and no closeted passion for . . . a Jewish homeland in the barren and remote sands of Palestine. So it was not surprising that the first rumblings of Nazism, swelling to a roar of hate in the 1930s, did not send them scurrying for the nearest frontier (1996:xxii–xxiii; see also Hoge 1997).

Indeed, Dippel says, "some Jews, especially those in the armaments business . . . [fared] embarrassingly well under a resurgent Nazi Germany" (1996:xxiii).[37]

Enloe argues that the strategies a nation-state uses to reduce the influence of its component ethnic, racial, and alien nationality groups are "(1) cooptation (so that the ethnic group, for instance, still mobilizes resources but now channels them to serve state ends) . . . [and (2)] demobilization of the competitor." Thus, "the [American] state . . . has demobilized certain groups by encouraging a dependent relationship between members of the group and state agencies. . . . Such moves to create state dependency are often accompanied by state cooptation of the group's potential leaders, recruiting them into state agencies or making them responsible for state programs" (1981:132–133). Moreover, Enloe argues, the principle of *individualism* (the ultimate go-it-alone strategy) has been used by those who wield the American state power as a weapon with which to break up coalitions within and between various ethnic, racial, and foreign-nationality groups inside its boundaries: "For all ethnic groups in the United States, European, Indian, Black, Chicano, Chinese, the heavy hand of ideological individualism has thwarted ethnically-based mobilization or . . . converted it quickly into merely a collaborative effort by group members to acquire individual benefits" (1981:132).[38]

Influences on Coalition-Formation

What determines whether two groups (or two individuals) go-it-alone and compete with each other or go-it-together and cooperate with each other against some perceived common enemy? Let us consider some factors that go into answering this question.

First, to the extent that each group sees the other group as an important means to its own victory in its confrontation with some third opponent, its valuation of that other group will rise. Indeed, as the discussion of informational and propagandistic functions of intergroup descriptions earlier in this chapter has indicated, if the ingroup's perception of the outgroup as a strong competitive threat—whether in one competitive arena or several, and whether violent or non-violent—holds up, and especially if the ingroup regards the threat as posed in an "honorable" way (that is, a way that entails no significant loss of "face" to the ingroup if the threat is yielded to), the outgroup can, almost paradoxically, come to be regarded by the ingroup not only as a strong competitor, but as a potential cooperator (see the discussion of intergroup descriptions, above).[39]

Thus, "when ingroup members cannot easily think of themselves as superior on a certain dimension, differences between groups on this dimension will tend to be minimized or ignored" (Stephan and Rosenfield 1982:103). Similarly, Bleeke and Ernst, referring to multinational business coalitions, tell us that "The more equal the partnership, the brighter its future" (1993:2); Blalock claims that for a coalition to be formed between two groups, one group's members "must have competitive resources that make it advantageous for the [other group's] members to interact with them in preference to members of their own group" (1967:122; see also Carmichael and Hamilton 1967:242; Thompson 1967:34; Fanon 1968:73–95), and adds that "Minorities of substantial size constitute both a political threat to the dominant group and a potentially useful coalition partner. Depending on circumstances, they may be treated with either considerable respect or hostility, but they are rarely treated with indifference" (1982:56). (Note that for "substantial size," of course, one can readily substitute substantial wealth, substantial power, substantial knowledge, and/or substantial honor.)

Moskos outlines the impact that equalizing resources has had on coalition-formation between racial groups in the U.S. Army: "Throughout the Vietnam War race relations were terrible [in the Army. However,] the military of the 1970s recognized that its race problem was so critical that it was on the verge of self-destruction." Accordingly, "the Army's stated goal [became] absolute commitment to equal opportunity and non-discrimination regardless of race—with no qualifications." As the pivotal means to this end, "the Army developed the most extensive training and staffing program of equal opportunity anywhere," with the result that "rank and promotion in the enlisted ranks are [now] roughly equivalent between the races." In addition, "the tremendous emphasis on rank helps erode racial feelings by producing cross-race solidarity within ranks. It also breaks down racial solidarity across ranks." The outcome,

Moskos says, is that "the races do get on remarkably well [in the Army]. Under the grueling conditions of Desert storm not one racial incident occurred that was severe enough to come to the attention of the military police" (1991:16–20).[40]

In general, then, the probability of a cooperative coalition goes up as the difference between the groups' strengths goes down. This means that if the only outgroup available for coalition is so irremediably weak and dependent that it would drain away more ingroup resources than it could ever contribute to a coalition, then having *no* ally would be better than having such a one.[41] On the other hand, if the only outgroup available for coalition is perceived as being so powerful that it could win the intergroup competitions hands-down and all by itself, then, too, it would be better for the ingroup to go-it-alone because a coalition with such a powerful outgroup may only result in tying the ingroup's hands until the outgroup finds it convenient to crush it outright (see Simmel 1950:162–169; see also Machiavelli 1940:84; Carmichael and Hamilton 1967:80–81; Caplow 1968:152).

That coalitions are most often formed when the participants see each other as more or less equally strong in the relevant competitive arena is the unstated basis of Axelrod's argument that "continuing interaction is what makes it possible for cooperation based on reciprocity to be stable," and "Mutual cooperation can be stable if the future is sufficiently important [in the minds of the participants] relative to the present. This is because the [participants] can each use an implicit threat of retaliation against the other's defection—if the interaction will last long enough to make the threat effective" (1984:125, 126). Although Axelrod does not say so, only their being more or less equally strong can make reciprocity ("tit for tat") between participants possible, and only such equality can make a threat of retaliation from any participant effective against every other participant.

It is also true, of course, that the probability of coalition rises as the anticipated strength of the coalition itself rises relative to its opponents—which is just another way of saying coalitions are likely to be formed when their prospective participants think there is a good chance of winning with them.

The net outcome of these considerations is most important for the global species consolidation thesis: Once the first coalition is formed in a given competitive arena, the remaining competitors there will feel compelled either to *join* that first coalition or *gang up* on it (see Huntington 1996:231), whichever seems to offer them the best chance of winning (or at least not losing). The point is that either way, *competition leads to cooperative coalitions among the competitors* (see Simmel 1950:154–162).

This may seem paradoxical but there really is no paradox here; cooperation is just a very powerful competitive strategy. That is to say, people cooperate among themselves largely because they expect it to improve their chances in competing with people who are not in on the cooperation.

Competition and Coalitions; Coalitions and Competition

As a result of the competitive advantages of cooperation, then, coalitions are found virtually everywhere, not only among humans but at all levels of the unending competition among living organisms for survival. Indeed, Margulis and Sagan (1986; see also Spencer 1898, I:464–469) claim, in effect, that the Darwinian principle of evolution by *natural selection of competing organisms* (whether these be bacteria or people) should be augmented by a principle of evolution by *natural coalition of cooperating organisms* (my words, not theirs).

Applying the latter principle to human societies—specifically, societies in equatorial Africa—Vansina tells us that although persistent separation among these societies was "more striking," nevertheless,

one sees time and time again a breakdown of regional equilibria when one or another society became more powerful than its neighbors because it could mobilize more people more often or because it incorporated more people than its neighbors. . . . Once the equilibrium was broken on one point in a given area, people in the neighboring districts . . . had to react, either by adopting the structural innovations of the successful group or by inventing new institutions of their own that would restore the balance of power or give them an advantage. This . . . produced in some regions an acceleration over time in the growth of the scale of political societies. To cite the most extreme case: in the southwest, Kongo societies passed from groupings of perhaps 500 inhabitants by A.D. 500 to 500,000 by 1400, a 1,000-fold growth in less than a millenium (1990:252–253).

Confining his remarks to a much narrower frame of reference but drawing very similar conclusions, Gomes-Casseres observes that "cooperation among [busi-ness] firms has grown rapidly since the early 1980s, as alliances have proliferated in one industry after another" (1996: 1; see also Alter and Hage 1993:259). Bleeke and Ernst add that "For most global businesses, the days of flat-out, predatory competition are over. . . . [Businesses] have learned that fighting long, head-to-head battles leaves the companies financially exhausted, intellectually depleted, and vulnerable to the next wave of competition and innovation. In place of predation, many multinational corporations are learning that they must collaborate to compete" (1993:1). Even Huntington, who insists that "civilizations" mostly "clash," admits that "in politics a common enemy creates a common interest" (1996:185; see also Smith's discussion of "Pan-nationalisms" and "families of cultures" 1991:171–172). And, most importantly, Axelrod notes that "the overall level of cooperation tends to go up and not down. In other words, the machinery for the evolution of cooperation contains a rachet" (Axelrod 1984:177).

It is not, however, that competition simply gives way, once and for all, to coalition; instead, competition and cooperation alternate, as though they were feet climbing an evolutionary stair. Thus, the first coalitions in a given arena compete with each other until they give rise to coalitions of the first coalitions. Then these coalitions compete with each other until they, too, give rise to coalitions—and so on up: "alliances at one level [shape] the groups that compete against outsiders at another, higher level" (Gomes-Casseres 1996:2,3; see also 4–5).

With this simple but universally applicable and therefore immensely powerful little two-step, evolution bootstraps whatever original entities it works on to higher and higher levels of organizational complexity and survival strength (within limits set, for example, by the nature of the entities and of their environment).

Seen in this perspective, then, the succession of coalitions different-iated along family, kinship, ethnic, racial, and nationality lines—as discussed in connection with Figure 2.4—form a stairway, perhaps not to the stars, but at least to global species consolidation. (But maybe to the stars, too; see chapter 6.)

Coalitions and Equality

Now to the idea (also discussed in connection with Figure 2.4) that every group of individuals is a coalition and every group of such groups is a coalition on a higher, more inclusive, level let us now add that every coalition introduces an element of subjective equality among its participants that they did not have prior to its formation. That element is the simple equality of awareness of being members of the same coalition. This is what Weber is pointing to when (as we have already seen here), he says "The sense of ethnic honor is . . . accessible to *anybody* who belongs to the subjectively believed community of descent."

Bear in mind that equality of *membership* is not the same as equality of *members*. Members of the same coalition may know that they are widely unequal in wealth, power, knowledge, and/or honor at the same time that they are equal in the bare fact of their coalition membership. In forming a coalition, it is as though each member puts on eyeglasses that tint the perception of all coalition members uniformly while tinting their common enemies (and others) differently.[42]

This is what Simmel has in mind when, after arguing that a society consisting of objectively equal individuals is inconceivable and that the objective inequalities among individuals must lead to exploitation if given free rein, he concludes that "Equality, after being destroyed by freedom, can be re-established only through the ethical renunciation to utilize natural gifts [through adding]. . . . to freedom and equality a third requirement: fraternity" (1950:65, 66–67). By adding this third requirement, the exploitation that would result from full freedom of competition among individuals who are objectively unequal is reined-in by the ethical restriction that such freedom must not be practiced inside the coalition of same-descent siblings (including purely fictive siblings, of course). Beliefs in an equally shared "brotherhood," and "sisterhood," then, are the eyeglasses that tint all members of a given coalition equally—thereby significantly (but never completely) counter-balancing their objective inequalities and protecting each of them from the others' exploitation.

But, obviously, equality and inequality are *objective* as well as subjective properties of human societies. Therefore, let us now consider the bearing of coalitions on the objective equality of their participants. We begin, again, by noting that by forming a coalition members pool their wealth, power, knowledge, and/or honor. This means that in addition to members' subjective sense of being equally members, coalitions also enhance their members' objective equality by giving them all some access to the pooled resources of the coalition and some share in the winnings or losses—access and shares they would not have if they did not belong. In addition, the weakest member of a coalition may often successfully demand a disproportionately large share of whatever winnings there may be—thereby enhancing objective equalization among members of the coalition still more—if that member's participation is anticipated by the other members to be essential to the coalition's winning (see Simmel 1950:154–169; Caplow 1968).

So it seems fair to conclude that coalitions work for the objective as well as the subjective equalization of their members. And almost needless to add, the two equalizations feed on each other. Coalition members' subjective belief that they are all equally on the same side strengthens their tolerance of, and indeed their interest in, each other's objective equality if that becomes a condition of continuing the coalition. Their objective equality, in turn, strengthens their subjective belief that they are, and need to be, all equally on the same side.

In this way, the social structural *inclusiveness* of coalitions interacts with the cultural structural *universalism* of their norms; each strengthens the other (see the discussion of mutually strengthening cultural structural and social structural strategies earlier in this chapter).[43]

But it follows from all this that if a species-inclusive and species-universalistic coalition (that is to say, global species consolidation) is indeed emerging before our very eyes, there should be some evidence of it in the objective and subjective equalizations of the world's people. Does such evidence exist?

Equalization in the Emerging Global Coalition

It appears that after 200-to-400 thousand years of prehistory in which an objective near-equality probably prevailed among members of the species Homo sapiens with respect to wealth, power, knowledge, and honor, the Neolithic Revolution initiated ten thousand years of rapid decline in that objective equality (accompanied by an extremely rapid rise in the absolute levels of those resources). Recently, however, it seems fair to say that some basic upturns in species-wide objective equality have become visible.

Consider power: If one regards formally democratic government as a significant (though still imperfect) equalization of decision-making power when compared with the characteristic inequality of power present in all formally autocratic governments, then McColm's observation that whereas there were only twelve countries counted as democratic in 1942, a mere fifty years later there were "91 democracies and another 35 countries in some form of democratic transition—a staggering 126 out of the 183 nations evaluated—compared to forty-four democracies in 1972 and 56 in 1980" (1992:47) documents a striking rise in power equalization. Karatnycky updates these findings: "there are now [in 1995] 117 democracies [representing] just over 61 percent of the world's 191 countries. . . . Ten years ago, less than 42 percent of the world's countries were formal democracies. Today, 3.1 billion persons out of a world population of 5.7 billion live under democratically elected governments. While not yet a universal standard, democracy has deepening and widening roots in all parts of the world" (1996:4–5).

Consider knowledge: UNESCO reports that "Over a billion young people—nearly one-fifth of the world's population—are enrolled in formal education today, compared to around 300 million or one-tenth of the world's population in 1953, the earliest year for which UNESCO has global estimates of enrolment" (1995:19), and the United Nations reports that "Between 1960 and 1991 net enrolment at the primary level increased by nearly two-thirds—from 48 percent to 77 percent [in the developing countries of the world]" (1996:20). UNESCO also says that the percent illiterate in the world's population aged 15 year and older declined from 30.5 percent in 1980 to 22.6 percent in 1990—the corresponding figures are 42.0 percent and 29.6 percent for developing countries, including 59.8 percent and 43.2 percent for sub-Saharan African countries (see UNESCO 1996:2–9). Even allowing for inflation in these figures, it still seems likely that some increase in the global distribution of knowledge is occurring (see the percentage increases, quoted on page 66, in TV and radio receivers in various parts of the world). Moreover, any inflation that exists may testify to a fundamental change in attitude, just during the last hundred years or so, toward the global equalization of knowledge.

Consider honor: Chapter 3 discussed the Universal Declaration of Human Rights adopted by the UN General Assembly in 1948, and its assertions that "recognition of the inherent dignity and of the equal and inalienable rights of all members of the human family is the foundation of freedom, justice and peace in the world," and that "All human beings are born free and equal in dignity and rights. . . . and should act towards one another in a spirit of brotherhood" (United Nations 1994:1, 2). Recall, also, the reference earlier in this chapter, to The United Nations Genocide Convention (signed December 9, 1948) and its prohibition of "acts committed with intent to destroy in whole or in part, [any] national, ethnical, racial or religious group' by killing members of the group, causing them serious bodily or mental harm, creating conditions calculated to bring about their physical destruction, preventing births, or forcibly transferring children to another group." Such declarations bespeak what it seems no exaggeration to call a revolutionary turn toward the species-wide equalization of honor, on paper at least. And paper declarations need not be sneered at (especially when they are of such radically innovative character) on the ground that they have not yet grown the fangs of implementation. The

Declaration of Human Rights is certainly only a first step in a long journey, but it has been said that there is no better way to begin a long journey than with a first step.

When we come to wealth, however, the situation is altogether differrent: Although "The more than 7% average annual per capita income growth rate of East Asia in the 1970s and 1980s is the most sustained and widespread economic development miracle of the 20th century, perhaps all history" (Patel et al., quoted in United Nations Development Programme 1996:12), nevertheless, "the ratio between income in the richest one fifth of countries and the poorest one fifth has widened from 30 to 1 in 1960 to 61 to 1 in 1991" (Brown 1996: 3–4; see also Falk 1992:21–29; compare Waters 1995:71; Huntington 1996:85). Thus,

were all humanity a single nation-state, the present North-South divide [between developed and developing nations] would make it an unviable, semi-feudal entity, split by internal conflicts. Its small part is advanced, prosperous, powerful; its much bigger part is underdeveloped, poor, powerless. A nation so divided within itself would be recognized as unstable. A world so divided should likewise be regarded as inherently unstable (Report of the South Commission 1990:2).

Needless to say, people living in the territorially self-segregating developed nations—for all their proud democracy and loud avowal of human equality—take the perpetuation of such a world division to be their sovereign and inalienable right, whereas people living in the segregated underdeveloped countries are more apt to regard it as unspeakably inhumane and duplicitous. Indeed, Arjun Makhijani concludes that "the structure of the world economy is in its most essential ways like that of apartheid in South Africa"; it is, he says, "global apartheid" (quoted in Falk 1992:3). Similarly, Homer-Dixon et al. find "causal links between scarcities of renewable resources and violence." To prevent the latter, they argue that "rich and poor countries alike must cooperate to restrain population growth, to implement a more equitable distribution of wealth within and among their societies, and to provide for sustainable development" (1993:45). And at that point, one recalls Deutsch's idea that "if the world's population could be brought up to $4800 per capita income yearly, we could expect that most of the world most of the time would no longer have an *economic* motive for fighting . . . [and this would be] something unheard of to this day" (1969:185). The setting of a global minimum income (or preferably the setting of a maximum allowable gap between maximum and minimum incomes) remains an idea whose time has not yet come, but it almost surely will come.

Meantime, with the continuing exception of wealth, world equalization of the objective possession of the resources of human life seems to be well under way. Indeed, it seems that at the very same historical moment that we are learning how atmospheric and water pollution, war, and genocide in one locality can pose an active threat to other localities around the world, we may also be learning that the same applies to poverty—and to autocracy, ignorance, and dishonor as well. All these, too, are global in their potential consequences and require global, species-wide, solutions—about which, more in the next chapter.

Before opening that closing chapter, however, let us complete our examination of coalitional strategies by considering the middleman strategy (a type of go-between relationship of migrants to different groups of hosts that combines elements of going-it-alone with going-it-together), and then intermarriage (a type of coalition that, because of its special role in forging the chain of birth cohorts that we call human history, is both an indicator of past and present trends toward global species consolidation, and a predictor of future trends in that direction).

The Go-Between Strategy

"Middleman minorities," Bonacich tells us, "tend to constitute a separate and distinct community from the surrounding society," but they remain in contact with that society insofar as "they play the role of middleman between producer and consumer, employer and employee, owner and renter, elite and masses" (1973:583; see also Sowell 1996:27–35). For example, Spence says, "under Dutch rule in Indonesia, the Chinese served profitably as tax collectors, working under contract, and as managers of the Dutch-controlled opium monopoly" (1990:211), and Schermerhorn notes that the laborers who were "imported as indentures from India into Natal remained in South Africa . . . [and] came to occupy an intermediate racial position between whites and Africans" (1978:112). Note, also, that middleman minorities may operate not only between those who live in affluence and those who live in poverty, but also between those of much knowledge and those of little knowledge; between those of great political power and those of little political power; and between those of high honor and those of low honor, or all of these, combined.[44]

Middleman groups are often selected and self-selected for being ethnically distinct from the groups they mediate for at least two reasons. First, they are not likely to be subject to the same taboos that the mediated groups may have (Wirth points out that the Jewish middleman group in medieval Europe "performed useful functions such as trade and commerce in which the creed of the dominant group would not allow its own members to engage" [1945:355]), and second, ethnic difference reduces the likelihood of coalition between the middleman group and the subordinate group against the dominant group.

Two types of middleman roles seem possible. In the first type, the middleman group is strong enough to act independently and directly in its own interests, without allying itself with any of the mediated groups (see Spencer 1898, I:494–497; Simmel 1950:154–169). For example, in a discussion that admittedly bears on ethnic, racial, or nationality groups only by analogy, Burnham predicted not long ago that people who have managerial occupations (and who, therefore, mediate between owners and production workers) would soon "exploit the rest of society" (1942:126; see also Berle and Means 1939:84,

85, 124). A lastingly independent middleman position, however, appears highly unlikely in view of the advantages of going-it-together and the disadvantages of going-it-alone (discussed previously) and, as a result, middleman minorities tend to gravitate toward the second type of middleman role. Here the middleman group serves as a protective ally of, and a cat's-paw for, the dominant group. For example, "in the top [Thai] echelons, the more wealthy Chinese [middlemen] not only have close connections with the Thai rulers and the nobility, but often bring the latter into business partnership [so that] the Thai upper classes could win financial gain without expending much effort while the Chinese managers win protection" (Schermerhorn 1978:151, 153, 55).

In the presence of this high probability middleman-upperman coalition, "the merchant, bargaining over prices, comes to symbolize [to the subordinate group] the manufacturing elite; the overseer or tax collector, the large landholder or plantation owner; the small-time money lender, the large financial interests" (Blalock 1967:81). The result is that "where middlemen are an ethnically distinct group—the Chinese in Southeast Asia, the East Indians in Uganda, and the Ibos in Nigeria—that ethnic group is hated by the masses who deal with them. The Jews are the classic example of such a group in such occupations. . . . [They] typically lived together, and with the . . . rise of militant Christianity, they were forced to do so " (Sowell 1981:72).

For all these reasons, the middleman position is precarious: "in times of prosperity and reduced class conflict, the middleman finds himself relatively secure under the protection of the elite group. . . . [and] may gradually become assimilated and amalgamated with the elite group." But in times of adversity and heightened class conflict, the middleman is apt to suffer: "he becomes a natural scapegoat. . . . During periodic crises, such as major depressions, peasant uprisings, or epidemics such as the Bubonic Plague, the Jew has been turned upon in a kind of temporary coalition between the two other groups. . . . In effect, the price the minority pays for protection in times of minimal stress is to be placed on the front lines of battle in any showdown between the elite and [subordinate groups]" (Blalock 1967:81–83). Indeed, "periodic crises or depressions, during which they serve as convenient scapegoats, may *lock such minorities into these middleman positions for a very long period:* just as tensions begin to subside, as the minority begins to adopt less 'foreign' ways and to disperse itself through the economy, a new crisis arises for which it is blamed, forcing its members to retreat inward, to reduce contacts with members of the 'host' community" (Blalock 1982:55, italics added; see also 108).[45]

Perhaps paradoxically, the long-term locking-in of which Blalock speaks may be of special benefit to eventual global species consolidation by focusing radically different kinds of pressures on the middleman group: On the one hand, there is pressure to nurture contact and deepen familiarity with each of the mediated outgroups, but on the other hand, simultaneously, to nurture the separate identity of the middleman ingroup. Middleman groups, then, have continuously to cultivate close familiarity with a minimum of two outgroups, and often many more, plus their own. It follows that the middleman situation is an inherently privileged one from the standpoint of global species consolidation. Groups in that situation experience the multiculturalist transition (see chapter 6) as a long-term way of life and accumulate intergroup mediation skills. Thus, speaking of the middleman Ibo (preferably, Igbo) mentioned above, Cole and Aniakor report that both trade and oracles

took Igbo well beyond their own borders where interaction with other people doubtless provided "feedback" in cultural and material terms for homeland areas. In return for ivory and slaves (many thousands of whom were Igbo) came a variety of European trade goods: cloth, cowry shells, brass manillas and rods, and later, iron, beads, mirrors, gun powder, and alcoholic drinks. Many of these items were also currencies. The most famous slave and commodity traders were the Aro . . . who established "colonies" in many other communities, where they serviced a remarkably broad and efficient trading network. Their famous oracle . . . at Arochukwu . . . seved as the base of their power, wealth, and prestige. . . . With their oracle and their trading acumen, the Aro exploited and intimidated other Igbo as well as neighboring non-Igbo peoples. . . . [Other Igbo groups] were long-range professional traders as well, bringing foreign goods and ideas back to their own peoples and helping to foster a measure of cultural continuity throughout the various Igbo regions (1984:6–7).

Most prominent among intergroup mediation skills are literacy and numeracy, and the ability to spot connections between previously disparate realms of human experience that these two skills, both separately and together, so effectively engender (see Simmel 1955:115–116; Ong 1982). (Literacy was not one of the skills of the Igbo—nor was it essential for a middleman group in sub-Saharan Africa—but numeracy was.) Such mediation skills come in handy for host societies when, as a result of processes discussed in chapter 4, previously separate ethnic and/or racial groups find themselves in close contact inside those societies. Regarding just such a situation, Lipset and Raab report that "The American playwright Joseph Addison wrote in 1712 that the Jews were 'the pegs and nails in a great building, which, though they are but little value in themselves [sic] are absolutely necessary to keep the whole frame together'" (1995:13).

It almost goes without saying that the same mediation skills come in just as handy when global species consolidation is at stake as when local nationality consolidations are at stake.

Now let us bring another factor into the picture—namely, the general decline, at various speeds in different places and among different nationality groups, of fixed ascriptive labeling and the rise of changeable achievement labeling (discussed further in chapter 6). This change frees members of the middleman group to carry skills long accumulated inside the middleman group outside that group, into the host society. Individual members of the middleman group find these skills welcomed by their hosts now on purely pragmatic, non-traditional, grounds, and the middleman individuals, in their turn and for the same reasons, discover useful skills among their hosts—skills that they themselves formerly regarded as alien. Thus, Lipset and Raab document how increasingly large numbers of American Jews (and American non-Jews) have reaped benefits of the shift toward achievement labeling rather than ascriptive labeling in the host society and of their group's long, varied, and arduous training in the skills of middlemanship (see 1995:14–28).[46] The result is the welcome acceleration of consolidation between these middleman migrants and their hosts:

By the end of the 1994 elections, there were 43 Jews in the U.S. Congress (ten of whom were in the Senate), making up about 8 percent of the Congress, a proportion almost four times higher than that of Jews in the population. . . . During the last three decades Jews have made up 50 percent of the top two hundred intellectuals, 40 percent of American Nobel Prize winners in science and economics, 20 percent of professors at the leading universities, 21 percent of high level civil servants, 40 percent of partners in the leading law firms in New York and Washington, 26 percent of the reporters, editors, and executives of the major print and boadcast media, 59 percent of the directors, writers, and producers of the fifty top-grossing motion pictures from 1965 to 1982, and 58 percent of directors, writers, and producers in two or more primetime television series (Lipset and Raab 1995:142, 26–27).

In sum, "American Jews are steadily becoming more thoroughly integrated into the intellectual, economic, and public life of the society. Their social and geographic mobility is increasing, as is their interaction with other Americans and their cultures. . . . Jews express greater acceptance of other Americans and their cultures, just as other Americans express greater acceptance of Jews and their culture. The rate of intermarriage, already above the halfway mark, is still accelerating."

While they present this picture not without some trace of approval, Lipset and Raab call it "bleak" and assure their readers that "no one is saying that American Jewry will vanish, or that some core of strongly committed Jews will not remain" (1995:192, 47).[47] It should be clear by now, however, that the present book finds neither this nor any other *voluntary* consolidation picture bleak. This is because the reference-point of this book is *species* survival over the long-haul future—although anyone adopting that reference-point should recognize (with sympathy but without grief) that global species consolidation is indeed bleak from the standpoint of every ethnic, racial, and nationality group entering that consolidation, for in it they will *all* "vanish"—and indeed they *are* all, at various speeds, vanishing.[48]

And that comment conveniently points us toward the final topic of this chapter:

Intermarriage

Wedding ceremonies confer political and often religious legitimation on many coalitions at the same time: one coalition between the spouses as individuals, and the others between the families, kinship groups, ethnic, racial, and nationality groups to which the spouses belong and which they, in some sense, represent. For this reason, intermarriage rates can tell us which way, and how strongly, the consolidation wind is blowing now, and which way it is likely to be blowing in the immediate future. As Coleman puts it, "Patterns of marital choice ultimately determine whether a society continues to be characterized by sub-divisions of religion, region or ethnicity, or whether instead a more homogeneous culture develops or is preserved. . . . In an open society, the freedom to choose a marriage partner is taken for granted. . . . Achieved characteristics such as educational and occupational level become more important than ascribed characteristics such as religious, class, regional or ethnic origin" (1992:208–209).

Currently, in the United States at least, "all the evidence suggests that ethnicity is a declining barrier to love and marriage, a development that nationalistic barriers cannot conceivably survive" (Waters 1995:139), and "If the trend of interethnic marriages continues, an ultimate effect may be *the end of ethnicity as we know it today*. There will be too many 'anomalous' individuals around to maintain clear-cut distinctions" (Ericksen 1993:159, italics added). Analyzing this trend, Lieberson and Waters point out that "A substantial and growing segment of the white population [of the United states] is of mixed ethnic ancestry; in 1980, 37 percent of those giving at least one specific ancestry gave a multiple one" (1988:249). These researchers also claim that "a substantial segment of the white population [of the United States] are 'unhyphenated whites' . . . [who] either report themselves as 'American' or are unable to indicate their ancestry," and warn that we should "expect a shift toward a new white subset of the population who are essentially unaware of their European origins" (1988:50).

A popular news magazine has summed up recent data on intermarriage in the United States:

The profusion of [American] couples breaching the once impregnable barriers of color, ethnicity and faith is startling. Over a period of roughly two decades, the number of interracial marriages in the U.S. has escalated from 310,000 to more than 1.1 million. . . . The incidence of births of mixed-race babies has multiplied 26 times as fast as that of any other group. Among Jews the number marrying out of their faith has shot up from 10% to 52% since 1960. Among Japanese Americans, 65% marry people who have no Japanese heritage; Native Americans have nudged that number to 70%. In both groups the incidence of children sired by mixed couples exceeds the number born into uni-ethnic homes (Smolowe 1993:64).

Moreover, the specifically Black-White intermarriage rate increased more than four-fold between 1960 (51,000 marriages) and 1988 (218,000 marriages) (U. S. Bureau of the Census 1990:44; 1991:44) and a recent report (Holmes 1996) claims that whereas in the past, "interracial unions tended to occur later in life and . . . [may thereby have] obviated the possibility of having and raising children, always the most problematic issue in an interracial marriage," a new study shows that "35.4 percent of white women married to black men said they planned to have children, [compared to] the 29 percent of white women married to white men who said they wanted children." The same report notes that "in 1990 . . . nearly two million children live in homes where the primary adults were of different races . . . more than four times the number in 1970." In addition, Goldstein points out that "the voluntary union of two individuals ramifies to create involuntary, but nonetheless real, social relations between kin," and estimates that "about 1 in 7 Whites, 1 in 3 Blacks, 4 in 5 Asians, and more than 19 in 20 American Indians are closely related to someone of a different racial group. Despite the fact that only about 1% of Americans are married to someone of a different race, approximately 20% count someone from a different race among their extended family" (1995:2, 1).

Reporting on intermarriage in Western European countries, Coleman says "Trends from 1927 to 1982 in the proportion of foreigners' marriages with French nationals solemnised in France show an upward trend for all nationalities until 1980, after which those of North Africans have fallen. The rate for Italian men (the highest) has been just over 80% since the early 1980s, suggesting that there may be an upper limit to this process . . . which, without immigrant reinforcement, will lead to the rapid disappearance of any minorities experiencing such levels of out-marriage, unless they 'capture' the spouses and children. . . . By 1988 there were over 327,000 people of mixed origin in Britain, 13% of the total ethnic minority population. . . . The age structure shows that [mixed] birth have become an increasing proportion of all ethnic minority births. In 1985–87 children of mixed origin comprised 19.1% of 0–4–year-olds, 9.3% of 20–24–year-olds and 4.8% of 30–34–year-olds" (1994:126–128). Regarding Germany, Kane tells us that "Between 1961 and 1980 . . . the proportion of all marriages that are mixed (i.e., between Germans and foreigners) has almost doubled . . . because of the increase in the relative size of the foreign population to German nationals accompanied by an increase in the absolute number of intermarriages" (1989:139–140).[49]

Intermarriage data are scarce or nonexistent for the rest of the world. In Japan, however, Kim reports that "Koreans in Japan form the largest of the alien populations living in that country. . . . About 47% of total marriages of Koreans during the period 1965–79 comprised a husband and wife of different nationality. The proportion of Korean-Japanese marriages was higher than that of Korean-Korean marriages in recent years. Attitudes of Koreans in Japan are likely to favor intermarriage with Japanese . . . [suggesting] that mixed marriages of Koreans and Japanese will continue to increase" (1985:445). And in China, Shuzhang and Weijiang report that "fifty-five ethnic groups [not counting the dominant Han group] have been identified" and claim that as a result of a 1978 change in government policies toward these groups, many children born of intermarriages involving members of the Han group began to claim their [non-Han] ethnic identity (see 1992:9–10)—thereby indicating the existence of such intermarriages.

Now, on the foundation the preceding chapters have tried to build, the final chapter sets forth some guesses chiefly about the next couple thousand years (that drop in the bucket again!), and then reaching toward the really distant future. But please note: None of these guesses will be *predictions* for, as Niels Bohr, or was it Casey Stengel, rightly warned us all, "It is very difficult to make accurate predictions, especially about the future."

NOTES

1. "Winning" (and "losing") may be defined by comparing the ingroup's perceived present success level (1) to that of some competing outgroup: Are we as well off as they are? (2) to its own past level of success: Are we better off than we used to be? (3) to a past difference in level of success between it and some competing outgroup: Have we caught up to them, drawn ahead of them, or fallen behind them? and (4) to some arbitrarily set absolute end: Can we do this or that, independently of what other groups can do and independently of what we used to do)?

2. Ogbu also argues that the "collective orientation [of such students] is anti-academic success" (Ogbu 1991:16, 22), to which Fordham and Ogbu add that it is pro-athletics, which, they say, "are regarded as 'black activities'" (1986:202). Fordham adds that the orientation is also pro-resistance as such: "resistance is used as cultural mortar to reclaim, create, and expand African-American humanness" (1996:283).

3. For discussions of the distinction and relationship between cultural structure and social structure, see Wallace 1983, 1988, 1997.

4. On this conceptualization of norms, see Rajecki 1982:33 (he calls them "attitudes"); Wallace 1983:97–109.

5. Jones says: "group A members see group A as more heterogeneous than group B members do, and B members see group A as more homogeneous than A members do: Protestants believe Hassidic Jews are more similar to each other than Hassidic Jews do; Hassidic Jews, on the other hand, see greater Protestant homogeneity than Protestants do" (Jones 1990:101). Why should this be so? The hypothesis Jones prefers "takes into account the probable quality or variety of interactions that we have with ingroup versus outgroup members. . . . [Protestants] see hatted and bearded Hassidic Jews walking down [the street] . . . but [Protestants] do not enter into their lives to see them laugh and cry and get angry in a variety of different circumstances" (1990:103). Thus, stereotypes are often said to be "overgeneralized" and/or "based on too little experience or knowledge" (Rajecki 1982:202; Stephan and Rosenfield 1982:92).

6. Ross and Nisbett refer to "People's inflated belief in the importance of [other, observed, people's] personality traits and dispositions, together with their failure to recognize the importance of situational factors in affecting [those observed people's] behavior" as the "fundamental attribution error" (1991:4). Regarding the opposite tendency in assessing one's own behavior see Ross and Nisbett 1991:140–141. In using this concept to understand group stereotypes, Jones says "instead of attributing negative actions to understandable cultural differences, childhood training, or economic circumstances, [stereotypes] are overly inclined to attribute such actions to underlying dispositions that are so stable as to be irremediable if not actually genetic" (1990:96).

7. Note that each individual is his/her own closest, most intimate, "ingroup"; all other individuals are seen by him/her as, to one degree or another, "outgroups." (The degree of "outness" that the individual assigns to other individuals is called their "social distance" from the individual.) This seems so because the individual cannot be as well acquainted with other individuals' differences among themselves as s/he can be with the difference between him/herself and those others. The outgroup homogeneity component of group stereotypes may thus be grounded in the elementary tendencies of human individuals to distinguish between themselves and others on the basis of a familiarity gradient.

8. Although prejudices are sometimes said to be "characterized by *negative* valuations" (Stephan and Rosenfield 1982:93, italics added), this is only the half of it; prejudices that refer to the ingroup are characterized by strongly *positive* valuations.

9. Smith notes "the role of ethno-history, its myths, values, memories and symbols, in assuring collective dignity (and through that some measure of dignity for the individual) for populations that have come to feel excluded, neglected or suppressed in the distribution of values and opportunities" (1990:182), but one certainly should not limit this effect to disadvantaged populations. Degler, for example, cites "the early [American] colonists' discrimination against the outlander" (1959:66) as having helped shape these colonists' behavior toward both African-American slaves and the American Indians they tried to enslave.

10. Espenshade says "little has changed in how immigrants [to the U.S.] are perceived. At least since the 1880s, immigrants have been assumed to take jobs away from and to lower wages of native workers, to add to the poverty population, and to compete for education, health and other social servives. . . . All that seems to have changed are the origins of migrants and the terms used to describe them. Seldom are new immigrants today referred to as they were in 1920 as the melting pot's 'unsightly indigestible lumps'" (1995:201)—which must be regarded as a terminological change in the direction of consolidation.

11. The same distinction holds for readiness to think or feel a certain way versus the actual thinking or feeling that way (e.g., anticipating the enjoyment of a particular food, and the actual enjoyment of it).

12. Carmichael and Hamilton's discussion of "individual racism and institutional racism" (see 1967: 4–5) seems to combine two different claims: (1) that actual discriminatory behavior may issue from individuals acting independently of each other or from individuals acting cooperatively, and (2) that after discriminatory behavior has brought about residential segregation (that is, after the consumer housing market has been racially segmented—see below), further discriminatory behavior need not be driven by racist norms but may be driven (equifinally—see chapter 1, note 10) by nonracist norms (for example, capitalist entrepreneurs' profit motives, or politicians' support motives). Incidentally, the latter claim seems to be the unspoken basis of Wilson's claim that the significance of race is declining while that of class is increasing (see 1978:1–23).

13. I have adapted this quotation: where I say "migrants" and "hosts," Hannan and Freeman say "organizations."

14. Note the reference to perception here. As Espenshade points out, although "At least since the 1880s, immigrants have been assumed to take jobs away from and to lower wages of native workers" (1995:201), "'studies of labor market impact [in the U.S. during recent years] have found that the effects of immigrants (both legal and undocumented) on the wages and earnings of other labor force groups are either nonexistent or small (and sometimes positive)'. . . . [and that] the overall empirical findings are more consistent with the position that undocumented workers hold jobs that other groups find unattractive" (1995:208, 209).

15. Lieberson and Waters point out that "Blacks provide the most extreme example of immigration barriers [in the United States]. . . . Until the beginning of this century, there was no decade in which more than 900 immigrants came from Africa or more than 35,000 from the West Indies. . . . Asians were also specifically excluded by U.S. immigration law. . . . [T]here was a relatively brief period when Chinese and Japanese were allowed into the United States, but the flow was shut off in 1882 and 1907, respectively" (1982:29–30). Dower notes that "the Chinese [were] singled out by name as undesirable immigrants in no less than fifteen federal laws, or parts of laws, passed between 1882 and 1913—a dishonor done to no other nationality. . . . Where the Chinese in particular were concerned . . . thirty Congresses over a period of sixty years had actively or passively found exclusion appropriate" (1986:165). That these conditions have changed is a measure of the melt to which I have been referring.

16. By contrast, van den Berghe's distinction between "paternalistic" and "competitive" types of race relations (see 1967:28–30) seems to imply that the former is categorically different from the latter and not, as I would claim, merely a variety of the latter.

17. Fernandez-Kelly identifies the gender-based market-segmenting referred to in these last two points as persisting into the current stage of economic globalization: "the definition of women as specialized home-makers and men as providers is being replaced by an understanding of individuals with an obligation to participate in the labor market regardless of gender and/or domestic responsibilities. . . . [but women have been] targeted . . . as a preferred labor force. . . . [by relying] on a reserve of definitions about the proper behaviors and natural predispositions of the sexes. Notions of domesticity, manual ability and conformity were used to explain the incorporation of women into low-skill, low-wage operations" (1994:263, 265).

18. Cox would say "caste-like" (see 1970:67; compare Warner 1953:70–71).

19. In discussing the history of several split labor markets, and noting their link to migration, Castles and Miller say "In the latter half of the nineteenth century, slaves were replaced [in the Americas] by indentured workers as the main source of plantation labour. . . . British colonial authorities recruited over 30 million from the Indian sub-continent. . . . Some were taken to Trinidad, Guyana and other Caribbean countries to replace the labour of emancipated slaves in the sugar plantations. Others were employed in plantations, mines and railway construction in Malaya and eastern Africa. . . . Indenture epitomised the principle of divide and rule, pitting one colonised people against another. Indentured workers were used to undercut the wages of free workers (sometimes former slaves). . . . A number of post-colonial interethnic conflicts (for

example, hostility against Asians in Africa, against Chinese in South East Asia, against Indians in Fiji) have their roots in the divisions brought about by indenture" (1993:49).

20. The same strategies (total exclusion, partial exclusion through market-segmenting, and partial exclusion through market-splitting) are available, also, to entrepreneurs in the economic, political, scientific-educational-technological, and religious markets. For example, Porter proposes "three generic strategic approaches to outperforming other firms in an industry: (1) overall cost leadership, (2) differentiation, and (3) focus" (1980:35). The "focus" strategy pursues total exclusion insofar as it is "built around serving a particular target very well," thereby driving all other competitors out of the market represented by this target—which may be "a particular buyer group, segment of the product line, or geographic market"; and insofar as this strategy "seeks out countries where governmental restraints exclude global competitors . . . . [thereby encouraging the firm to place] extreme attention on the host government in order to insure that protection remains in force" (1980:38, 294–295). The "overall cost leadership" strategy pursues partial exclusion through market-splitting insofar as the firm seeks to produce an equally acceptable product for less cost which it can then sell at a lower price (see Porter 1980:35–37). Finally, the "differentiation" strategy pursues partial exclusion through market-segmenting—that is, by "creating something that is perceived industry-wide as being unique" and that "achieve[s] customer loyalty" which "often [requires] a perception of exclusivity" (1980:37, 38).

21. The economic entrepreneur market may also be partitioned along the same lines (with entrepreneurs belonging to one group being barred from investing in kinds of business in which other groups are welcome to invest, or with one group reaping a lower return on the same investment in the same kind of business than other groups). The same goes for entrepreneurial markets devoted to knowledge, power, and honor.

22. Pinney also notes that "in 324 B.C., the Rhodian Antimenes invented the first system of insurance mentioned in history. He guaranteed owners against the flight of slaves for an annual premium of 8 percent of the value of the slave" (1972:33). Regarding the force applied to slaves in Ancient Greece and Rome, and flight and other resistance among such slaves, see Pinney 1972:33–39; Phillips 1985:27–29.

23. For present purposes, the data here are, of course, limited. My own rough estimate is that the data on about 95% of the cultures in the *Atlas* pertain to dates ranging only from 1800 to 1960, and that there are only perhaps a half-dozen cultures whose *Atlas* data pertain to any time prior to the Christian era.

24. Patterson, in recognizing cases in which members of the slaveholding group itself were enslaved (see 1982:105, 148), argues that the slave's outsider status (which he calls "natal alienation") may come about in two ways—by the slave being brought in from some other group, and by the slave being expelled from the slaveholding group itself (see 1982:38–44).

25. For a review of slavery in, among other places, China, Korea, India, Thailand, Burma, the Philippines, Nepal, Malaya, Indonesia, and Japan, the pre-Columbian New World, England, Scandinavia, France, Germany, Poland, Lithuania, Russia, Arabia, Pakistan, the Ottoman Empire, and sub-Saharan Africa, see Hellie 1991: 286–288.

26. The word "slave" is still applied (as a proper noun) to "a group of Athabascan-speaking Indians of Canada, originally inhabiting the western shores of the Great Slave Lake, the basins of the Mackenzie and Liard rivers, and other neighbouring riverine and forest areas. The name, Awokanak, or Slave, was given them by the Cree, who plundered and often enslaved numbers of them, and this name became the familiar one used by the French and English" (Anonymous 1991).

27. Fortunately, judging from the record of slave rebellions in every known slaveholding society, at least some humans—and, indeed, also some horses, cattle, and dogs (and, Capek predicts, robots as well)—will always remain undomesticated (see Childe 1942:257; Patterson 1982:173; Phillips 1985:14, 19–20, 210–215).

28. Compare Burnham: "Ownership means control; if there is no control, then there is no ownership" (1941:92). When one sees slavery as a primarily *political* relationship it becomes easy to understand how slaves could sometimes be better off economically, educationally, and honorifically than free persons. For example, Finley notes that "Slaves drawn from culturally advanced peoples, such as the Hellenized Syrians in Rome, were regularly employed in such occupations as medicine and education" (1968:309); and Phillips cites the claim that "the free poor . . . not the slaves, occupied the lowest rungs of the Roman social ladder. The slaves were assured that their masters were obliged to provide for their needs; the free poor were alone in facing a hostile world. . . . [E]xposure or sale of children because they could not be supported was done by the free, not the slaves" (1985:28); and Pinney remarks that in the Roman Empire, "There were times when it must have seemed a happier state to be a rich man's slave than a freeborn but poor citizen" (1972:42; see also Childe 1942:256–257, 272; Patterson 1982:182–186, 299; Watson 1980:8).

29. Viewed in this light, one immediate effect, for the freedmen, of Emancipation in the U.S. was the substitution of a mainly categoric and largely economic subordination for a mainly personal and essentially political subordination.

30. The slave-master relation may exist between, as well as within, countries. Entire countries may be partially excluded from regional and/or global producer and consumer markets, and may be forcibly denied decision-making power in those markets—as imperial England once tried to deny to its economically taxed but politically unrepresented middle North American colonies. Seen in this perspective, the American Revolution was a kind of slave revolt.

31. Although no research evidence comes to mind, a similar perception of moral cheapening may apply, in varying degrees, to inheritance and gambling luck as well as theft, counterfeiting and professional misreprepresentation, extortion, profit-making on insider information, special pleading, nepotism, etc. Interpretations of gender, racial, and ethnic affirmative action that (1) disregard that the resources required for social mobility have changed over time, and (2) refuse compensatory damage awards for the unjustified denial of access to earlier mobility resources would put such action in this category as well.

32. Actually, the truth or falsity of the definition is irrelevant; the concept of a self-fulfilling prophecy is easily extended to initial definitions that are true, and to those whose truth or falsity is unknown. The key point is that in all these cases, we have a

mental prophecy that molds the thinker's behavior (his/her action) into conformity with that prophecy—either by generating the conforming action or by sustaining it after it has been generated by some other influence.

33. Thompson says "to the extent that [a coalition] is operative, the organizations involved act as one with respect to certain operational goals." He adds, however, that "Coalition not only provides a basis for exchange but also requires a commitment to future joint decision-making" (1967:36)—a constraint I do not find necessary beyond a commitment to the decision immediately at hand.

34. One effect of American slavery—regarded as a physically coerced master-and-slave coalition—was to strengthen slaveholding European Americans in their competition with European Americans who did not hold slaves (see Fogel and Engerman 1974:5; Finley 1968:310), and with American Indians.

35. Compare the variabilities described above with Gamson's much narrower definition of coalitions as "temporary, means oriented, alliances. . . . [requiring] tacit neutrality of the coalition on matters which go beyond the immediate prerogatives [of the coalition]" (1961a:374). This definition specifies variability neither in the scope of matters within the coalition's prerogatives, nor in the inclusiveness of its membership, nor regarding its permanence. In addition, by requiring coalitions to be "*means* oriented," it ignores that coalitions are almost always *goal*-oriented—that is, formed to pursue some common goal by whatever means are available rather than to use some common means in pursuit of whatever goal turns up.

36. See, for example, Gerlach 1992:xiii–xv, 248, 252–253, 258–262.

37. Dippel also says "Lines were drawn in Germany and elsewhere . . . between those who reaffirmed their allegiance to their country and those who fell under the sway of other attachments—to Marx, 'blood,' race, or the volk. German Jews were divided in these polarities, too" (1996:29).

38. In the same manner, when one joins Weiner's claim that (1) "Most of the world's population flows since World War II did not merely happen; they were made to happen. For the governments of sending countries. . . . [e]migration can be a solution to the problem of cultural heterogeneity. It can be a device for dealing with political dissidents, including class enemies. And it can be a mechanism for affecting the domestic and foreign policies of other states," with his claim that (2) "How governments treat their own populations—once regarded as primarily an internal affair—has become an issue of international relations not simply because human rights are now a global matter but because governments [that violate those rights] may create refugee burdens for others" (1995:29, 15), one can conclude that those governments which support human rights may do so less out of their claimed humanitarianism than out of self-interested defense against being called upon to accept unwanted new refugees.

39. Moskos and Butler say "Race relations can best be transformed by an absolute commitment to nondiscrimination, coupled with uncompromising standards of performance. To maintain standards, however, paths of opportunity must be created—through education, training, and mentoring—for individuals who otherwise would be at a disadvantage" (1996:13).

40. Cohen and Lotan find that if a low-status elementary school student's competence is evaluated highly, and—of equal importance—if that competence is shown to be useful toward some collective achievement by the class, then the "net result . . . will be higher participation and influence on the part of the low-status group members relative to that of the high-status group members [without depressing the participation and influence of the high-status members]." Cohen and Lotan add that "Research has shown the power of these newly assigned expectations for competence to transfer to new task situations" (1995:103–104)—that is, to generalize, eventually, to the whole person and, potentially, to the entire status group to which the student belongs.

41. Of course, the ally in question may be regarded in such an ethnocentric, racist, or nationalistic way as to be treated as a throw-away-after-single-use. In such cases, slavery and genocide are combined. Examples are the labor forcibly commandeered by Nazi Germany, Imperial Japan, and the Stalinist Soviet Union, and on the Caribbean slave sugar plantations during the 18th century.

42. Alba claims that a coalition (which he calls inclusively "European American") is now forming among Americans of many different European origins as they seek to defend their established positions of wealth, power, knowledge, and honor against what they regard as a common enemy—namely, recent Asian, Latin American, Caribbean, and African immigrants: "identities that once separated The English, Irish, Italians, Jews, and Scots now bring individuals with these ancestries together, based on putative memories of ancestors who contributed to [a] common history [of immigration and social mobility in America]" (1990:311, 312).

43. Parsons contrasts universalistic norms with particularistic norms as follows: "'honor thy father and thy mother' is. . . . particularistic, namely, for each child, toward *his particular* parents. If the rule were, on the other hand 'pay honor to parents because of their quality of parenthood as such, regardless of whose parents they are,' it would be a universalistic norm" (1951:63). Applying this idea to the universalism within coalitions, we may say that it consists in paying equal honor (and/or wealth, power, knowledge) to all members of the coalition, or more realistically, that it consists in paying higher, and more nearly equal, honor to members of the coalition than to individuals and groups that are not members of the coalition. As Chapter 2 has already argued, all nations are, in varying degrees, inclusive of different ethnic, different racial, and different nationality groups. Two outstanding examples of such inclusion, within the United States nation, come to mind from the history of the American labor movement during the 19th century—namely, the Knights of Labor, and the Industrial Workers of the World ("Wobblies"). Jones says "the Knights sought to unite all 'toilers' in one grand association, irrespective of occupation, race, nationality, or sex. . . . Thus the unskilled were welcomed along with craftsmen; so were farmers and even capitalists. Only lawyers, bankers, liquor dealers, and professional gamblers were excluded" (1995:311; see also Dulles and Dubofsky 1984:121, 129–130; Higham 1955:70–71). "Wobblies," Dubofsky says, "concentrated upon those workers neglected by the mainstream of the labor movement: . . . exploited eastern and southern European immigrants, racially excluded Negroes, Mexicans, and Asian Americans. . . . Basically, the IWW did what

other American unions refused to do. It opened its doors to all: Negro and Asian, Jew and Catholic, immigrant and native" (Dubofsky 1969:148, 151).

44. Note, also, that entire nations may play middleman roles between other nations from which they are compelled to remain separate (see also note 30). Wallerstein refers to this situation when he says "In a world economy [such as capitalism] . . . besides the upper stratum of core states and the lower stratum of peripheral states, there is a middle stratum of semiperipheral ones. . . . The existence of the third category means precisely that the upper stratum is not faced with the unified opposition of all the others because the middle stratum is both exploited and exploiter" (1979:23, italics removed; see also Blalock 1982:30). In addition, note the special case of middleman minorities cited by Goody's remark that "states existed side by side with zones inhabited by 'uncontrolled,' stateless or tribeless peoples, whom they could raid for human booty without fear of reprisals" (1980:24, see also 27).

45. Middleman groups, of course, are in contact with different groups within the host community (that is the essence of their middleman role) and, despite the obstacles set up against it by ethnic differences, members of middleman groups may enter coalitions with one or the other of these host groups. Thus, Lipset and Raab emphasize the "interest in the welfare of the disadvantaged" that continues to be manifested by American Jews: In a 1984 poll, "60 percent of Jews said that government spending on the poor should be increased, as against 40 percent of the general population, although Jews reported a much higher income level than that of the general population and stood to gain the least from such programs, and to pay the most for them in higher taxes" (1995:147). Moreover, "American Jews have had a sense of shared fate with blacks, in terms of both their own history of oppression and of common enemies in this country. . . . Jews have been the main white supporters of the civil rights and racial equality causes. . . . [Although on occasion] the perceived defensive needs of Jews have conflicted with [this sense]" (Lipset and Raab 1995:155).

46. For discussion of some general theoretical considerations involved in the claim made in the text here regarding the achieved skill consequences of combining the middleman position with ethnic distinctiveness, see, first, Spencer 1898, I:533–538 and Simmel 1950:147–153, and then Mead 1962:152–154 and Mannheim 1955:5–13. The first two imply that mediation (whether of goods and services or information) requires the taking of multiple viewpoints, and the second two hypothesize that such multiplicity generates certain intellectual skills that are not available without it. See Lipset and Raab 1995:12 for what may be regarded as an application—unexplicated as such—of these considerations to Jews as a traditionally middleman group.

47. In striking similarity, Mazrui, after asking "Why should Ibo names be used only by the Ibo, and Zulu names only by the Zulu?" and after arguing that "A special commission of the Organisation of African Unity could. . . . encourage African parents to adopt trans-ethnic names," almost bites his tongue off: "If this process went too far it would, however, be culturally disastrous. African names would cease to signify and reflect the rich plurality of Africa's ethnic heritage. But fortunately only a small minority of parents is ever likely to adopt . . . names from groups other than their own" (1986:255).

48. Friedman reports on one response to this vanishing: "The Israeli Government is worried that as the ring of hostility around it falls, and Israel assimilates with its neighbors and the world, Israel's secular majority will lose its Jewish identity. While business and Asian studies classes at the Hebrew University are booming, Jewish studies enrollment has declined by 30 percent in the last decade. . . . No wonder all Israeli religious parties voted against the peace process—not on security grounds but because they think it will destroy Israel's Jewish character. They do not believe that 'Peace Now' and 'Jewish Now' are compatible" (1995). Simmel explains: "A state of conflict . . . pulls the members so tightly together and subjects them to such a uniform·impulse that they must either completely get along with, or completely repel, one another. This is the reason why war with the outside is sometimes the last chance for a state ridden with inner antagonisms to overcome these antagonisms, or else to break up definitely" (1955:92–93). See also Lipset and Raab 1995:136–137.

49. Botev claims "the popular notion that ethnic intermarriage was widespread in the former Yugoslavia . . . [is] an exaggeration. Rather, ethnic endogamy has been the norm in Yugoslavia . . . [and] Yugoslavia has never been fully integrated: Thus, there is no mystery in that country's disintegration" (1994:476, 477).

6

WHAT NEXT?

The near-future guesses offered here double as answers to some questions that are almost surely still nagging the reader: Does global species consolidation mean cultural *uniformity*? Can, and should, global species consolidation be *forcibly imposed*? What *societal conditions* have to be met in order for that consolidation to be achieved? (A big question.) Isn't there some way to *avoid* global species consolidation? Finally, if and when it is achieved, what seem likely to be some of the principal *benefits and costs* of that consolidation?

CULTURAL UNIFORMITY AND CONSOLIDATION

Bear in mind that the global species consolidation projected here is limited to ethnic, racial, and nationality consolidation. It is sometimes easy to forget that culture comes in many more flavors than just ethnic, racial, and national. There are thousands of vocational and avocational varieties, as well as gender, age, geographical (coastal, valley, mountain, tropical, temperate, frigid, and so on), and ideological varieties—each with its own ideals, its own lingo, and its own way of doing things.

The factors that guarantee perpetual heterogeneity, competition, and innovation among human individuals and groups are many, but they all boil down to the fact that no two things (in the macro world, at least) are absolutely identical and such non-identity, when perceived by two or more individuals, can lead to competition and innovation among them. And the individuals themselves: No two individuals (even clones) or groups can be influenced (from within or from without) by exactly identical sets of forces. Even the grains of sand on a beach are somewhat different from one another and so are we, and each of us reacts to the same stimulus somewhat differently. It comes as no surprise, therefore, to read that globalizing forces of all kinds "tend to become *indigenized* in one or another way: this is true of music and housing styles as much as it is true of science and terrorism, spectacles and constitutions" (Appadurai 1990:294, italics added; see also Hannerz 1990:237; Childe 1942: 2–23; and Ahmed and Donnan 1994:3). No surprise, either, is Braudel's observation that

with the speeding up of communications, the triumphant spread of the French language . . . with the industrial growth of the nineteenth century, and finally the extraordinary and unprecedented prosperity of the 'thirty glorious years' 1945–75, it would be logical to suppose that such mighty forces would have . . . at least spread a thick coat of mono-chrome paint over the mosaic with its hundreds and thousands of coloured fragments. But not at all . . . for progress, marching with giant steps throughout the land, turns out to have changed one *pays* more than its neighbour, or perhaps to have changed it in a par-ticular way, creating a new difference (1988:39, 41).

So the projection of global species consolidation should not be mis-taken to imply any deadeningly homogeneous or static state of human culture. For example, although the world seems to be gradually moving toward a single heterodox (but perhaps mainly English) language, there are apt to be constantly changing locational, vocational, avocational, gender, age, and other sorts of "indigenized" usages of that language which will keep it alive and lively.[1]

FORCE AND CONSOLIDATION

The high valuation that has come to be placed on voluntary "self-deter-mination" from the level of internation coalitions right down to individual persons (together, one must add, with the global diffusion of modern military technology), puts enforced consolidation entirely out of the question. Indeed, it seems clear that the central theme of the fifty-plus years from 1933 to 1989—encompassing the rise and fall of fascist and communist consolidationisms in Europe—was not that consolidation is doomed but that *enforced* consolidation is doomed. The same is true on the global level: "in the twentieth century [we] have . . . moved from a phase dominated by the unidirectional impact of one civilization [the Western] on all others to one of intense, sustained, and multidirectional interactions among all civilizations." During this time, "'the expansion of the West' ended and 'the revolt against the West' began. Unevenly and with pauses and reversals, Western power declined relative to the power of other civilizations" (Huntington 1996:53).

In other words, present trends toward the global equalization of power, knowledge, and honor (and the likely future trend toward globally equalizing wealth) mean that the days of empire are over. Global species consolidation can (and should—in the interests of species survival) now be achieved only to the extent that it is regarded on all sides as an uncoerced voluntary choice.[2] So when Rudolph argues that many of today's conflicts arise from groups' fears that they are culturally endangered species, that enemies seek their cultural, if not physical, annihilation. Such fears drive the militant Sikhs, Sinhala Buddhists, Kurds, Hutus, Andean Indians, and Bosnian Serbs and provide motive and fuel to domestic conflicts in Punjab, Sri Lanka, Guatemala, Turkey, Bosnia and Rwanda. Identities, including religious identities and the esteem conferred by them are at stake (1996:27),

one replies that not universal force but universal implementation of human rights, a transitional multiculturalism supported by a democratic world government, plus convincing demonstrations of global consolidation's benefits and of the forbiddingly escalating costs of ethnocentrism, racism, and nationalism, can allay such fears as these.

Among other things, this means those ethnic, racial, and national groups that have, within recent memory and resentment, exploited others are likely to become persuaded—in their own interests—to offer reparations and apologies to the exploited groups. Germany's reparations to Israel, on behalf of all Jews, for Nazi Germany's genocide can serve as a model here, as can Hungary's 1993 "Act on the Rights of National and Ethnic Minorities" (Republic of Hungary Office for National and Ethnic Minorities 1993),[3] the United States government's recent monetary compensation and public apology to the survivors of the Tuskegee experiment (see Mitchell 1997), and that government's current formal consideration of making apology for 350 years of slavery in the United States. With reparations and apologies of this sort, slates can be wiped as clean as can be reasonably expected in any one or two generations.

Some of the exploited groups, however, will wish to secede from coalitions with groups that have long subordinated them in order to bring that subordination to an unambiguous end and prepare themselves, as well as their former superordinates, for eventual global consolidation on the basis of the equality of all human individuals (Nagel says "In many of the new republics of the former Soviet Union, nationalist mobilizations are built as much on a backlash against Russia and local Russians . . . than on a strong historic pattern of national identity" [1994:158]). Indeed, widespread separatism may turn out to be a boon to the formation of a democratic world government: A well-established large nation—possessing expensive weapons, communications, transportation, and other systems—can better stand alone against attack. A small, weak, and new nation is likely to have greater need of protection by a collective world government.

In any case, it seems clear that, as chapter 1 mentioned, only those separatisms that advocate mass suicide by their members actually favor *complete and permanent* separation. All other separatisms favor some degree of interdependence in their relations with other groups and are thereby open to the eventuality of global species consolidation. (Thus, as chapter 5 indicated, we have strategies of total and partial *self*-exclusion as well as strategies of total and partial *other*-exclusion.) Modern separatisms of this kind, McNeill tells us, are fueled by

population growth on the one hand and new forms of communication on the other [that] brought disruption to local use and wont on a massive scale, creating personal uncertainty, isolation, and disappointment more often than not. Resulting distress can and often does find expression in fundamentalist movements that counteract uncertainty by emphatic affirmation of eternal truths, and counteract isolation and disappointment by forming supportive communities of fellow believers (1993:567, 561).

Needless to add, separatism does not always choose peaceful means—any more than imperialism has chosen such means. Thus, Huntington notes that "separately, terrorism and nuclear weapons are the weapons of the non-Western weak. If and when they are combined, the non-Western weak will be strong" (1996:187–188, see also 192), and Huntington believes they will soon be so combined. One would be shocked but not surprised if that turned out true.

Separatisms of various kinds (both within and between nations) may characterize the next several decades of human history—as reactions to the world's recent and still well-remembered centuries of enforced local and regional consolidations. This is, of course, a reaction that has happened before: "The collapse of the Austro-Hungarian, Ottoman, and Russian empires at the end of World War I stimulated ethnic and civilizational conflicts among successor peoples and states. The end of the British, French, and Dutch empires produced similar results after World War II. The downfall of the communist regimes in the Soviet Union and Yugoslavia did the same at the end of the Cold War" (Huntington 1996:261–262). To this McNeill adds that "more than anything else, reaffirmation of Islam . . . means the repudiation of European and American influence upon local society, politics, and morals" (1993: 569; see also Waters 1995:139; Huntington 1996:53, 81–101, 183–206).

In my judgment, however, the probably large extent to which humankind realizes the economic, political, scientific-educational-technological, and religious conditions to be discussed next will overcome all such separatisms voluntarily (but not overnight), thereby permitting us to complete humankind's first turn around the Grand Cycle and to continue readying ourselves for the second turn.

SOCIETAL CONDITIONS OF GLOBAL SPECIES CONSOLIDATION

Scientific-Educational-Technological Conditions

I put the applied science conditions ahead of all others required for global species consolidation for reasons that will soon become clear. The conditions themselves include: (1) the invention and universally global diffusion of ways to access and transmit massive amounts of cheap, safe, clean, easily usable, and virtually inexhaustible energy; (2) the invention and global diffusion of ways to control world population growth and depletion of the ecosystem; (3) the invention and global diffusion of ways to minimize the production, distribution, and use of arms; (4) the full globalization of the scientific-educational-technological institution itself.

Accessing Cheap, Safe, Clean, Energy. White has formulated the classic argument concerning the bearing of energy resources on human history in general:

Culture never would have exceeded the peaks already achieved by [the beginning of the Christian era] had not some way been devised to harness additional amounts of energy per capita per year by tapping the forces of nature in a new form. [This new form was fossil fuels, namely,] coal, and, later, oil and gas . . . harnessed by means of steam and internal combustion engines (1969:373).

"It is energy," White declares, "that, at bottom, carries the culture process onward and upward" (1969:376)—and who can doubt it?

But because the world's fossil fuel (coal, oil, gas) reserves have absolute limits and, at the rate we are using up these reserves, we shall reach those limits after only another few hundred years at most (see Perutz 1989; Starr et al. 1992), "We must ask ourselves whether . . . the supply of available energy, which has been rising steadily all through human history, will finally peak and begin to decline, and whether that will carry down with it human civilization" (Asimov 1979:315).

Fortunately, however, solar energy technology, wind energy technology, and nuclear fusion technology all seem likely to yield practical applications within the next hundred years or so. Then, not many centuries thereafter, it seems reasonable to expect a switchover, on a massive scale, to some still more inexhaustible, still cheaper, safer, and cleaner outer space solar energy technology (see Criswell, 1985:52, 60–75; Jones and Finney, 1985:91).[4] Meanwhile, Brown reports that "wind power, using the new, highly efficient wind turbines to convert wind into electricity, is poised for explosive growth in the years ahead. . . . The potential is enormous, dwarfing that of hydropower, which provides a fifth of the world's electricity. In the United States, the harnessable wind potential in North Dakota, South Dakota, and Texas could easily meet national electricity needs" (1996:15).

The consequences of introducing new energy sources may be expected to cascade ("Increases in the amount of energy harnessed result in technological progress all along the line, in the invention of new tools and in the improvement of old ones" [White 1969:376]) just as the tool-invention-and-improvement consequences of the large-scale use of fossil fuels are still cascading in waves that we know as the industrial, electrical, electronic, and information revolutions. These have already diminished or wiped out many inequalities among townships, provinces, states, cantons, prefectures, *within* countries. Accessing new energy sources of the sort just described can potentiate further leveling at a high level, not only within but *among* countries.

With such advances, together with robotized and customized production, at last, the enormous economic inequalities between the developed and the developing countries of the world will be finally wiped out.

This is not meant to imply that such inequalities cannot be ameliorated prior to the advent of these new energy sources and the production mentioned above, but the complete *erasure* of these inequalities seem clearly to depend on the production, globally, of not merely abundant wealth but *superabundant* wealth. Wealth has to become as plentiful as the air we breathe (as difficult to imagine as that may be) before it is likely to give up its role as perhaps the prime motivator of competition and the prime differentiator between winners and losers.

Take air, indeed. Breathable air is an item of wealth that is even more indispensable than drinkable water, digestible food, wearable clothes, land, or even television sets and cellular phones. Without air (oxygen), every one of us is dead in a matter of a very few frantic minutes. If we take into account only this fact, we would expect air to be the object of the most intense and universal competition—but that is not the case. The reason is that air is normally superabundant. It is only when air becomes abnormally scarce that its effects on social life change radically (I once read, somewhere that is now lost to my recall, a description of shatteringly convincing *post factum* evidence of intense competition for the last drafts of air in concentration camp gas chambers), and the same, it seems, is true of any other item of wealth as well.

Reducing Population Growth and Ecosystem Depletion. The second desperately needed applied science contribution to global species consolidation is the invention of effective and safe ways of reducing the growth of the world's population and the exhaustion of the world's ecosystem.

The arithmetic of global population growth has become numbingly familiar: 1 billion in 1800, 2.5 billion in 1950, and 5.5 billion today. In the past four decades more people have been added to the globe than in all of history before the middle of this century. And growth continues unabated. The world's population is now expanding at the unprecedented rate of nearly 1 billion per decade, and the United Nations and the World Bank project an additional 6 billion inhabitants by the end of the next century. Virtually all of this growth is expected to occur in Africa, Asia, and Latin America (Bongaarts 1994: 771).

But Brown notes that "thirty countries now have stable populations, including most of those in Europe plus Japan. . . . Collectively, these 30 countries contain 819 million people or 14 percent of humanity. . . . The challenge is for the countries with the remaining 86 percent of the world's people to reach stability. The two large nations that could make the biggest difference in this effort are China and the United States" (1996:12). Brown also points out that "the world economy is growing even faster [than world population]. It has expanded from $4 trillion in output in 1950 to more than $20 trillion in 1995" but adds that

the demand for natural resources has grown at a phenomenal rate. Since 1950, the need for grain has nearly tripled. Consumption of seafood has increased more than four times. Water use has tripled. Demand for . . . beef and mutton has also tripled since 1950. Firewood demand has tripled, lumber has more than doubled, and paper has gone up sixfold. The burning of fossil fuels has increased nearly fourfold, and carbon emissions have risen accordingly. These spiraling human demands for resources are beginning to outgrow the capacity of the earth's natural systems (1996:3–4).

Clearly, global species consolidation is conditional on all these accelerations being braked before they reach levels that set off a global (in both the developed and the underdeveloped world) population crash and all the nearly unthinkable horrors that would imply.

Ending Military Violence. To give it its due, as I have tried to do, war (like the ethnic, racial, and nationality differences that have both sustained it and been sustained by it) has, in the past, conferred major benefits on the evolution of human society as a whole.[5] These benefits have continued to accrue even up through the Cold War in the form of certain well-known technological advances—perhaps most notably the rapid development of electronic computing and rocket propulsion. And Dower reminds us of another, quite different, but important (and mixed) contribution: "It was [the military actions of the Japanese that] . . . destroyed the myths of white supremacism and shattered the European and American colonial structure in Asia in a way that proved . . . to be beyond repair. The Japanese inspired countless millions of Asians with their audacity, even as they inspired hatred for their own overweening arrogance" [1986: 178–179].)

But because "men have gained control over the forces of nature to such an extent that with their help they would have no difficulty in exterminating one another to the last man" (Freud 1961:92), military violence must soon end, and other ways of adjudicating disputes must replace it to at least the same degree that it has been replaced in relations between such one-time mercilessly warring enemies as, say, Massachusetts and Mississippi—and more recently, France and Germany, and Japan and the United States.[6]

Indeed, the very existence of these successes, standing out dramatically against the killing and maiming that immediately preceded them, assure us that a global end to military violence is possible and that it is becoming increasingly feasible. This seems to be the case (despite the fact that "since mid-century, warfare has spread. From fewer than 10 wars at any one time during the fifties, the number of major ongoing conflicts stood at 34 in 1993") because "more than 92 percent of all conflicts since World War II have occurred in developing countries" (Kane 1995:139–140), which means that the most highly developed countries, at least, have turned sharply away from warfare. Moreover, "the nature of war itself is changing. . . . According to the United Nations, of the 82 armed conflicts in the world between 1989 and 1992, only 3 were between countries" (Kane 1995:142). So it seems fair to say that while Robertson's claim that "the world 'learned' something about what has been called 'mutually expected self-restraint' during the Cold War period" (1992:118) applies not yet to the whole world but chiefly to the developed world and especially the so-called Great Powers, that is itself a gigantic step in the right direction.

Of course, war's harm derives not only from actual fighting but from preparation for actual fighting. That preparation, too, seems to be declining:

In 1991, the latest year for which figures are available, the number of troops worldwide totaled 26 million, a drop of 2.7 million, or 10 percent, from 1987. The proportion of the world's population under arms fell to 4.8 from 5.7 over the same period. . . . Arms exports declined by 62 percent between 1987 and 1991 . . . [and] military expenditures worldwide in 1991 were $1,038 trillion, a 14 percent decrease from the peak in 1987. . . . The steepest declines were in the developed world—nearly 20 percent from 1987 levels. [However,] in the developing world, where some two dozen wars are raging . . . spending during the same period actually rose 9 percent to $241.7 billion (Anonymous 1994:A16; see also Glossop 1987:3–4; Huntington 1996:89; Broder 1997).

In conclusion on this point, one remembers Deutsch's reference to "the gradual atrophy of war" (1969:173; see also Keohane and Nye 1977:227); Hollins, Powers, and Sommer's claim that "the era of armaments [may be] drawing to a close," and that "for the greater part of a century, a broad consensus has been building across national and social boundaries heretofore thought insurmountable that war as an institution has outlived its usefulness (if it ever had any)" (1989:196, 1).

Globalizing the Scientific-Education-Technological Institution. Under present circumstances, when the organizational scale, spatial extension, ethnic, racial, and nationality consolidation of human society are all being rapidly globalized, each individual participant's firsthand knowledge of that society is confined to a rapidly shrinking proportion of the whole. A scientific-educational-technological institution that is globalized at all levels of knowledge and skill can counteract this confinement, spread awareness of all manner of alternatives in human concerns, and develop sensitively accurate ways of recording choices among those alternatives—and in all these ways enhance our species' survival chances.

Simmel cites the following historically pivotal, but localized, precedent for the globalization of this institution: "The period of the Renaissance demonstrated most clearly the power of intellectual and educational interests to bring together in a new community like-minded people from a large variety of different groups. Humanistic interests broke down the medieval isolation of social groups and of estates. They gave to people who represented the most diverse points of view and who often remained faithful to the most diverse occupations, a common interest" (1955:135–36; see also Mannheim 1955:5–13), and Waters updates these ideas to our own time: "Cultural flows are primary examples of trans-national connections, links between collective actors and individuals that subvert state frontiers. . . . Satellite broadcasting in particular denies the possibility of national sovereignty over the airwaves" (1995:149).

Regarding the need to globalize the pursuit, as well as the diffusion, of scientific knowledge, Mernissi goes straight to the heart of the matter. The West, she says,

holds a quasi-monopoly on decision-making in matters of science and technology. It alone decides if satellites will be used to educate Arabs or to drop bombs on them. It is understandable and even excusable that the Third World . . . unable to participate in the celebration of science, seeks to find its way by drawing on myths and historical memory. *But when the West, which is opening the way toward the galactic era, trots out tribal flags and Bibles to inaugurate man's exploration of the moon, it does not help the excluded . . . feel they are partners in this universality* (1992:146, italics added).

Weinberg's conclusion follows inexorably:

the radical attack on science [may be] one symptom of a broader hostility to Western civilization. . . . Modern science is an obvious target for this hostility; great art and litera-ture have sprung from many of the world's civilizations, but ever since Galileo scientific research has been overwhelmingly dominated by the West. . . . In the end this issue will disappear. Modern scientific methods and knowledge have rapidly diffused to non-West-ern countries like Japan and India and indeed are speeding throughout the world. We can look forward to the day when science can no longer be identified with the West but is seen as the shared possession of humankind (1992:190).

The day Weinberg forecasts, fortunately, seems on its way, for recent reports tell us that "nowhere is [the pursuit of scientific knowledge] being applied with more enthusiasm today than in the so-called Tigers of Asia—South Korea, Taiwan, Hong Kong, and Singapore—and in China, the region's emerging superpower" and that "Asia's investment in science and technology has skyrocketed over the past decade. . . . Today, the Asian Tigers spend close to $80,000 a year on each research scientist and engineer, about two-thirds the amount in Japan and over half the amount in the United States" (Kinoshita 1993:348). In addition, Moseley reports on a course, called "Human-Computer Interface Technology," now being offered simultaneously, in real time, at Princeton, Stanford, and San Jose universities: "A faculty member of one of the institutions lectures to all the students, who can see each other, engage in discussion and question the lecturer. 'Since the system is interactive,' says [the instructor], 'we've even been able to have lecturers from two different campuses in the same session' " (1996:1, 3). It requires little imagination to see such courses, reaching to and from every part of the world, eventually transforming all the sciences into a single, genuinely global and species-wide, enterprise whose participants will eventually rank as far above our present average in knowledge and technological instrumentation as the present average is above that of ten thousand years ago.

Regarding the globalization of communication in general, Schramm stresses the effects of mass education on government: when "people went to school . . . they learned to read and became more deeply interested in their governments and in the world beyond the realm of their eyes and ears. The growth of popular governments required people to inform themselves and helped them to do so by providing schools and facilitating the distribution of newspapers" (1972:49–50). Swatos helps make the connection to individual freedom by arguing that as part of its universal dissemination of information, "the media can have a tremendously decharismatizing effect by providing 'instant analysis'—that is, criticism—of any figure or event. The extraordinary and the everyday are so merged here as to become indistinguishable, and of course, one may at any time turn the dial elsewhere or the tube off" (1984:206).

Moreover, insofar as decharismatizing special individuals is tanta-mount to charismatizing ordinary individuals equally, the result is that "the dignity of the individual, irrespective of the groups of which he is a part" (Merton 1976:190; see also Simmel 1950:282) is becoming a prime support of global species consolidation.

Voluntary Associations. Another strong contributor to global species consolidation, closely related to the globalization of communications, is the proliferation of voluntary associations that cut across (and thereby help break down) lines of ascribed ethnicity, race, and nationality by catering to achieved human interests, skills, and beliefs. Of such associations, Hannerz says, "It is really the growth and proliferation of such cultures and social networks in the present period that generates more cosmopolitans now than there have been at any other time" (1990:241). Gleick reports on the new technologies that such voluntary cultures and social networks now have at their disposal:

At any given moment, several dozen people in the United States, Britain, Taiwan, Hong Kong, Norway, Sweden, and a handful of other countries can be found . . . playing bridge with one another on [the Internet]. . . . In the past, people with [certain] special interest[s]—medieval fabrics or military-strategy games or expressionist art—made their way to cities or universities, the only places that accumulated critical masses of like-minded people. Now the possibilities are richer. . . . We are learning . . . to maintain new forms of "virtual community" or "community without propinquity" (1993:62, 64; see also Rheingold 1993).

And we should not forget to include those voluntary associations that deliberately promote some particular social change or social persistence (see Lauer 1976:xiii; McAdam, McCarthy, and Zald 1988:695). Even though some of these movements seek to strengthen ethnic, racial, and nationality boundaries, the fact that they reach across such boundaries to do so is not entirely without benefit for consolidation. Wirth says, "In this shrunken and interdependent world, social movements of all sorts assume a progressively universal character and recruit their supporters and adversaries among peoples near and far, irrespective of national boundaries (1945:347).

Economic Conditions

Leontiades tells us, "One of the most important phenomena of the twentieth century has been the international expansion of industry. Today virtually all major firms have a significant and growing presence in business outside their country of origin" (1985:3; see also Clarke 1985:1–16; Kotabe 1992:1; Sider 1992:237; Kennedy 1993:54; Portes and Walton 1981:187). Of course, as Kennedy points out, this globalization is heavily dependent on modern science and technology: "Without the vast increase in the power of computers, computer software, satellites, fiber-optic cables, and high-speed electronic transfers, global markets could not act as one, and economic and other information—politics, ideas, culture, revolutions, consumer trends—could not be delivered instantaneously to the more than 200,000 monitors connected to this global communications system" (1993:50–51).

Economic globalization extends to the labor force as well, but in addition to the increasingly free global migration of the human labor force that has already been discussed here, one can also see signs of the time that Marx envisioned—the time when the labor force will no longer consist of a class, occupation, and job division of labor among humans but of a fundamentally new division of labor—between humans on one side and machines on the other. The machine side, he predicted, will be carried out by "an automatic system of machinery . . . set in motion by an automaton, a moving power that moves itself; this automaton consisting of numerous mechanical and intellectual organs" (1973:692, italics removed). And on the human side,

the human being . . . [will] relate more as watchman and regulator to the production process itself. . . . He steps to the side of the production process instead of being its chief actor. . . . The free development of individualities   . . . [based on] the general reduction of the necessary labour of society to a minimum, which then corresponds to the artistic, scientific etc. development of the individuals in the time set free, and with the means created, for all of them (Marx 1973:705, 706; see Kennedy 1993:82–94).

Whatever other, secondary, and, in many cases, failed predictions Marx made, this primary one seems increasingly borne out in these years of industrial robotization. Indeed, Rifkin, writing little more than a century after Marx, says "now, for the first time, human labor is being systematically eliminated from the production process. . . . [and] within thirty years as little as 2 percent of the world's current labor force 'will be needed to produce all the goods necessary for total demand'" (1995:3, 239). A few centuries more, and all basic economic production seems likely to be carried out by an array of highly differentiated, customizing, robotically operated, world-distributed and world-serving wind-and/or fusion-powered, public utilities—joining those other public utilities that now provide people in the developed countries with superabundant, cheap, safe, clean drinking water.

As this transformation comes to pass, the problem will become less that of finding economically productive work for people than of distributing goods that are robotically produced among the world's overwhelmingly nonworking (but not unemployed) people and training them in whatever may then be regarded as the "productive" use of what we now regard as "leisure" time (compare Rifkin 1995:239, 257–258).

Recreation. Only in extreme circumstances, and then only rarely, has the individual's daily life been totally without respite from work, so we should not overlook the importance of play, entertainment, recreation—especially as work-for-a-living releases its ancient and at last aging grip.

Schramm (writing in 1957) notes that "only fifty years ago there [was] no radio and no television; movies were represented by a few nickelodeons; newspapers were a combination of party papers and yellow press." But, Schramm asks, "What would people have thought 50 years ago, if someone had told them that in the future most homes would contain a relatively inexpensive little box into which one could look and see and hear the Metropolitan Opera, the New York Music Hall stage, the Olympic games in Melbourne, the meetings of the United Nations, the fighting in a distant part of the world, and the candidates for national office?" (1972:53, 54). And what may people a thousand years, a million, a hundred million years from now have at their disposal for what we call recreation and what Marx calls "the artistic, scientific etc. development of . . . individuals"? Who can tell what instantaneous, user-friendly, unobtrusively portable, individualized, and interactive access they may have to all the transcribed and imaged information ever collected by humankind, to all the play and recreation of AI-generated virtual worlds as well as of the real world, and to participation in an endless variety of ethnicity, race, and nationality-transcending voluntary associations extending all around this planet and beyond?

Political Conditions

Waters notes "the possibility of a borderless world is enhanced to the extent that there is a common political culture across societies" and that "the main developments [toward the global predominance of liberal democracy] occurred within . . . the accelerated phase of globalization, the last third of the twentieth century. . . . The number of liberal-democratic states in the global system . . . doubled between 1975 and 1991 so that about 60 of the world's largest societies are now liberal democracies (1995:118, 119, 120).

However, democracy in separate and autonomous societies is no guarantee in itself that military violence will cease. Indeed, it seems that a principal military function of the state in advanced industrial democracies today is coming to be the defense of its national borders and international interests against refugees and illegal immigrants from the underdeveloped societies (just as one function of the economy in those advanced democracies is selling arms to those same societies—see Sivard 1991:17). So, even when it is democratic, the territorially sovereign nation-state "might . . . just be the final bastion of resistance to globalizing trends and the key indicator of their ultimate effectivity" (Waters 1995:122)—but perhaps not the *last* final bastion (as will be discussed below).

Nevertheless, one should certainly count international organizations among the most important factors now undermining the sovereign nation-state. Boli and Thomas, indeed, assert that "for a century and more, the world has constituted a single polity. By this we mean that the world has been conceptualized as a unitary social system, increasingly integrated by networks of exchange, competition, and cooperation, such that actors have found it 'natural' to view the whole world as their arena of action and discourse." Their study of "international non-governmental organizations" finds that "following [World War II, the number of] international organizations exploded. By 1947 over 90 organizations a year were being founded, a pace that was maintained and even surpassed through the 1960s [and into the 1970s]," and that "five basic world-cultural principles . . . underlie [international non-governmental organization] ideologies and structures: universalism, individualism, rational voluntaristic authority, human purposes of rationalizing progress, and world citizenship" (1997:172, 177, 180). McNeely identifies some of the polity-globalizing practices of these organizations:

Through their standard-setting instruments, . . . through their designation of collective authority and recognition, and through various types of aid and resources . . . international organizations help to effectively establish and implement world ideological accounts and practices. . . . [Such organizations] have fixed procedures for decision making, and states utilizing international organizations to achieve certain goals must take those measures into account. . . . [In this way,] international organizations . . . [act] to formulate and construct world level norms and values, relating the nation-state to the international system in terms of structure, practice, and ideology (1995:151, 152, 153; see also 160).

Almost needless to add, the extent to which such international organizations possess genuinely global memberships is also significant, and McNeely notes that "the International Confederation of Free Trade Unions, the World Confederation of Labor, and the World Federation of Trade Unions could be viewed as nascent global labor movements and trade unions" (1995:152).[7]

To all this we must remember to add the continuing impact of migration on political globalization. Coleman says "Migration since the Second World War, much of it organised during Europe's rapid economic growth up to 1973, has created a population of 14 million foreigners living in Western European countries. In the EC there are about 5 million citizens of other European countries. . . . In addition, Third World immigration streams of various origins have established substantial colonies within almost all European countries, differing in colour, language, religion, and economic and political background from the host population. Altogether in the EC these number about 8 million foreigners of various non-European origins, of whom almost 5 million are Muslim" (1994: 107). Weiner concludes that

the venerable notion of state sovereignty . . . is being transformed under the new reality of international population movements. It is old news that states are becoming interdependent and face more and more international constraints on domestic policies. Global trends in international transporttation, technologies, weapons, and the structure of the global economy have eroded earlier notions of sovereignty. What is unique about international migration, however, is that it changes the very composition of a country's population. . . . It brings the outside in, as it were, even as it also involves sending insiders out. The result is not merely an impersonal interaction involving monetary systems, trade flows, or acid rain but deeper, affective interactions involving human beings (1995: 130).[8]

(What better portrait of emerging global species consolidation could one want?)

Multiculturalism. Now as chapter 1 suggested, the idea of global species consolidation can be used (misused) as a sly velvet glove disguising the iron fist of global species *dominance* by some particular ethnic, racial, and/or nationality group. Indeed, Huntington claims that "the concept of a universal civilization helps justify Western cultural dominance of other societies. . . . Universalism is the ideology of the West for confrontations with non-Western cultures," and that "the argument that [modern societies will merge] rests on the assumption that [such societies] must approximate a single type, the Western type" (1996:66, 69; see also 109; see also Schermerhorn 1978:14; see also 66).

By contrast with a onesided and closed consolidation (read domination), of this sort, a many-sided and open consolidation does not presume the dominance of any *particular* ethnic, racial, or nationality group, and remains open to contributions from all conceivable sides. However, note that *some* such dominance (changing over time and varying over space) seems likely on purely probabilistic grounds. Just as chapter 2 explained the sociocultural founder effect shown in Figure 2.5 on the ground that absolute identity of any two things is, in principle, extremely unlikely because out of all the vast number of different relationships that the two things may have to one another only *one* of this vast number is identity. The same holds for the absolute *equality* of any two things. It, too, is extremely unlikely, while inequality between the two things—at every single point in time—is extremely likely. In a permanently open and manysided consolidation, although the prediction that *some* contribution will be more salient than others is assured, *which* contribution that will be is an altogether separate, and virtually unpredictable, question. It is like knowing, for sure, that in a fair toss of a fair die—that is, one that is equally open to any number from one to six showing up on a given toss—*one* of these numbers is bound to show up, but *which* one is completely uncertain.

Currently, the most popular defense against loaded dice (i.e., a prematurely closed and onesided global consolidation) is "multiculturalism," a kind of halfway house that combines consolidation in some aspects of social life with continued separation in other aspects. Rex, for example, defines multiculturalism as advocating "the acceptance of a single culture and a single set of individual rights governing the public domain . . . [but] a variety of folk cultures in the private domestic and communal domains" (1996:18).[9] Among the supporters of multiculturalism are Mernissi, who believes that in it, "all cultures can shine in their uniqueness" (1992:174) and Huntington, who argues that "avoidance of a global war of civilizations depends on world leaders accepting and cooperating to maintain the multicivilizational character of global politics" (1996:21).[10]

Of Mernissi, however, one must ask Shine *for how long*? and of Huntington Avoid *for how long*?—for it seems likely that "even a modest degree of structural separation will tend always to [generate] . . . a low, endemic degree of prejudice among the various ethnic groups" (Gordon 1964:238) and such prejudice will steer those groups back into the same vicious circle of attack and counterattack that has so bloodied human history until now.[11]

In short, multiculturalism does not seem to be a stable alternative to global species consolidation. It may still be a useful transition, however, in getting us from where we are now to a symmetrically open global species consolidation. That is to say, insofar as multiculturalism protects ethnic, racial, and nationality cultures whose societies are technologically weaker from being steamrollered by more powerful cultures, its role seems parallel to environmentalism, which aims to protect currently endangered biological species and ecologies until they can get on their feet.

World Government. For the same reason, some transition from the present political system of autonomous and intrinsically warlike nation-states may be useful until the open global species consolidation referred to above can get on its feet.[12] Stinchcombe points out that "Universalistic laws making contracts between [strong and weak] strangers binding, reliable negotiable instruments so that one can trust the paper and not the man, ethics of achievement according to impersonal standards in occupational life, rather than interpenetration of occupational and kinship life, all clearly make it easier to construct social systems out of groups of strangers" (1965:149).[13] A world government seems clearly the place to look for such laws.

To this, one must add the importance of such a world government being a democratic one whose principal officeholders are popularly elected by a global constituency. Given the continuing (though diminishing) bearing of geographical territory on ethnicity, race, and nationality—coupled with the still uneven distributions of power, knowledge, honor and wealth across those territories—local political constituencies are likely to breed localist (i.e., ethnocentrist, racist, and nationalist) political leaders. Global constituencies, by contrast, stand a better chance of breeding globalist political leaders, and it is from such leaders, answering to such constituencies, that we should expect the "universalistic laws" to which Stinchcombe refers.

In any case, the prospect of eventual global species consolidation permits us to look forward, in Tilly's neat phrase, to "obituaries for the state" (1975b:683)—a future that seems already nascent in, among other places, the worldwide system of international organizations that are independent of such states (discussed earlier), and also in the United Nations. Indeed, we may look forward to a democratic world federation of nations in which all persons will hold equal citizenship; to which they will as willingly pay global income taxes as we now pay federal, state, and local income taxes—which is certainly not all that willingly, but we do it, and we know it makes a big difference in the quality of our own and our fellow-citizens' lives.[14]

With such a world government in place, the world's citizens will soon come and go across all former national boundaries as freely, and causing as little social disruption, as Americans now come and go across the Mason and Dixon line. And in the same way that the latter coming and going (though once mortally dangerous) has, within barely two lifespans, become not worth remarking upon—even for African Americans—so the former will be, in time.

A world government, then, standing above all national governments but dividing jurisdictions with them as the latter now (and will then) divide jurisdictions with state and local governments—can facilitate the transition from our present system of largely (though diminishingly) autonomous nation-states to global political consolidation (see also Alter and Hage 1993:293).

At this point, one might ask What might such a truly global political consolidation look like? Here, Waters offers a speculation that I find attractive:

A globalized polity can have the characteristics of a network of power centres. . . . In principle such power centres might be coordinated because their controllers share common norms and common interests and sought to move toward consensus on such issues. . . . Regional groupings of states, such as the [European Union], and a wide range of special interest associations already coordinate their activities on just such a basis. However such an outcome is less likely than a polity organized as a market, or more precisely as multiple markets. Here processes of allocation (e.g., of welfare, economic development, peace and security, pollution, cultural performances) would be governed by competition between power centres much in the way that global flows of finance or of information are the consequences of multiple and complex decisions (1995:111).

Thinking along the same lines, Naisbitt says "just as the Internet is a network of about 25,000 networks . . . [the] world is moving from a collection of nation-states to a collection of networks" in which "no one is in charge; the marketplace is. [In such a system,] each of the parts functions as though it were the center of the network [and each individual can] experience being in the center, just as does each of the other 50 million users of the Internet" (1996:21, 23, 22).

Religious Conditions

"For many centuries, the great universalizing religions of the world, Buddhism, Christianity, Confucianism, Islam and Hinduism offered adherents an exclusivist and generalizing set of values and allegiances that stood above both state and economy" (Waters 1995:125). Such religions, however, have supported only *incoming* conversions. The lowering of barriers to individuals freely choosing to *leave* as well as to join, and also to *cross, straddle,* and *combine*, different religious faiths should be regarded as furthering the long-term trend toward transforming religious faith from an ascribed characteristic conferred at birth and not easily changed thereafter to an achieved characteristic that anyone, at any time, may freely choose, change, construct, or reject. Coleman's comment refers to a modern emergence of freedom of this sort: "Today, for many people in Western Europe, religious affiliation no longer determines social contacts or marital choice. Old local cultural isolates have substantially broken up. . . . By the early 1970s a majority of marriages solemnised in Roman Catholic churches in England and Wales were mixed marriages, not counting marriages involving Catholics solemnised elsewhere" (1992:213). (Intermarriage as such is discussed later in this chapter.)

Thus, when Dulles (commenting as a Catholic on the Second Vatican Council of 1962–1965) predicts that "the coming decades . . . will witness the maturation of a broadly ecumenical theology in which adherents of different religions and ideologies can fruitfully collaborate" (1980:40), that collaboration is apt to enhance individual freedom to choose among various combinations of such collaborators and to increase thereby the chances for global species consolidation. A similar opinion has been expressed by another Catholic leader: "As far as the future goes, only one thing is certain: At the end both of human life and the course of the world Buddhism and Hinduism will no longer be there, nor will Islam nor Judaism. Indeed, in the end Christianity will not be there either. In the end no religion will be left standing, but the one Inexpressible, to whom all religions are oriented" (Kung 1988:255). Then there are the still more radical words of Lukas Vischer, director of the Secretariat of the Commission on Faith and the Constitution of the World Council of Churches, in which he suggests an emergent religious agnosticism: "A strange new community [among different faiths] has come into being, a community of questioning and search-ing, a community of fundamental agreement and, in many respects, also of fundamental uncertainty" (1979:105).

It would seem, however, that our species still has many centuries of adherence to an assortment of fundamental *certainties* before Vischer's community of uncertainty can come to pass worldwide. Indeed, it seems likely that global religious consolidation may be the *really* final institutional bastion of resistance to globalizing trends mentioned earlier— because what is at stake in loyalties to religious certainties is, by definition, both beyond all conceivable empirical disconfirmation and transcendant of all other conceivable values.

Any conclusion regarding the religious conditions of global species consolidation should definitely find a place for Durkheim's now 80-year-old claim that "a social life of a new sort is developing. It is this international life which has already resulted in universalizing religious beliefs" (1965:493); for Spencer's 120-year-old claim that there are two types of religion—"the religion of enmity and the religion of amity"—and that the first type is "supreme at the beginning [of history]" while the second "will be supreme at the end" (1961:161); and also for Wuthnow's more recent comment that "when individual and national authority are understood . . . in the context of social relations that affect all of humanity, then a broader, more encompassing, and even more transcendent sense of the sacred becomes necessary" (1991:36).

AVOIDANCE OF GLOBAL SPECIES CONSOLIDATION

Now, given the societal conditions of global species consolidation (and not one of them seems simple or easily accomplished) that have just been discussed, let us consider two other questions: First, since it seems so difficult, do we have to go as far as *consolidating* all the ethnic, racial, and nationality groups into which our species is presently divided? Can't we *repair* the existing system of ethnicity, race, and nationality well enough to go on, indefinitely, *un*consolidated? Second, If we do have to consolidate, can't we just consolidate the developed world and *leave the underdeveloped world out of it*?

Ascribed and Achieved Group Membership Labeling

To begin approaching the first question, consider the nature of the labels used to denote membership in ethnic, racial, and nationality groups. Anthropologists and sociologists call such labels "ascribed"—meaning that they are assigned to the individual at birth and are generally fixed-for-life.[15] (Note that such labels were more fixed in the past than they are now; many exceptions have evolved over time, including trans-ethnic, trans-racial, and trans-national adoption, name-changing, place-changing, and other techniques of "passing," and, most important of all, what is whimsically referred to as the "naturalization" of immigrants. I shall argue that these exceptions to the rule give us important clues regarding the direction in which the labels themselves are changing.)

The crucial thing about the fixed-for-life character of ascribed labels is that *conversion* of a group defined according to such labels is, in principle, not possible. If one is competing against such a group, the only way to beat it is to *exterminate* it, or seal it off until it dies out on its own. Facing each other across ascribed boundaries, to use Huntington's expression, "Each side . . . eventually attempts to transform this distinction into the [difference] between the quick and the dead" (1996:266; see also Browning 1992:162). So it was that the anthropologist Earnest Hooton, pursuing his belief that criminal tendencies are genetically determined, therefore present at birth and fixed-for-life, concluded that "the elimination of crime can be effected only by the extirpation of the physically, mentally, and morally unfit, or by their complete segregation in a socially asceptic environment" (quoted in Marks 1995:244; see also Hooton 1939:392–393, 396–398).

By contrast, when group membership labels are applied according to achieved, experientially changeable, criteria, it is *conversion* rather than extermination that is the strategy of choice. Indeed, it is the ever-present potentiality of conversion that makes possible political democracy and its characteristically peaceful transfer of power: The party that loses one election knows it may win the next—not by killing off its opposition and thereby weakening the entire society over which it seeks rulership but by persuading members of the opposition as well as uncommitted participants to change their views and come over to its side. With conversion rather than extermination as their mechanism of leadership change, democratic societies preserve and build their strength.

The intrinsically exterminative bias (chapter 5 called it a total exclusionist strategy) of ascribed membership labels, then, is the primary feature that has made such labels too hot to handle in the present world—a world equipped to implement that bias with an ultimately species-extinguishing vengeance. The second prohibitive feature of ascribed membership labels is their close tie to the partial exclusion techniques of market-segmenting and market-splitting that were also discussed in chapter 5 (see also Durkheim 1984:310–322). When fixed-for-life membership in a particular ascribed group does not mark outsiders for extermination, it locks individuals into particular social statuses, roles, and careers—regardless of the personal abilities they may be capable of developing during their lifetimes. Such gross inefficiency can only diminish the species' chances for continued survival.[16]

For these reasons, I argue that the system of ascribed ethnic, racial, and nationality groups that once so well served humankind's survival, has now outlived its usefulness and is holding us back from further strengthening our species survival powers. This system, in a word, is past repair; it has become fit only for junking.

Indeed, the proliferation of exceptions (mentioned earlier) to the fixity of ascribed membership labels suggest that the system has been increasingly over-ridden by achievement labels—and in this sense, it has been gradually moved over to the junkpile of history—for some time now. Gans, for example, argues that "the ethnic role [in the United States] is today less of an ascriptive than a voluntary role that people assume alongside other roles," and "the behavioral expectations that once went with identification by others have declined sharply, so that ethnics have some choice about when and how to play ethnic roles" (1979:7–8). "People," Gans says, "are less and less interested in their ethnic cultures and organizations—both sacred and secular—and are instead more concerned with maintaining [the sociopsychological elements of] their ethnic identity, [namely,] the *feeling* of being Jewish, or Italian, or Polish" (1979:7, italics added). Nagel adds to this by arguing that since the individual changes his/her ethnicity (and Nagel includes race in that term) according to the situation,

the individual carries a portfolio of ethnic identities that are more or less salient in various situations and vis-a-vis various audiences. As audiences change, the socially-defined array of ethnic choices open to the individual changes. . . . [In this manner,] ethnic identity is *both* optional and mandatory, as individual choices are circumscribed by the ethnic categories available at a particular time and place. That is, while an individual can choose from among a set of ethnic identities, that set is generally limited to socially and politically defined ethnic categories with varying degrees of stigma or advantage attached to them (1994:154, 156).

Gans' and Nagel's analyses refer to late-twentieth century American ethnicity. However, the extent to which the flexibility and choice they have in mind is now gathering momentum in the world seems a clear indication of breakdown in ascriptive fixity-for-life labels and the emerging dominance of achievement labels.[17]

        To appreciate fully the negative view of the future usefulness of ascription being presented here it may be helpful to compare it with a more positive view. Patterson tells us that "The incapacity to make any claims of birth or to pass on such claims is considered a natural injustice among all peoples, so that those who were obliged to suffer it had to be regarded as somehow socially dead" (1982:8). One can have no quarrel with the first part of this as an empirical statement about how much people have cherished, and still do cherish, ascribed membership labels—i.e., "claims of birth." But Patterson, by identifying an incapacity to make or pass on such labels with "social *death*" (he also says "the definition of the slave, however recruited, [is] as a socially dead person. Alienated from all 'rights' of claims of birth, he ceased to belong in his own right to any legitimate social order" [1982:5]), asks us to associate ascriptive fixity-for-life with *social life* as such in "*any* legitimate social order." In sharp contrast, I argue that such fixity is intimately associated with socially exterminative tendencies, and that a social order in which all such claims are replaced by claims of achievement is altogether preferable in the interests of species survival—and of course social life (see also Durkheim 1984:310–316).

        One must admit, however, that ascribed membership labels have, in the past, provided security, warmth, and a sense of "home" to ingroup members (while at the same time radiating forbiggingly alien threat to outgroup members).[18] So we must ask whether discarding such labels would cost personal psychological disorientation and physical disruption.

There is simply no denying that it would entail such costs, and the only comfort (apart from the basic comfort of species survival) is that every leaving of one's home to encounter the wider world entails some temporary psychological disorientation (culture shock) and some temporary physiological disruption. But on the other hand, there are the explorer's pleasures of "crossing boundaries and charting new territories" (Said 1993:317; see also Mannheim 1955:154–164), and eventually our descendants will feel completely comfortable saying, with Wole Soyinka, "In my head, that's where home is" (quoted in Jaffrey 1997:C10). In any event and whether we like it or not, many kinds of boundary-crossing are growing daily and seem unstoppable: Modern "technologies are able to uncouple culture from its territorial base so that, detached and unanchored, it pulsates through the airwaves to all those with the means to receive it." The result is that "more people than ever before [are] becoming involved with more than one culture" and "matters which in the past were considered only by the well-informed few [are] now debated in markets, at village wells and in tea houses [in the Muslim world]" (Ahmed and Donnan 1994:4, 17).

There is at least one other possible objection to trading-in ascribed labels for achieved ones. Ascribed labels have been an essential part of that interethnic, interracial, and international competitiveness from which so much human innovation has sprung. Would we have to do without that as well?

In considering this question, one notes that, after reporting that both Black and White soldiers believe competitive friction between their races is much lower in the Army than in civilian life,[19] Moskos and Butler go on to claim that this does not mean *all* intergroup and interpersonal friction comes to an end; it simply moves elsewhere: "Friction in the Army arises [now] not so much between the races as between lower-ranking soldiers and sergeants, between enlisted men and officers, between line units and staff units" (1996:6).

Indeed, it seems a reasonable guess that we shall have intergroup and interpersonal friction and competition with us *always* (much longer than we shall have poverty with us)—as indispensable sources of new human history. What we can no longer afford to have with us always are group membership labels that rely on the extermination-disposing, and grossly inefficient, fixities of ethnic, racial, and nationality ascription.

Partial Global Species Consolidation?

Now let us turn to the second avoidance question—namely, Why shouldn't the more developed countries and peoples simply *write-off* the under-developed ones? Why not think of the underdeveloped part of the species as like the booster stage of a rocket, to be deliberately jettisoned once it lifts the second stage high enough? Or, to put the same question differently: *We've got ours*; let the underdeveloped peoples get theirs (not including, of course, *taking* it—even though that's how we got a lot of ours). If they don't, it's just *too bad for them*. Period.

To name some names so that there can be no doubt regarding who we are talking about here, the "them" include, in the first place, all the under-nourished, underempowered, undereducated, and dishonored *Africans*, both those now living in sub-Saharan Africa and the hyphenated Africans living elsewhere—the African Americans, African English, African French, African Germans, African Haitians, African Guyanans, African Jamaicans, and so on. And include also all the other underdeveloped racial, ethnic, and nationality groups of the world—all the Nicaraguans, Azerbaijanis, Yemenis, Bangladeshis, Bhutanis, Indians, Nepalese, Pakistanis, Tajikistanis, Laotians, Vietnamese, Mongolians, and Albanians, for starters.[20]

More than twenty-five years ago, Yette put this question (his focus was then narrowly on African Americans, but the question easily stands extending to the entire underdeveloped world) as follows: "black Americans are obsolete people . . . in the minds and schemes of those who, with inordinate power and authority, control the nation. . . . [To them,] black Americans have outlived their usefulness. . . . Once an economic asset, they are now considered an economic drag. . . . [Black Americans] want to survive, but only as men and women—no longer as pawns or chattel. *Can they?*" (1971:14, 15; italics changed).

More recently, Wilson has narrowed the focus of this question to inner-city Blacks (and his analysis, too, is readlily extended to the entire under-developed world inside the United States—which is composed of Whites as well as Blacks, and also Browns, Reds, and Yellows—and to the much vaster underdeveloped world outside the United States): "The economy has churned out tens of millions of new jobs in the last two decades. In that same period, joblessness among inner-city blacks has reached catastrophic proportions. Yet in this Presidential election year, the disappearance of work in the [Black] ghetto is not on either the Democratic or the Republican agenda." Wilson goes on to explain why work is so crucial to the character of a person's entire life: "Work is not simply a way to make a living and support one's family. It also constitutes a framework for daily behavior because it imposes discipline. . . . In the absence of regular employment, life, including family life, becomes less coherent." As a consequence, Wilson says,

High rates of joblessness trigger other neighborhood problems that undermine social or-ganization, ranging from crime, gang violence and drug trafficking to family breakups. . . . As the neighborhood disintegrates, those who are able to leave depart in increasing numbers; among these are many working- and middle-class families. The lower popula-tion density in turn creates additional problems. Abandoned buildings increase and often serve as havens for crack use and other illegal enterprises that give criminals—mostly young blacks who are unemployed—footholds in the community. Precipitous declines in density also make it even more difficult to sustain or develop a sense of community (1996:27, 30, 28, 29)

Now as chapter 5 has already indicated, the basic strategies open to the developed world are (1) to *exclude* (either totally or partially) the presently underdeveloped world from the wealth, power, knowledge, and honor that the developed world enjoys, and apply all the particularistic stereotypes, prejudices, and discriminatory behavior dispositions that support such exclusion, or (2) to *include* the underdeveloped world in the global species coalition on an entirely equal basis with itself, and apply the universalistic norms that support such inclusion.

Yette's quotation from a press interview with sociologist and demographer Philip Hauser refers to these basic alternatives—and, once again, they apply beyond the underdeveloped world inside the United States to the much larger underdeveloped world outside the United States, as well: "As [Hauser] sees it America . . . can make the heavy 'investment in people' which will have to be made to transform the underprivileged into responsible citizens; or it can suppress its rebellious minorities. 'If we are not prepared to make the investment in human resources that is required,' according to Hauser, 'we will be forced to increase our investment in the Police, National Guard, and the Army. And possibly—it can happen here—we may be forced to resort to concentration camps and even genocide'" (1971: 177–178; see also Wilson 1996:48–54 for more specific, and more recent, proposals regarding investment in American human resources).[21]

Suppose the developed world were to decide in favor of *excluding* (in Hauser's term, suppressing) the underdeveloped world—and not just for now but *forever.*

At least five types of costs, to the developed world of such an investment come to mind: (1) the costs of running all the organizations that would be required to carry out that worldwide exclusion; (2) the costs in terrorist acts that would be inflicted by an increasingly embittered underdeveloped world together with its inevitable allies and suppliers of increasingly sophisticated weapons; (3) the costs of sustaining a permanent polarization inside the developed world—a polarization dwarfing that generated in the United States by the Viet Nam war—and a permanent exclusion there of all who oppose excluding the underdeveloped world; (4) the costs of sacrificing all the manysided sociocultural and individual potentials of the underdeveloped world;[22] (5) the costs of bestializing the developed world itself (here, one recalls Spencer's warning that "Fellow-feeling, habitually trampled down in [such] conflicts, cannot at the same time be active in the relations of civil life," and his conclusion that "Nothing like a high type of social life is possible without a type of human character in which the promptings of egoism are duly restrained by regard for others" [1961:179]).

In sum, then, the predictable costs to the developed world of writing-off the underdeveloped world and thereby avoiding global species consolidation would require a catastrophic degradation of its own wealth and power, its own knowledge, and its own honor—including its developing self-honor or moral conscience.[23] It would be not only "too bad for *them*," but too bad for the rest of the world, as well.

But now suppose the developed world were to choose the other strategy and make whatever investment in human resources the world over would be required to include the underdeveloped world, on an absolutely equal basis with itself, in all future development of the human species' wealth, power, knowledge, and honor. What would some principal benefits be?

Before considering a possible answer to that question, an aside: The developed world might begin pursuing the inclusion strategy with a publicly expressed commitment—again, in its very own self-interest (the way Moskos says the United States Army did, regarding race relations; see Chapter 5), to achieve global equalization with all deliberate speed and to measure all other choices we may be called upon to make against that paramount criterion. Obviously, the developed world does not yet have either the leadership or the followership for such a commitment (but then neither did the United States Army twenty-some years ago). What a transforming moment in human history it will be when we do have them! May this book hasten that moment.

Some Likely Benefits of Global Species Consolidation

I have argued that ever since the Neolithic Revolution (but most likely not before that), the main dangers to the survival of any given population of our species have arisen from *inside* the species—in particular, from the often lethal competition among family, kinship group, ethnic, racial, and/or nationality populations. It is for this reason that John Jay cited "dangers from *foreign arms and influence*" as the primary threat to the safety of the American people (see Hamilton et al. 1961:42, italics added).[24] I have also argued that whenever two or more human family, kinship, ethnic, racial, or nationality groups (or parts thereof) have identified some other human group as a common enemy, the typical response has been to form a coalition against that enemy and face it with their pooled resources.

But our perception of the main danger to any given human population and, indeed, to the human species itself, may already have begun to take an epochal turn away from a focus *inside* the human species to a focus *outside* the human species, in the natural environment. Such a turn would be the result of the conjunction of two distinctively late-twentieth century developments: on the one hand (as we have already seen here) a sharp decline in perceived danger from war, and on the other hand, dramatic gains in scientific understanding of the scale and ineluctability of the dangers to all humankind that emanate from the natural environment. (One has only to recall comet Shoemaker-Levy's 1994 collision with planet Jupiter, which, had it occurred to planet Earth, would have spelled The End for every single one of us.)

Thus, in precisely the same way that ten thousand years of ingrained belief that the main danger to any given group of people originates in neighboring "other people" has justified all sorts of localized coalitions until now, so a growing awareness of the still more terrible and far more implacable dangers that we face from the natural environment (which neighbors us all, everywhere and always) justifies global species consolidation.

Modern astrophysicists seem unanimous in the view that the universe at large is, has always been, and will continue to be extremely hostile to life. Times and places that can support life, and especially life complex enough to be called intelligent and social, are inordinately rare when compared to the times and places that cannot support such life (although the former places seem sure to be far more widespread than is conceived in naively Earth-centered cosmologies—see, for example, Ferris 1992:19; Gribbin 1993:45–79). Even when and where life exists it remains forever embattled—highly vulnerable to incursions from the life-denying extremes of temperature, pressure, momentum, and radiation that are so nearly universal in the cosmos. Consider Earth itself: It is the only place that we now know life exists, yet 99 percent of all the species of life that have ever existed here have gone extinct (see Ferris 1988:387), whether by reason of climate change, tectonic and volcanic activity, asteroidal collision, cosmic radiation, predation by other species, or some perhaps still unrecognized natural danger.

But if all this is too general to be convincing, let us briefly focus on just three types of foreseeable natural environmental dangers.

Microbiological Epidemics. Garrett quotes D. H. Henderson, a scientist who once led the eradication of smallpox, to the effect that "there is a growing belief that mankind's well-being, and perhaps even our survival as a species, will depend on our ability to detect emerging diseases. . . . Where would we be today if HIV were to become an airborne pathogen? And what is there to say that a comparable infection might not do so in the future?" Henderson therefore urges a program for global preparedness and asks "Can we afford to invest in such a program? A better question is whether we can afford *not* to invest in a program that could be a determinant in our own survival as a species" (Garrett 1994:602, 604–605; see also 619–620). Garrett concludes that "rapid globalization of human niches requires that human beings everywhere on the planet go beyond viewing their neighborhoods, provinces, countries, or hemispheres as the [limits] of their personal ecospheres. Microbes, and their vectors, recognize none of the artificial boundaries erected by human beings" (1994:618).

Climate Change. "The earth has entered a period of climatic change that is likely to cause widespread economic, social and environmental dislocation over the next century if emissions of heat-trapping gases are not reduced, according to experts advising the world's governments" (Stevens 1995:A1). Thus begins a recent report which, after noting that although "the experts are now more confident than before that . . . at least some of the warming is due to human action" they are not sure how much, goes on to cite some "possible early effects." These include a rise in average sea levels around the world ("At the most likely rate of rise, some experts say, most of the beaches on the East Coast of the United States would be gone in 25 years"). A second early effect would be an "increase in extremes of temperature, dryness and precipitation in some regions" leading to more droughts, heat waves, floods, and woodland fires. Third, a "retreat of mountain glaciers," leading to diminished river and stream flows in some regions. In some regions, there would be milder winters and faster crop growth, but others, "especially sub-Saharan Africa, South and Southeast Asia and tropical Latin America—could suffer loses in their harvests. Deserts are expected to expand, and the heartlands of continents to become drier. . . . Northern temperate regions would experience more rain and less snow in winter. In summer, water would evaporate faster, drying the soil" (Stevens 1995:A1; see also Stone 1995).

Volcanic Eruptions and Collisions with Asteroids and Comets. Wilson tells us that "Krakatau . . . an island the size of Manhattan located midway in the Sunda Strait between Sumatra and Java, came to an end on Monday morning, August 27, 1883. It was dismembered by a series of powerful volcanic eruptions," and goes on to note that "an 1815 eruption in Tambora, 1,400 kilometers to the east of Krakatau . . . lifted five times as much rock and ash as Krakatau. . . . About 75,000 years ago a still greater eruption occurred in the center of Sumatra. . . . An event the size of the Krakatau explosion happens once or twice a century. An eruption as big as the one [in the center of Sumatra] is far rarer but, over millions of years, probably inevitable" (1992:16, 24–25).

Regarding collisions with debris from outer space, a NASA astronomer is quoted as saying "'The day will surely come when the sheltering sky is torn apart with a power that beggars the imagination. It has happened before. Ask any dinosaur, if you can find one. This is a dangerous place'" (Ferris 1997:49; contrast this late twentieth century quotation with James Fenimore Cooper's early nineteenth century, naive, and highly localized belief in "the holy calm of nature"). In the same vein, a science writer tells us that nowadays

the Chicken Little crowd, which once drew smiles by suggesting that Earth could be devastated by killer rocks from outer space, is suddenly finding its warnings and agenda taken seriously now that Jupiter has taken a beating in recorded history's biggest show of cosmic violence. . . . Astronomers already know of more than 100 [major comets or asteroids] whose paths occasionally cross Earth's orbit and estimate as many as 2,000 may be speeding through space on such paths and are big enough to do global damage. . . . [A 1990 NASA study] said that at worst, the impact of a large comet or asteriod would be similar to many thousands of nuclear warheads going off simultaneously at the same spot, creating a global pall of dust that could block sunlight, disrupt the climate and possibly end civilization (Broad 1994; see also Matthews 1992).

(In addition to those "more than 100," an estimated one hundred *billion* potential comets in the Oort cloud surrounding the solar system are liable to many sorts of accidental gravitational disturbances which can shift—and may already have shifted—some of them to paths that will take them toward the inner solar system, where dwells Earth.) Following up more recently, Broad reports that "the Federal Government has assumed a serious role in . . . scanning the skies for speeding rocks from outer space that could slam into the planet to cause widespread destruction and death. It is the first such governmental search in the world. . . . It is estimated that among the many thousands of comets and asteroids speeding through the solar system, up to 1,700 of those crossing Earth's path might be big enough to wreak global havoc" and reports that the White House science adviser says the government "should have a full map of the most interesting objects in the next couple of decades" (1996:C1; see also 1997:C1).

Even limiting ourselves to just these three types of danger, then, it seems clear that here—in the very same Nature which is our origin and our continuingly indispensable sustenance—lies the perpetual common danger that is the ultimate justification for global species consolidation.[25]

So when Moskos and Butler point out that "the Army treats good race relations as a means to readiness and combat effectiveness—not as an end in itself" (1996:53), and when they argue that "an overarching, common American identity must override cultural diversity" and that "sharing the obligations of citizenship will act as a solvent for many of the differences among [participants in a program of national service, analogous to voluntary military service]" (1996:53, 58, 134), one anticipates the broadening of this same approach, sooner or later, beyond race relations to ethnic and nationality relations as well; beyond the United States Army, beyond the United States, and beyond national service to the United States, to all members of the perpetually endangered species Homo sapiens, and to universally global service in its defense.

A POSSIBLE DISTANT FUTURE

The physical sciences seem agreed that our 4.6 billion-year-old Sun is now approaching the middle of the journey of its life, with somewhat more years than this to go before its death throes—first fire, then ice—render the Earth unfit for any life at all (see Bartusiak 1986:33–34). Someone (I have forgotten who) has said that if the distance from the tip of one's nose to the tip of one's outstretched middle finger were taken to represent the age of the Earth so far, then the first rasp of a nail file on the nail of that finger would erase all *past* human history and prehistory. But one should add that something like a nose-to-other-middle-finger distance represents the potential span of *future* human history on this planet.

So there may well be tens, hundreds, even thousands, of millions of years left in which the increasingly self-directed evolution of our species may continue its struggle for survival beyond Earth and beyond solar system to whatever may turn out to be our species' ultimate limits. Viewed in such a perspective, the full story of Homo sapiens may involve a second, and even a third, turn around the Grand Cycle after, and perhaps overlapping with, the full achievement of our present consolidation stage.

The explanation proposed in chapter 2 for the first turn may hold for future turns as well. Our species has powerful drives to secure the resources of its member organisms' lives—including more and more pure and applied scientific knowledge of the universe, and greater and greater dispersion of the species therein. In the latter connection, Bartusiak suggests that "direct imaging of more Earth- or Jupiter-like bodies outside our solar system could come with future generations of infrared telescopes launched into space in the 1990s and the 21st century. . . . [Such images] could be the bait that finally lures humankind itself out of the solar system" (1986:26) and, at this writing, we seem to be drawing very close, both to that imaging and to robotic exploration of some of the solar system sites thus imaged.

Seen this way, the past and the present together become but prologue— and we stand, not at the end but at the end of the beginning of human history.

Thus, Dyson, arguing that the "the expansion of life over the universe is a beginning, not an end," tells us that "At the same time as life is extending its habitat quantitatively, it will also be . . . [experimenting] with intelligence in a million different forms" (1979:237)[26]—and that thought's reply to Lincoln's whither-are-we-tending question (with which this book began), can lift all our lives clear of the nasty and brutish, if not also the short.

NOTES

1. Parshall says "'We [English-speakers] have the most cheerfully democratic and hospitable language that ever existed. . . . Other people recognize their language in ours'. . . . The Oxford English dictionary lists more than 600,000 words; German has fewer than one third that number, French fewer than one sixth. What makes English mammoth . . . is its great sea of synonyms"—many of which have been borrowed from other languages (1995:48). One suspects, however, that any 'cheerful hospitality' the English language has may originate in the successes of a not-so-cheerful imperialism—as did the widespread usage of the Roman Empire's Latin.

2. Orbell and Dawes support the 'should' in that statement: "(1) When individuals are free to accept or reject play in Prisoner's Dilemma games, social or aggregate welfare increases. (2) This increase in welfare occurs because intending cooperators are more willing to enter such games than are intending defectors, which increases the probability of socially productive cooperate-cooperate relationships. (3) [T]he welfare of intending cooperators relative to that of intending defectors also increases, providing intending cooperators with a potential absolute advantage" (1993:797–798).

3. I am indebted to Professor Kim Lane Scheppele for information about this legislation, which identifies "Armenians, Bulgarians, Croats, Germans, Greeks, Gypsies, Poles, Romanians, Ruthenians, Serbs, Slovaks and Ukranians" as presently "qualifying as national or ethnic groups living in Hungary" and provides for the later addition of other groups numbering 1000 or more. "Being fully aware that the harmonious co-

existence of national and ethnic minorities with the majority nation forms an integral part of international security, [the National Assembly] declares that it considers the right of national and ethnic identity as a part of universal and human rights, and recognizes the specific individual and collective rights of national and ethnic minorities as fundamental civil rights and will assert these rights in the Republic of Hungary." Among other things, the Act says "Anyone may use one's mother tongue anywhere and at any time in the Republic of Hungary. [This] possibility . . . shall be ensured by the state"; that "Minorities living in the Republic of Hungary have a constitutional right to organize self-government at both local and national level"; that "Persons belonging to a minority have the right to maintain relations both with the governmental and communal institutions of the mother countries or language nations and with minorities living in other countries"; and that "Minorities and their organizations are entitled to develop and maintain wide-ranging and direct international relations." To these ends, the Act authorizes financial grants to the national self-governments of the 13 minorities mentioned above—grants made in a manner corresponding to "compensation coupons" issued by the Republic of Hungary "in partial compensation for properties . . . confiscated or nationalized prior to 1949 and later during the communist regime" (Republic of Hungary Office for National and Ethnic Minorities 1993:27, 2. 23, 5, 7, 9, 29). An international clearing house for information regarding practical steps toward global ethnic, racial, and nationality consolidation would be useful.

    4. For discussion of the prospects for fusion power, including the report that "the United States, the European Community, Japan and Russia [have] agreed to a $1.2 billion, six-year effort to design the International Thermonuclear Experimental Reactor, under the direction of the International Atomic Energy Agency, headquartered in Vienna, Austria," see Anonymous (1993:62). And regarding the possibility of switch-over to collecting energy in outer space, see Dyson (1988:115).

    5. Comte says "war had great moral and political utility as a preparation" (1975:451).

    6. Spencer anticipated this reversal of war's significance for consolidation from positive to negative—but for different reasons (see 1961:178–180).

    7. Moreover, the "provision of experts [by international organizations]. . . . plays a significant role in the construction and operationalization of state practices and interests . . . [partly] because their existence allows for implicit regulation in a way that minimizes the need for direct political intervention" (McNeely 1995:161).

    8. Weiner's book, however, closes on a strangely inconsistent and shortsighted note: "But at the end of the day," he says "states will not and cannot allow others to decide who will permanently live and work in their own societies" (1995:222). One wishes his calendar had more days on it.

    9. Rex here echoes Booker T. Washington's comment at the Atlanta Exposition of 1895: "In all things that are purely social we [Blacks and Whites] can be as separate as the fingers, yet one as the hand in all things essential to mutual progress" (1971:6); see also Lipset and Raab's quotation of Rabbi Leeser's 1850s comment that "In the Synagogue and congregational meetings, we want Jews; in public matters only American citizens" (1995:140). Rex also argues that "law, politics and the economy" are in the

public domain, while "the family, morality and religion" are in the private domain, with education residing in both domains (see 1996:18–25).

10. Huntington precedes this sentence by asserting that "The survival of the West depends on Americans reaffirming their Western identity and . . . uniting to renew and preserve [Western civilization] against challenges from non-Western societies" (1996:20–21). In this way, he makes it clear that his main concern is with preserving "Western" civilization in some delusionally pure state, unmixed with the other (Latin American, African, Islamic, Sinic, Hindu, Orthodox, Buddhist, and Japanese) civilizations he identifies, and that maintaining the "multicivilizational character of global politics" is, for him, primarily a tactical means to that end under circumstances that increasingly rule out Western domination of global politics. Somehow, however, Huntington overlooks the estimate he himself presents that the percent Non-Hispanic White in the American population will drop to 53% by the year 2050 (and the fact he does not mention—namely that although they comprise only 3% of the U.S. population at present, Asians are the fastest growing American minority), thereby rendering this "Western" nation nearly half *non*-Western in its population origins (assuming, as Huntington does, that Latin America is not part of the "West"—see 1996:26–27).

11. Weiner, too, points out that "even as multiculturalism can be a positive acceptance of cultural diversity, it can also be a form of enforced separation, a way of inducing minorities to return to their country of origin. For example, the German government has been particularly reluctant to assimilate its Turkish and Yugoslav migrants, hoping that many of them will return home" (1995:47).

12. It seems noteworthy that Burnham, writing during the early days of World War II, argued against continuing "the existence of a large number of sovereign nations"; they are, he says, "incompatible with contemporary economic and social needs. The system simply does not work" (1942:173). Burnham concluded, however, that a "single world state" is "extremely doubtful'" and proposed, instead, that "a comparatively small number of great nations, or 'super-states,' . . . will divide the world among them" (1942:175). It seems clear that Huntington (1996), is Burnham's intellectual descendant here. But then Burnham also believed "the mechanism whereby this new political system will be built is and will be war. . . . There is not the slightest indication—certainly not at the opening of 1941!—that any other [mechanism] is going to replace it" (1942:176). Times seem to have changed since 1941 on this count.

13. "In time to come," Spencer says, "a federation of the highest nations, exercising supreme authority (already foreshadowed by occasional agreements among 'the Powers'), may, by forbidding wars between any of its constituent nations, put an end to the re-barbarization which is continually undoing civilization" (1898, III:610). And Wriston emphasizes another, complementary, mechanism for achieving this outlawing of war: "One of the fundamental prerogatives assumed by all sovereign governments has been to pursue their national interests by waging war. Today this prerogative is being severely circumscribed by information technology. No one who lived through America's Vietnam experience could fail to understand the enormous impact that television had in frustrating the government's objective in Southeast Asia" (1992:13).

14. Smith argues that nations will persist into the indefinitely distant future because they serve three functions. "Perhaps the most important [is that identification] with the 'nation' in a secular era is the surest way to surmount the finality of death and ensure a measure of personal immortality. . . . [Second, nationalism] promises [that] . . . the world will recognize the chosen people and their sacred values [he does not say which "chosen people" he has in mind]. . . . A third function of national identity is the prominence it gives to . . . fraternity" (1991:160–162). Chapter 6 will argue for a better way of performing all these functions—with the exception of the second function. No matter which "people" Smith might name as "chosen," the hideous examples so recently set by those who would have had the world recognize "Aryans," the "Yamato race," or the "CPSU" as the "chosen people" bearing "sacred values" can only fill one with shock and revulsion at the proposal of some other, *any* other, to take their places.

15. In his seed statement on ascribed and achieved statuses, Linton says "achieved statuses. . . . are not assigned to individuals from birth but are left open to be filled through competition and individual effort." However, "reference points for the ascription of status. . . . are always of such a nature that they are ascertainable at birth. . . . The simplest and most universally used of these reference points is sex. Age is used with nearly equal frequency. . . . Family relationships . . . are also used in all societies. . . . Lastly, there is the matter of birth into a particular socially established group, such as a class or caste. [T]hese reference points . . . serve to delimit the field of [the individual's] future participation in the life of the group" (1936:115–116). This delimiting, plus the exterminative tendencies to be mentioned below, render ascribed statues grossly dysfunctional for the long-term future of humankind.

16. Most, if not all, ascribed statuses start out as achieved statuses. Thus, ethnic and racial, and later nationality, groups (and membership status therein) originated in different dispersion and settlement patterns (hence the sociocultural founder effect and territorial luck discussed in chapter 2), but these statuses became ascribed when passed on to the descendants of the participants in those patterns. Similarly, the statuses of king and slave started as achieved but were then ascribed to the heirs of those who held these statuses—as Degler implies when defining the slave status as "lifetime servitude [plus] inheritable status" (1959:53). This means that to argue for the elimination of ascribed statuses (as I do) is to argue against the inheritance of social statuses (as I also do). Speaking of inheritance, the family is a mixed achieved-ascribed case insofar as membership in a nuclear family is achieved by the spouses, as is their parent status there, but ascribed to the children of those spouses.

17. For example, U.S. Census data indicate that the 1991 median money income of Black persons (male and female) who were 25 years old and over and had achieved an educational level of BA or better was $20,933 higher than that of Blacks in the same age group but who had achieved an educational level of less than 9th grade (the comparable difference for Whites was $23,395). By comparison, the unweighted average 1991 median money income of Black persons in this age group who had achieved the indicated levels of education was $3,053 less than that of White persons of the same age group and the same educational achievement levels (computed from Bennett 1992:42–43, 46). Judging from these data, one's ascribed race still counts for a significant amount

in one's income, but for not nearly as much as one's achieved education—a complete turnaround from one or two hundred years ago in the United States—although one's achieved education itself remains subject to ascribed racial constraints.

18. Note that Patterson applies his claim to "*any* legitimate social order," not only *past* legitimate social orders. In the past, the absence of "claims of birth" has indeed meant "social death" (or something close to it, for Patterson himself shows repeatedly that neither slaves nor masters considered slaves socially *dead*—any more than they considered working horses, cattle, oxen, or dogs socially dead).

19. "[B]lacks [in the Army] are three times more likely to say that race relations are better in the Army than [they are to say such relations are better] in civilian life. Whites are five times more likely to say so" (1996:5).

20. This list comprises all the non-African countries listed on the World Population Data Sheet as having had per capita GNPs in 1994 of $500 or less (see Population Reference Bureau 1996). Note that, very probably, not *all* members of the groups listed in this paragraph are drastically undernourished, underempowered, under-educated, and dishonored; it is a matter of the *average* of these groups being so. Indeed, one measure of the extent to which ascription has lost its grip is that few if any of the world's ethnic, racial, or nationality groups may be characterized in these ways in their entireties.

21. Note that one sees, nearly 30 years after Hauser's remark, a huge invest-ment in the U.S. prison system: "In August 1995, the Justice Departmnent counted 1,053,738 inmates in the state and federal prison systems of the United States. . . . In 1992, just over half of the inmates in state and federal prisons were black and 14 percent were hispanic. Black men were eight times as likely to be imprisoned as white men. . . . [and in 1990] 25 percent of black men in the 25 to 29 age group were in prison, on probation, or on parole. . . . By 1995, that number had risen to 32 percent" (Anonymous 1996:1,2).

22. A tiny part of these potential costs may be inferred from Brimmer's estimate that "The disparate treatment of blacks cost the American economy about $241 billion in 1993. This figure is equal to roughly 3.8 percent of that year's gross domestic product. . . . While part of the loss can be attributed to the lag in blacks' educational achievement, the bulk of the shortfall appears to be related to continued discrimination, which limits their access to higher-paying jobs. Furthermore, over the last quarter-century, the relative cost of discrimination seems to have risen" (1997a:24; see also 1997b).

23. In addition, Reich points to "the inability of [highly paid individuals] to protect themselves, their families, and their property from the depredations of a larger and ever more desperate population outside" (1992:303), and Kennedy answers the question, "Why should rich societies care about the fate of far-off poor people?" as follows: "It is that economic activities in the developing world . . . are adding to the damage to the world's ecosystem. . . . the prospect that human economic activities are creating a dangerous greenhouse effect of global warming. . . . would inevitably concern Wisconsin and Jutland as well as Bombay and Amazonia" (1993:96, 105; see also Lenssen 1993:106; Passell 1995).

24. Jay gave second place to "dangers of the *like kind* arising from domestic causes" (Hamilton et al. 1961:42), a point elaborated on by Hamilton in the sixth Federalist Paper (see Chapter 1 here).

25. Note, then, that Homo sapiens has been spared major microbiological epidemics (a possible contributor to the extinction of *Homo neandertalensis*, one of our immediate hominid predecessors), and major collisions with asteroids and comets (such as is now generally agreed to have at least contributed to the extinction of the dinosaurs sixty-five million years ago). Indeed, regarding the latter, it seems likely that the luck of the territorial (here, planetary) draw—for example, the shield provided us by the large outer planets Jupiter, Saturn, Uranus, and Neptune has afforded our evolutionary line a four million-year window of opportunity to prepare itself genetically, socioculturally, and technologically for the titanic confrontations with Nature that are sure to await us in the future.

26. Ferris says "Within the range of our telescopes lie perhaps one hundred billion galaxies, each home to a hundred billion or so stars. Astronomers estimate that at least half those stars have planets. If so, [and if] intelligent life has arisen on but one planet in a billion, then fully ten thousand billion planets have given birth to intelligent species" (1992:19). And one notes that evidence of ten or more stars in our galaxy that have planets has been collected in just the past few years.

REFERENCES

Adams, Robert McC. 1966. *The Evolution of Urban Society*. Chicago: Aldine.

Ahmed, Akbar S., and Hastings Donnan. 1994. "Islam in the Age of Post-modernity." In Akbar S. Ahmed and Hastings Donnan (eds.), *Islam, Globalization and Post-modernity*. London, England: Routledge, pp. 1–20.

Alba, Richard D. 1990. *Ethnic Identity: The Transformation of White America*. New Haven, CT: Yale University Press.

Alba, Richard D., and Gwen Moore. 1982. "Ethnicity in the American Elite." *American Sociological Review* 47 (June): 373–383.

Alexander, Jeffrey C. 1980. "Core Solidarity, Ethnic Outgroup, and Social Differentiation: A Multidimensional Model of Inclusion in Modern Societies." In Jacques Dofny and Akinsola Akiwowo (eds.), *National and Ethnic Movements*. Newbury Park, CA: Sage, pp. 5–24.

Allport, Gordon W. 1954. *The Nature of Prejudice*. Garden City, NY: Doubleday.

Alter, Catherine, and Jerald Hage. 1993. *Organizations Working Together*. Newbury Park, CA: Sage.

Anonymous. 1991. "Slave." *New Encyclopaedia Britannica (Micropaedia)*, p. 873.

Anonymous. 1993. "Nuclear Fusion." *CQ Researcher* 3 (22 January): 49–72.

Anonymous. 1994. "The World's Shrinking Armies." *The New York Times*, May 30, p. A16.

Anonymous. 1996. "The Incarceration Mania." *The Social Change Report* 6, no. 1: 1–4.

Appadurai, Arjun. 1990. "Disjuncture and Difference in the Global Cultural Economy." In Mike Featherstone (ed.), *Global Culture*. Newbury Park, CA: Sage, pp. 295–310.

Arnold, Benedict. 1991. *Imagined Communities*. London: Verso.

Asimov, Isaac. 1979. *A Choice of Catastrophes*. New York: Fawcett Columbine.

Axelrod, Robert. 1984. *The Evolution of Cooperation*. New York: Basic Books.

Ayala, Francisco J. 1995. "The Myth of Eve: Molecular Biology and Human Origins." *Science* 270 (22 December): 1930–1936.

Barinaga, Marcia. 1992. "'African Eve' Backers Beat a Retreat." *Science* 255, no. 7 (February): 686–687.

Barker, Ernest. 1952. *The Politics of Aristotle*. London, England: Oxford University Press.

Barry, Kathleen. 1995. *The Prostitution of Sexuality*. New York: New York University Press.

Barth, Ernest A. T., and Donald L. Noel. 1972. "Conceptual Frameworks for the Analysis of Race Relations: An Evaluation." *Social Forces* 50 (March): 333–348.

Barth, Fredrik. 1981. *Process and Form in Social Life: Selected Essays*. Boston: Routledge & Kegan Paul.

Bartusiak, Marcia. 1986. *Thursday's Universe*. New York: Times Books.

Bauman, Zigmunt. 1990. "Modernity and Ambivalence." In Mike Featherstone (ed.), *Global Culture*. Newbury Park, CA: Sage, pp. 143–169.

Bennet, James. 1997. "Medals of Honor Awarded at Last to Black World War II Soldiers." *The New York Times*, January 14, pp. A1, A12.

Bennett, Claudette E. 1993. *The Black Population in the United States: March 1992*. U.S. Bureau of the Census, Current Population Reports, P20-471 U.S. Government Printing Office, Washington DC.

Berle, Adolph A., Jr., and Gardiner C. Means. 1939. *The Modern Corporation and Private Property*. New York: Macmillan.

Birch, Anthony H. 1989. *Nationalism and National Integration*. Boston: Unwin Hyman.

Blalock, Hubert M., Jr. 1967. *Toward a Theory of Minority-Group Relations*. New York: Wiley.

———. 1982. *Race and Ethnic Relations*. Englewood Cliffs, NJ: Prentice-Hall.

Blau, Judith R., and Peter M. Blau. 1982. "The Cost of Inequality: Metropolitan Structure and Violent Crime." *American Sociolological Review* 47 (February): 114–129.

Blaut, James W. 1993. *The Colonizer's Model of the World: Geographical Diffusionism and Eurocentric History*. New York: Guilford.

Bleeke, Joel, and David Ernst. 1993. "The Death of the Predator." In Joel Bleeke and David Ernst (eds.), *Collaborating to Compete*. New York: Wiley, pp. 1–9.

Boli, John, and George M. Thomas. 1997. "World Culture in the World Polity: A Century of International Non-Governmental Organization." *American Sociological Review*. 62 (April): 171–190.

Bonacich, Edna. 1972. "A Theory of Ethnic Antagonism: the Split Labor Market." *American Sociological Review*. 37 (October): 547–559.

———. 1973. "A Theory of Middleman Minorities." *American Sociological Review*. 38 (October): 583–594.

Bongaarts, John. 1994. "Population Policy Options in the Developing World." *Science* 263 (11 February): 771–776.

Borjas, G. J. 1989. "Economic Theory and International Migration." *International Migration Review* 23: 3.

Botev, Nikolai. 1994. "Where East Meets West: Ethnic Intermarriage in the Former Yugoslavia, 1962 to 1989." *American Sociological Review* 59 (June):461–480.

Braudel, Fernand. 1988. *The Identity of France*. Vol. 1. London: Collins.

Brimmer, Andrew Felton. 1997a. "Blacks in the American Economy: Summary of Selected Research." In Thomas D. Boston (ed.), *A Different Vision: African American Economic Thought, Vol. I*. London: Routledge, pp. 9–45.

———. 1997b. "The Economic Cost of Discrimination Against Black Americans." In Thomas D. Boston (ed.), *A Different Vision: African American Economic Thought, Vol. II*. London: Routledge, pp. 1–13.

Broad, William J. 1993. "Millions Converse Daily on a System of Linked Computers That Shrinks Space and Time." *New York Times*, May 8, pp. C1, C10.

———. 1994. "When Worlds Collide: A Threat to the Earth Is a Joke No Longer." *The New York Times*, August 1, pp. A1, A12.

———. 1996. "For Killer Asteroids, Respect at Last." *The New York Times*, May 14, pp. C1, C7.

———. 1997. "Earth Is Target for Space Rocks at Higher Rate Than Thought." *The New York Times*, January 7, pp. C1, C8.

Broder, John M. 1997. "In Washington, It's Never Farewell to Arms." *The New York Times*, May 11, sec. 4, p. 16.

Brooks, George E. 1977. "European Relations with Africa before 1870." In Phyllis M. Martin and Patrick O'Meara (eds.), *Africa*. Bloomington: Indiana University Press, pp. 114–131.

Brown, Lester R. 1996. "The Acceleration of History." Worldwatch Institute, *State of the World 1996*. New York: Norton, pp. 3–20, 189–192.

Browning, Chistopher R. 1992. *Ordinary Men*. New York: HarperCollins.

Burnham, James. 1941. *The Managerial Revolution*. Westport, CT: Greenwood.

Caldwell, Wallace Everett. 1949. *The Ancient World*. New York: Rinehart.

Campbell, Bernard. 1985. *Human Evolution* 3d. edition. New York: Aldine.

Caplovitz, David. 1963. *The Poor Pay More*. New York: Free Press.

Caplow, Theodore. 1968. *Two Against One*. Englewood Cliffs, NJ: Prentice-Hall.

Carmichael, Stokely. 1966. "What We Want." *The New York Review of Books*. (September 22), pp. 5–8. Reprinted in Peter I. Rose (ed.). 1970. *Americans from Africa: Old Memories, New Moods*. New York: Atherton, pp. 237–246.

Carmichael, Stokely, and Charles V. Hamilton. 1967. *Black Power: The Politics of Liberation in America*. New York: Vintage.

Carneiro, Robert L. 1981. "The Chiefdom: Precursor of the State." In Grant D. Jones and Robert R. Kautz (eds.), *The Transition to Statehood in the New World*. Cambridge: Cambridge University Press, pp. 37–79.

Castles, Stephen, and Mark J. Miller. 1993. *The Age of Migration*. New York: Macmillan.

Childe, V. Gordon. 1942. *What Happened in History*. Harmondsworth, England: Penguin.

———. 1951. *Man Makes Himself*. New York: New American Library.

Clarke, Ian M. 1985. *The Spatial Organisation of Multinational Corporations*. New York: St. Martin's Press.

Cohen, Elizabeth G., and Rachel A. Lotan. 1995. "Producing Equal-Status Interaction in the Heterogeneous Classroom." *American Educational Research Journal* 32, no. 1 (Spring): 99–120.

Cole, Herbert M., and Chike C. Aniakor. 1984. *Igbo Arts: Continuity and Cosmos.* Museum of Cultural History, Los Angeles: University of California.

Coleman, D. A. 1994. "Trends in Fertility and Intermarriage Among Immigrant Populations in Western Europe as Measures of Integration." *Journal of Biosocial Science* 26:107–136.

Coleman, David. 1992. "Ethnic Intermarriage." In A. H. Bittles and D. F. Roberts (eds.), *Minority Populations: Genetics, Demography and Health.* Hampshire, England: Macmillan, pp. 208–240.

Comte, Auguste. 1975. *Auguste Comte and Positivism: The Essential Writings.* Edited by Gertrud Lenzer. New York: Harper.

Cox, Oliver Cromwell. 1970. *Caste, Class, and Race.* New York: Modern Reader Paperbacks.

Crane, Jonathan. 1991. "The Epidemic Theory of Ghettos and the Neighborhood effects on Dropping Out and Teenage Childbearing." *American Journal of Sociology* 96, no. 5 (March): 1226–1259.

Criswell, David R. 1985. "Solar System Industrialization: Implications for Interstellar Migrations." In Ben R. Finney and Eric M. Jones (eds.), *Interstellar Migration and the Human Experience.* Berkeley, CA: University of California Press, pp. 50–87.

Curtin, P., S. Feierman, L. Thompson, and J. Vansina. 1978. *African History.* Boston: Little, Brown.

Daniels, Roger. 1990. *Coming to America.* New York: Harper.

Darwin, Charles. 1968. *The Origin of Species.* New York: Penguin.

Davidson, Basil. 1974. *Africa in History.* New York: Macmillan.

_____. 1980. *The African Slave Trade.* Revised and expanded. Boston: Little, Brown.

_____. 1992. *Africa in History.* London: Orion.

Davis, David Brion. 1984. *Slavery and Human Progress.* New York: Oxford.

Dawkins, Richard. 1987. *The Blind Watchmaker.* New York: Norton.

De Beer, Gabriella. 1966. *José Vasconcelos and His World.* New York: Las Americas.

Decalo, Samuel, Kennell A. Jackson, Jr., Kenneth J. Perkins, and Harmut S. Walter. 1993. "Africa." Chicago: *World Book Encyclopedia*, Vol. 1, pp. 98–136.

Degler, Carl. 1959. "Slavery and the Genesis of American Race Prejudice." *Comparative Studies in Society and History* II (October), pp. 49–66.

_____. 1971. *Neither Black Nor White.* New York: Macmillan.

Desmond, Annabelle. 1975. "How Many People Have Ever Lived on Earth?" In Kenneth C. W. Kammeyer (ed.), *Population Studies: Selected Essays and Research.* Chicago: Rand McNally, pp. 18–32.

Deutsch, Karl W. 1969. *Nationalism and Its Alternatives.* New York: Knopf.

Diamond, Jared. 1987. "The Worst Mistake in the History of the Human Race." *Discovery* 8 (May): 64–66.

_____.1992. *The Third Chimpanzee.* New York: HarperCollins.

_____.1996. "Empire of Uniformity." *Discover* 17 (March): 78–85.

DiMaggio, Paul J., and Francie Ostrower. 1990. "Participation in the Arts by Black and White Americans." *Social Forces* 68: 753–778.

Dippel, John V. H. 1996. *Bound Upon a Wheel of Fire.* New York: Basic Books.

Dower, John W. 1986. *War Without Mercy*. New York: Pantheon.

Dubofsky, Melvyn. 1969. *We Shall Be All: A History of the Industrial Workers of the World*. New York: Quadrangle/The New York Times Book Company.

Du Bois, W. E. B. 1945. *Color and Democracy: Colonies and Peace*. New York: Harcourt Brace.

Dulles, Avery. 1980. "Ecumenicalism and Theological Method" in Leonard Swidler (ed.), *Consensus in Theology?* Philadelphia, PA: Westminster, pp. 40–48.

Dulles, Foster Rhea, and Melvyn Dubofsky. 1984. *Labor in America: A History*. 4th ed. Arlington Heights, IL: Harlan Davidson.

Durkheim, Emile. 1965. *The Elementary Forms of the Religious Life*. Glencoe, IL: The Free Press.

_____. 1984. *The Division of Labor in Society*. New York: Free Press.

Dyson, Freeman. 1979. *Disturbing the Universe*. New York: Basic.

_____. 1988. *Infinite in All Directions*. New York: Harper & Row.

Enloe, Cynthia. 1981. "The Growth of the State and Ethnic Mobilization: The American Experience." *Ethnic and Racial Studies* 4 (April): 123–136.

Espenshade, Thomas J. 1995. "Unauthorized Immigration to the United States." *Annual Review of Sociology 1995*. Palo Alto, CA: Annual Reviews.

Fagan, Brian M. 1984. *Clash of Cultures*. New York: Freeman.

_____. 1989. *People of the Earth: An Introduction to World Prehistory*. 6th ed. Glenview, IL: Scott, Foresman.

_____. 1990. *The Journey from Eden*. London: Thames and Hudson.

Fage, J. D. 1995. *A History of Africa*. 3rd ed. New York: Routledge.

Falk, Richard. 1992. *Economic Aspects of Global Civilization*. Princeton, NJ: Princeton University Press.

Fanon, Frantz. 1968. *The Wretched of the Earth*. New York: Grove.

Featherstone, Mike. 1990. "Global Culture: An Introduction." *Theory, Culture & Society* 7 (June): 1–14.

Fernandez-Kelly, Maria Patricia. 1994. "Making Sense of Gender in the World Economy: Focus on Latin America." *Organization* 1, no. 2: 249–275.

Ferris, Timothy. 1988. *Coming of Age in the Milky Way*. New York: Bantam.

_____. 1992. *The Mind's Sky*. New York Bantam.

_____. 1997. "Is This the End?" *The New Yorker*. January 27:44–55.

Finley, M.I. 1968. "Slavery." In David L. Sills (ed.), *The Encyclopedia of the Social Sciences* 14, New York: Macmillan, pp. 307–313.

Fogel, R. W., and S. L. Engerman. 1974. *Time on the Cross*. Boston: Little, Brown.

Fordham, Signithia. 1996. *Blacked Out: Dilemmas of Race, Identity, and Success at Capital High*. Chicago: University of Chicago Press.

Fordham, Signithia, and John U. Ogbu. 1986. "Black Students' School Success: Coping with the 'Burden of "Acting White"'." *The Urban Review* 18, no. 3: 176–206.

Frazier, E. Franklin. 1957a. *The Negro in the United States*. Revised. New York: Macmillan.

_____. 1957b. *Race and Culture Contacts in the Modern World*. New York: Knopf.

French, Howard W. 1994. "On Slavery, Africans Say the Guilt Is Theirs, Too." *The New York Times*, December 27, p. A4.

Freud, Sigmund. 1961. *Civilization and Its Discontents*. New York: Norton.

Friedman, Thomas L. 1995. "I Dial Therefore I Am." *The New York Times*. October 29, p. 13

Gamble, Clive. 1993. *Timewalkers: The Prehistory of Global Colonization.* Phoenix Mill, United Kingdom: Alan Sutton.

Gamson, William A. 1961a. "A Theory of Coalition Formation." *American Sociological Review* 26 (June): 373–382.

_____.1961b. "An Experimental Test of a Theory of Coalition Formation." *American Sociological Review* 26 (August): 565–573.

Gans, H. J. 1972. "The Positive Functions of Poverty." *American Journal of Sociology* 78: 275–289.

_____.1979. "Symbolic Ethnicity: The Future of Ethnic Groups and Cultures in America." *Ethnic and Racial Studies* 2, no. 1 (January): 1–20.

Garrett, Laurie. 1994. *The Coming Plague*. New York: Farrar, Straus and Giroux.

Gaur, Albertine. 1992. *A History of Writing*. London: The British Library.

Gellner, Ernest. 1983. *Nations and Nationalism*. Ithaca, NY: Cornell University Press.

Gerlach, Michael L. 1992. *Alliance Capitalism*. Berkeley, CA: University of California Press.

Gleick, James. 1987. *Chaos*. New York: Viking.

_____.1993. "The Telephone Transformed—Into Almost Everything." *New York Times Magazine,* 16 May, pp. 26–29, 50, 53–56, 62, 64.

Glossop, Ronald J. 1987. *Confronting War*. Jefferson, NC: McFarland.

Goldstein, Joshua R. 1995. "American Kinship Networks that Cross Racial Lines: The Exception or the Rule?" Paper presented at the Annual Meeting of the American Sociological Association, August 20, 1990.

Gomes-Casseres, Benjamin. 1996. *The Alliance Revolution*. Cambridge, MA: Harvard University Press.

Goodman, W. 1984. "American Jewish Groups Faulted." *The New York Times*, July 31, pp. A1, B4.

Goody, Jack. 1980. "Slavery in Time and Space." In James L. Watson (ed.), *Asian and African Systems of Slavery*. Oxford, England: Blackwell, pp. 16–42.

Gordon, Milton M. 1964. *Assimilation in American Life*. New York: Oxford University Press.

_____.1978. *Human Nature, Class, and Ethnicity*. New York: Oxford University Press.

Gouldner, Alvin W. 1976. *The Dialectic of Ideology and Technology*. New York: Seabury.

Gribbin, John. 1993. *In the Beginning*. Boston: Little, Brown.

Grier, William H., and Price M. Cobbs. 1968. *Black Rage*. New York: Basic Books.

Griffin, John Howard. 1977. *Black Like Me*. New York: Houghton Miflin.

Hall, E. T. 1966. *The Hidden Dimension*. New York: Doubleday.

Hamilton, Alexander, James Madison, and John Jay. 1961. *The Federalist Papers* New York: New American Library.

Hannan, Michael T., and John Freeman. 1977. "The Population Ecology of Organizations." *American Journal of Sociology* 82, no. 5 (March): 929–964.

Hannerz, Ulf. 1990. "Cosmopolitans and Locals in World Culture." *Theory, Culture & Society* 7 (June): 237–251.

Hartmann, William K. 1985. "The Resource Base in Our Solar System." In Ben R. Finney and Eric M. Jones (eds.), *Interstellar Migration and the Human Experience*. Berkeley, CA: University of California Press, pp. 26–41.

Hegel, G. W. F. 1967. *The Phenomenology of Mind*. New York: Harper Torchbooks.

Hellie, Richard. 1991. "Slavery." In *The New Encyclopaedia Britannica (Macropaedia)* Vol. 27. Chicago: Encyclopaedia Britannica, pp. 285–298.

Higham, J. 1955. *Strangers in the Land*. New Brunswick, NJ: Rutgers University Press.

Hofstadter, Douglas R. 1979. *Gödel, Escher, Bach*. New York: Viking.

Hoge, Warren. 1997. "Rare Look Uncovers Wartime Anguish of Many Part-Jewish Germans." *The New York Times*, April 6, p. 16

Hölldobler, Bert, and Edward O. Wilson. 1990. *The Ants*. Cambridge MA: Harvard University Press.

Hollins, Harry B., Averill L. Powers, and Mark Sommer. 1989. *The Conquest of War*. Boulder, CO: Westview.

Holmes, Steven A. 1996. "Time and Money Producing Racial Harmony in Military." *The New York Times*, April 5, pp. A1, B8.

_____.1996. "Study Finds Rising Number of Black-White Marriages." *The New York Times*, July 4, p. A16.

Homer-Dixon, Thomas F., Jeffrey H. Boutwell, and George W. Rathjens. 1993. "Environmental Change and Violent Conflict." *Scientific American* (February): 38–45.

hooks, bell. 1995. *Killing Rage*. New York: Holt.

Hooton, Earnest Albert. 1939. *Crime and the Man*. Cambridge, MA.: Harvard University Press.

Huntington, Samuel P. 1996. *The Clash of Civilizations and the Remaking of World Order*. New York: Simon & Schuster.

Inbar, Michael, and Chaim Adler. 1977. *Ethnic Integration in Israel*. New Brunswick, NJ: Transaction.

Jaffrey, Zia 1997 "Fighting Africa's Enemy Within." *The New York Times*, May 1, pp. C1, C10.

Jaynes, G.D. and R. M. Williams, Jr. (eds.) 1989. *A Common Destiny: Blacks in American Society*. Washington, DC: The National Research Council.

Jennings, Francis. 1993. *The Founders of America*. New York: Norton.

Jick, Leon A. 1993. "Holocaust." Chicago: *World Book Encyclopedia*, Vol. 9, p. 296.

Johnson, Daniel M., and Rex R. Campbell. 1981. *Black Migration in America*. Durham NC: Duke University Press.

Joly, Daniele, and Robin Cohen. 1989. *Reluctant Hosts: Europe and its Refugees*. Aldershot, England: Avebury.

Jones, E. E. 1990. *Interpersonal Perception*. New York: Freeman.

Jones, Eric M., and Ben R. Finney. 1985. "Fastships and Nomads: Two Roads to the Stars." In Ben R. Finney and Eric M. Jones (eds.), *Interstellar Migration and the Human Experience*. Berkeley: University of California Press, pp. 88–103.

Jones, LeRoi. 1963. *Blues People*. New York: Morrow.

Jones, Maldwyn A. 1995. *The Limits of Liberty: American History 1607–1992*. 2nd ed. New York: Oxford.

Jordan, Winthrop D. 1968. *White Over Black*. Baltimore, MD: Penguin.

Kane, Hal. 1995. "Leaving Home." Worldwatch Institute, *State of the World 1995*. New York: Norton, pp. 132–149, 231–235.

Kane, Thomas T., 1989. *Streams of Change*. New York: Garland.

Karatnycky, Adrian. 1996. "The Comparative Survey of Freedom 1995–1996; Democracy and Despotism: Bipolarism Renewed?" In Freedom House Survey Team, *Freedom in the World*. New York: Freedom House.

Kauffman, Stuart. 1995. *At Home in the Universe*. New York: Oxford University Press.

Kennedy, Paul. 1993. *Preparing for the Twenty-First Century*. New York: Random House.

Keohane, Robert O., and Joseph S. Nye. 1977. *Power and Interdependence: World Politics in Transition*. Boston: Little, Brown.

Kim, Yoon Shin. 1985."Marriage Pattern of the Korean Population in Japan." *Journal of Biosocial Science*. (17): 445–450.

King, Martin Luther, Jr. 1992. *I Have a Dream*. San Francisco: Harper-SanFrancisco.

Kinoshita, June. 1993. "Counting on Science to Compete." *Science* 262 (15 October): 348–350.

Klein, Richard G. 1989. *The Human Career*. Chicago: University of Chicago.

Kollock, Peter. 1993. "'An Eye for an Eye Leaves Everyone Blind': Cooperation and Accounting Systems." *American Sociological Review* 58 (December): 768–786.

Kotabe, Masaaki. 1992. *Global Sourcing Strategy*. New York: Quorum.

Kuhn, Thomas S. 1962 *The Structure of Scientific Revolutions*. Chicago: University of Chicago Press.

Kung, Hans. 1988. *Theology for the Third Millennium: An Ecumenical View*. New York: Doubleday.

Lamphear, John. 1977. "Two Basic Themes in African History: Migration and State Formation." In Phyllis M. Martin and Patrick O'Meara (eds.), *Africa*. Bloomington: Indiana University Press, pp. 83–97.

Lauer, Robert H. 1976. "Introduction. Social Movements and Social Change: The Interrelationships." In *Social Movements and Social Change*. Edited by Robert H. Lauer. Carbondale: Southern Illinois University Press, pp. xi–xxviii.

Leakey, Richard, and Roger Lewin. 1992. *Origins Reconsidered*. New York: Doubleday.

Leontiades, James C. 1985. *Multinational Corporate Strategy*. Lexington, MA: Lexington Books.

Lerner, Gerda. 1986. *The Creation of Patriarchy*. New York: Oxford University Press.

Lewis, John S. 1996. *Mining the Sky*. Reading, MA: Addison-Wesley.

Lewis, L. A., and L. Berry. 1988. *African Environments and Resources*. Boston: Unwin Hyman.

Lieberson, Stanley. 1961. "A Societal Theory of Race and Ethnic Relations." *American Sociological Review* 26 (December): 902–910.

Lieberson, Stanley and Mary C. Waters. 1988. *From Many Strands*. New York: Russell Sage Foundation.

Lincoln, Abraham. 1971. *The Essential Lincoln.* Edited by Keith W. Jennison. New York: Watts.

Linton, Ralph. 1936. *The Study of Man.* New York: Appleton-Century.

Lipset, Seymour Martin, and Earl Raab. 1995. *Jews and the New American Scene.* Cambridge, MA: Harvard University Press.

Locke, Alain, and Bernhard J. Stern. 1946 "In the Setting of World Culture." In Alain Locke and Bernhard J. Stern (eds.), *When Peoples Meet: A Study in Race and Culture Contacts.* Revised. New York: Hinds, Hayden & Eldredge, pp. 3–11.

Lorenz, Konrad. 1970. *Studies in Animal and Human Behaviour.* Vol. I. Cambridge, MA: Harvard University Press.

Machiavelli, Niccolo. 1940. *The Prince and The Discourses.* New York: Modern Library.

Malcolm X. 1966. *The Autobiography of Malcolm X.* New York: Grove.

Mann, Michael. 1986. *The Sources of Social Power.* Vol. I. Cambridge: Cambridge University Press.

Mannheim, Karl. 1955. *Ideology and Utopia.* New York: Harcourt Brace.

Manning, P. 1992. "The Slave Trade: The Formal Demography of a Global System." In J. E. Inkori and S. L. Engerman (eds.), *The Atlantic Slave Trade.* Durham, NC: Duke University Press, pp. 117–139.

_____.1996. "Introduction." In Patrick Manning (ed.), *Slave Trades, 1500–1800: Globalization of Forced Labor.* Aldershot, Hampshire, Great Britain, pp. xv–xxxiv.

Marger, Martin N. 1991. *Race and Ethnic Relations: American and Global Perspectives.* 2nd ed. Belmont CA: Wadsworth.

Margulis, Lynn, and Dorion Sagan. 1986. *Microcosmos.* New York: Summit.

Marks, Jonathan. 1995. *Human Biodiversity: Genes, Race, and History.* Hawthorne, NY: Aldine de Gruyter.

Marshall, Eliot. 1990. "Clovis Counterrevolution." *Science* 249 (17 August): 738–741.

Martin, B. G. 1977. "The Spread of Islam." In Phyllis M. Martin and Patrick O'Meara (eds.), *Africa.* Bloomington: Indiana University Press, pp. 98–113.

Marx, Karl. 1973. *Grundrisse.* New York: Vintage Books.

Marx, Karl, and Friedrich Engels. 1947. *The German Ideology.* New York: International.

_____.1969. *Selected Works.* 3 volumes. Moscow: Progress.

_____.1978. *The Marx-Engels Reader.* Edited by Robert C. Tucker. 2nd ed. New York: Norton.

Massey, Douglas S. 1993. "Latino Poverty Research: An Agenda for the 1990s." *Items* 47 (March): 7–11.

Massey, Douglas S., and Mitchell Eggers. 1990. "The Ecology of Inequality: Minorities and the Concentration of Poverty," *American Journal of Sociology* 95, no. 5 (March): 1158–1188.

Massey, Douglas S., and Nancy A. Denton. 1993. *American Apartheid.* Cambridge, MA: Harvard University Press.

Matthews, Robert. 1992. "A Rocky Watch for Earthbound Asteroids." *Science* 255 (6 March): 1204–1205.

Mazian, Florence. 1990. *Why Genocide?* Ames: Iowa State University Press.

Mazrui, Ali. 1986. *The Africans*. Boston: Little, Brown.

McAdam, Doug, John D. McCarthy, and Mayer N. Zald. 1988. "Social Movements." In Neil J. Smelser (ed.). *Handbook of Sociology*. Newbury Park, CA: Sage, pp. 695–737.

McColm, R. Bruce. 1992. "The Comparative Survey of Freedom 1991–1992: Between Two Worlds." In Bruce McColm (survey coordinator), *Freedom in the World: Political Rights and Civil Liberties*. New York: Freedom House, pp. 47–52.

McEvedy, Colin. 1980. *The Penguin Atlas of African History*. New York: Penguin.

McNeely, Connie L. 1995. *Constructing the Nation-State*. Westport, CT: Greenwood.

McNeill, William H. 1963. *The Rise of the West*. Chicago: University of Chicago Press.

_____.1976. *Plagues and People*. New York: Doubleday Anchor.

_____.1978. "Human Migration: A Historical Overview." In William H. McNeill and Ruth S. Adams (eds.), *Human Migration: Patterns and Policies*. Bloomington: University of Indiana Press, pp. 3–19.

_____.1985. *Polyethnicity and National Unity in World History*. Toronto: University of Toronto Press.

_____.1993. "Fundamentalisms and the World of the 1900s." In Martin E. Marty and R. Scott Appleby (eds.), *Fundamentalisms and Society*. Chicago: University of Chicago, pp. 558–573.

McNulty, Michael L. 1977. "The Contemporary Map of Africa." In Phyllis M. Martin and Patrick O'Meara (eds.), *Africa*. Bloomington: Indiana University Press, pp. 24–49.

Mead, George Herbert. 1962. *Mind, Self, and Society*. Chicago: University of Chicago Press.

Mernissi, Fatima. 1992. *Islam and Democracy*. Reading, MA: Addison-Wesley.

Merton, Robert K. 1957. *Social Theory and Social Structure*. Revised and enlarged. Glencoe, IL: Free Press.

_____.1976. *Sociological Ambivalence*. New York: Free Press.

Meyer, John W. 1995. "Foreword." In *Constructing the Nation-State*, by Connie L. McNeely. Westport, CT: Greenwood 1995, pp. ix–xiv.

Michael, Franz. 1986. *China Through the Ages*. Boulder, CO: Westview.

Mitchell, Alison. 1997 "Survivors of Tuskegee Study Get Apology From Clinton." *The New York Times* (May 17): 10.

Molnar, Stephen. 1992. *Human Variation*. 3rd ed. Englewood Cliffs, NJ: Prentice-Hall.

Morgan, David. 1987. *The Mongols*. New York: Basil Blackwell.

Moseley, Caroline. 1996. "Course Links Princeton, California." *Princeton Weekly Bulletin* (9 December): 1, 3.

Moskos, Charles. 1991. "How Do They Do It?" *The New Republic* (August 15): 16–20.

Moskos, Charles, and John Sibley Butler. 1996. *All That We Can Be*. New York: Basic.

Munson, Patrik J. 1977. "Africa's Prehistoric Past." In Phyllis M. Martin and Patrick O'Meara (eds.), *Africa*. Bloomington, IN: University Press, pp. 62–82.

Mussolini, Benito. 1955. Quoted in *Familiar Quotations by John Bartlett*. 13th ed. Boston, MA: Little, Brown, p. 926.

Nagel, Joane. 1994. "Constructing Ethnicity: Creating and Recreating Ethnic Identity and Culture." *Social Problems* 41, February: 152–176.

Nagel, J., and S. Olzak. "Ethnic Mobilization in New and Old States: An Extension of the Competition Model." *Social Problems* 30, December: 127–143.

Naisbitt, John. 1996. *Megatrends Asia*. New York: Simon & Schuster.

Negroponte, Nicholas. 1995. *Being Digital*. New York: Knopf.

Nicolas, G., and I. Prigogine. 1977, *Self-Organization in Nonequilibrium Systems*. New York: Wiley.

Nightingale, C. H. 1993. *On The Edge*. New York: Basic.

Ogbu, J. U. 1991, "Immigrant and Involuntary Minorities in Comparative Perspective." In M. A. Gibson and J. U. Ogbu (eds.), *Minority Status and Schooling*. New York: Garland, pp. 3–33.

Ong, Walter J. 1982. *Orality and Literacy*. New York: Methuen.

Orbell, John M., and Robyn M. Dawes. 1993. "Social Welfare, Cooperators' Advantage, and the Option of Not Playing the Game." *American Sociological Review* 58 (December): 787–800.

Palmer, R.R. 1973. "Equality." In Philip P. Wiener (ed.), *Dictionary of the History of Ideas*. Vol. III. New York: Scribner's, pp. 138–148.

Pan, Lynn. 1994. *Sons of the Yellow Emperor*. New York: Kodansha.

Pareto, Vilfredo. 1935. *The Mind and Society*. New York: Harcourt, Brace.

Park, Robert E. 1950. *Race and Culture*. Glencoe, IL: Free Press.

Park, Robert E., and Ernest W. Burgess. 1921. *Introduction to the Science of Sociology*. Chicago: University of Chicago Press.

Parshall, Gerald. 1995. "A 'Glorious Mongrel'" *U.S. News and World Report* (September 25):48.

Parsons, Talcott. 1951. *The Social System*. Glencoe, IL: Free Press.

Passell, Peter. 1995. "Why the Richest Nations Want to Insure the Rest." *The New York Times*, June 18, Sec. 4, p. 3.

Patterson, Orlando. 1982. *Slavery and Social Death: A Comparative Study*. Cambridge, MA: Harvard University Press.

Pennisi, Elizabeth, and Wade Roush. 1997. "Developing a New View of Evolution," *Science* 277(4 July):34–37.

Perutz, Max F. 1989. *Is Science Necessary?* New York: Dutton.

Peters, William. 1971. *A Class Divided*. New York: Doubleday.

Phillips, William D., Jr. 1985. *Slavery from Roman Times to the Early Transatlantic Trade*. Minneapolis, MN: University of Minneapolis Press.

Pinney, Roy. 1972. *Slavery: Past and Present*. New York: Thomas Nelson.

Population Reference Bureau. 1996. *World Population Data Sheet*. Washington, DC: Population Reference Bureau.

Porter, Michael E. 1980. *Competitive Strategy*. New York: Free Press.

Portes, Alejandro. 1995."Economic Sociology and the Sociology of Immigration: A Conceptual Overview." In Alejandro Portes (ed.), *The Economic Sociology of Immigration*. New York: Russell Sage Foundation, pp. 1–41.

Portes, Alejandro, and Ruben G. Rumbaut. 1996. *Immigrant America*. 2nd ed. Berkeley, CA: University of California Press.

Portes, Alejandro, and John Walton. 1981. *Labor, Class, and the International System*. New York: Academic.

Rajecki, D. W. 1982. *Attitudes: Themes and Advances.* Sunderland, MA: Sinauer Associates.

Reich, Robert B. 1992. *The Work of Nations: Preparing Ourselves for 21st-Century Capitalism.* New York: Vintage.

Republic of Hungary Office for National and Ethnic Minorities. 1993. *Act LXXVII of 1993 on the Rights of National and Ethnic Minorities.* Budapest, Hungary.

Rex, John. 1996. *Ethnic Minorities in the Modern Nation State.* New York: St. Martin's.

Rheingold, Howard. 1993. *The Virtual Community.* Reading, MA: Addison-Wesley.

Ridley, Mark. 1993. *Evolution.* Boston: Blackwell.

Rieder, Jonathan. 1985. *Canarsie: The Jews and Italians of Brooklyn Against Liberalism.* Cambridge: Harvard University Press.

Rifkin, Jeremy. 1995. *The End of Work.* New York: Putnam.

Roberts, D. F. 1992. "The Galton Lecture for 1990: The Price of Isolation." In A. H. Bittles and D. F. Roberts (eds.) *Minority Populations: Genetics, Demography and Health.* Hampshire England: Macmillan, pp. 35–67.

Roberts, Neil. 1984. "Pleistocene Environments in Time and Space." In Robert Foley (ed.), *Hominid Evolution and Community Ecology.* New York: Academic, pp. 25–54.

Robertson, Roland. 1992. *Globalization: Social Theory and Global Culture.* Newbury Park, CA: Sage.

Ross, Lee. 1977. "The Intuitive Psychologist and His Shortcoming: Distortions in the Attribution Process."In Leonard Berkowitz (ed.), *Advances in Experimental Social Psychology.* Vol. 10. New York: Academic Press, pp. 173–220.

Ross, Lee, and Richard E. Nisbett. 1991. *The Person and the Situation.* Philadelphia: Temple University Press.

Rudolph, Susanne Hoeber. 1996. "Transnational Religion and Fading States." *Items* 50 (June-September): 25–30.

Said, Edward W. 1993. *Culture and Imperialism.* New York: Knopf.

Schermerhorn, R. A. 1978. *Comparative Ethnic Relations.* Chicago: University of Chicago Press.

Schramm, Wilbur. 1972. "Its Development." In *Mass Media and Communication.* Edited by Charles S. Steinberg. New York: Hastings House, pp. 44–55.

Schwartz, Douglas W. 1985. "The Colonizing Experience: A Cross-Cultural Perspective." In Ben R. Finney and Eric M. Jones (eds.), *Interstellar Migration and the Human Experience.* Berkeley, CA: University of California, pp. 234–247.

Sears, David O., and Donald R. Kinder. 1971. "Racial Tensions and Voting in Los Angeles." In Werner Z. Hirsch (ed.), *Los Angeles: Viability and Prospects for Metropolitan Leadership.* New York: Praeger, pp. 51–88.

Segal, Ronald. 1995. *The Black Diaspora.* New York: Farrar, Straus and Giroux.

Sherif, Muzafer, and Carolyn W. Sherif. 1953. *Groups in Harmony and Tension.* New York: Harper.

Sherif, Muzafer, et al. 1961. *Intergroup Conflict and Cooperation.* Norman, OK: The University Book Exchange.

Shibutani, Tamotsu, and Kian M. Kwan. 1965. *Ethnic Stratification: A Comparative Approach*. New York: Macmillan.

Shimahara, Nobuo. 1984. "Toward the Equality of a Japanese Minority: The Case of Burakumin." *Comparative Education* 20, no. 3: 339–353.

Shuzhang, Yang, and Liu Weijiang. 1992. "Ethnic Population: A Macro Analysis of Population Growth of China's Ethnic Groups in the 1980s," *China Population Today* 9, no. 3:9–11.

Sider, Gerald. 1992. "The Contradictions of Transnational Migration: A Discussion." In Nina Glick Schiller, Linda Basch, and Cristina Blanc-Szanton (eds.), *Towards a Transnational Perspective on Migration*. New York: New York Academy of Sciences, pp. 231–240.

Simmel, Georg. 1950. *The Sociology of Georg Simmel*. Glencoe IL: Free Press.

_____.1955. *Conflict and the Web of Group-Affiliations*. New York: Free Press.

Simon, Herbert A. 1973. "The Organization of Complex Systems." In Howard H. Pattee (ed.), *Hierarchy Theory: The Challenge of Complex Systems*. New York: George Braziller, pp. 1–28.

Simpson, George Eaton, and J. Milton Yinger. 1985. *Racial and Cultural Minorities*. New York: Plenum.

Sivard, Ruth Leger. 1991. *World Military and Social Expenditures 1991*. 14th ed. Washington, DC: World Priorities.

Smith, Anthony D. 1986. *The Ethnic Origins of Nations*. Oxford: Blackwell.

_____.1990. "Towards a Global Culture?" *Theory, Culture & Society* 7 (June): 171–191.

_____.1991. *National Identity*. New York: Penguin.

_____.1995. *Nations and Nationalism in a Global Era*. Cambridge: Polity.

Smith, Malcolm, and Robert Layton. 1987. "Why Haven't We Speciated?" *New Community* 13, no. 3 (Spring): 367–372.

Smolowe, Jill. 1993. "Intermarried . . . With Children." *Time* 142, no.21 (Special Issue, Fall):64–65.

South Commission. 1990. *The Challenge to the South*. Oxford: Oxford University Press.

Sowell, Thomas. 1981. *Ethnic America*. New York: Basic.

_____.1996. *Migrations and Cultures*. New York: Basic.

Spence, Jonathan D. 1990. *The Search for Modern China*. New York: Norton.

Spencer, Herbert. 1898. *The Principles of Sociology*. 3 vols. New York: Appleton.

_____.1961. *The Study of Sociology*. Ann Arbor, MI: University of Michigan Press.

Stares, Paul B. 1996. *Global Habit: The Drug Problem in a Borderless World*. Washington, DC: Brookings Institution.

Starr, Chauncey, Milton F. Searl, and Sy Alpert. 1992. "Energy Sources: A Realistic Outlook." *Science* 265 (15 May): 981–987.

Staub, Ervin. 1989. *The Roots of Evil*. New York: Cambridge University Press.

Steele, Shelby. 1990. *The Content of Our Character*. New York: St. Martin's Press.

Steinberg, Stephen. 1989. *The Ethnic Myth*. Expanded. Boston: Beacon.

Stephan, W. G., and D. Rosenfield. 1982. "Racial and Ethnic Stereotypes." In A. G. Miller (ed.), *In the Eye of the Beholder*. New York: Praeger.

Stevens, William K. 1995. "Scientists Say Earth's Warming Could Set Off Wide Disruptions." *The New York Times*, September 18, pp. A1, A8.

Stinchcombe, Arthur L. 1965. "Social Structure and Organizations." In James G. March (ed.), *Handbook of Organizations*. New York: Rand McNally, pp. 142–193.

Stone, Richard. 1995. "If the Mercury Soars, So May Health Hazards." *Science* 267 (17 February): 957–958.

Stuckert, Robert P. 1976. "'Race Mixture: The Black Ancestry of White Americans." In Peter B. Hammon (ed.), *Physical Anthropology and Archaeology*. New York: Macmillan, pp. 135–139.

Swatos, William H., Jr. 1984. "Revolution and Charisma in a Rationalized World: Weber Revisited and Extended." In *Max Weber's Political Sociology*. Edited by Ronald M. Glassman and Vatro Murvar. Westport, CT: Greenwood, pp. 201–215.

Swisher, C. C., III, et al. 1996. "Latest *Homo erectus* of Java: Potential Contemporaneity with Homo sapiens in Southeast Asia." *Science* 274 (13 December): 1870–1874.

Taeuber, Karl E., and Alma F. Taeuber. 1966. "The Negro Population in the United States." In John P. Davis (ed.), *The American Negro Reference Book*. Englewood Cliffs, NJ: Prentice-Hall, pp. 96–160.

Thompson, James D. 1967 *Organizations in Action*. New York: McGraw-Hill.

Tilly, Charles. 1975a. "Reflections on the History of European State-Making." In Charles Tilly (ed.), *The Formation of National States in Western Europe*. Princeton, NJ: Princeton University Press, pp. 3–83.

_____.1975b. "Western State-Making and Theories of Political Transformation." In Charles Tilly (ed.), *The Formation of National States in Western Europe*. Princeton, NJ: Princeton University Press, pp. 601–638.

_____.1994. "A Bridge Halfway: Responding to Brubaker," *Contention*, Vol. 4, No. 1, Fall, pp. 15–19.

Tocqueville, Alexis de. 1945. *Democracy in America*. 2 vols. New York: Vintage.

Turner, Alan. 1984. "Hominids and Fellow-Travellers: Human Migration Into High Latitudes as Part of Large Mammal Community." In Robert Foley (ed.), *Hominid Evolution and Community Ecology*. New York: Academic, pp. 193–218.

Turner, Frederick Jackson. 1920. *The Frontier in American History*. New York: Holt.

UNESCO. 1995. *World Education Report 1995*. Paris: United Nations Educational, Scientific, and Cultural Organization.

_____. 1996 *Statistical Yearbook 1996*. Paris: United Nations Educational, Scientific, and Cultural Organization.

United Nations. 1993. *Statistical Yearbook*. New York: United Nations.

_____.1994. *Human Rights: A Compilation of International Instruments*. Vol. I (1st part). New York: United Nations.

United Nations Development Programme 1996 *Human Development Report 1996*. New York: Oxford University Press.

U.S. Bureau of the Census. 1990. *Statistical Abstract*. Washington, DC: U. S. Government Printing Office.

_____.1991. *Statistical Abstract*. Washington, DC: U. S. Government Printing Office.

_____.1996. *Statistical Abstract*. Washington, DC: U. S. Government Printing Office.

van den Berghe, Pierre L. 1967. *Race and Racism*. New York: Wiley.

_____. 1987. *The Ethnic Phenomenon*. New York: Praeger.

Vansina, Jan. 1990. *Paths in the Rainforests*. Madison: University of Wisconsin Press.

Vaughan, James H. 1977. "Environment, Population, and Traditional Society." In Phyllis M. Martin and Patrick O'Meara (eds.), *Africa*. Bloomington: Indiana University Press, pp. 9–23.

Vincent, Jack E. 1976. *A Handbook of the United Nations*. Revised. Woodbury, NY: Barron's Educational Series.

Vischer, Lukas. 1979. "An Ecumenical Creed?" In Hans Kung and Jurgen Moltmann (eds.), *An Ecumenical Confession of Faith?* New York: Seabury, pp. 103–117.

von Fritz, Kurt. 1973. "The Influence of Ideas on Ancient Greek Historiography." In Philip P. Wiener (ed.), *Dictionary of the History of Ideas*, Vol. II. New York: Scribners, pp. 499–511.

Wallace, Walter L. 1983. *Principles of Scientific Sociology*. Hawthorne NY: Aldine.

_____.1988. "Toward a Disciplinary Matrix in Sociology." In Neil J. Smelser (ed.), *Handbook of Sociology*. Newbury Park, CA: Sage, pp. 23–76.

_____.1994. *A Weberian Theory of Human Society: Structure and Evolution*. New Brunswick, NJ: Rutgers University Press.

_____.1997. "A Definition of Social Phenomena for the Social Sciences." In John D. Greenwood (ed.), *The Mark of the Social: Discovery or Invention?* Lanham, MD: Rowman & Littlefield, pp. 37–57.

Wallerstein, Immanuel. 1979. *The Capitalist World-Economy*. New York: Cambridge University Press.

Walters, F. P. 1952. *A History of The League of Nations*. London: Oxford.

Wardhaugh, Ronald. 1993. *Investigating Language*. Cambridge MA: Blackwell.

Warner, W. Lloyd. 1953. *American Life*. Chicago: University of Chicago.

Washington, Booker T. 1971. "The Atlanta Exposition Address, September—1895." In August Meier, Elliott Rudwick, and Francis L. Broderick (eds.), *Black Protest Thought in the Twentieth Century*. 2nd ed. New York: Bobbs-Merrill, pp. 4–8.

Waters, Malcolm 1995 *Globalization*. London and New York: Routledge.

Watson, James J. 1980. "Slavery as an Institution, Open and Closed Systems." In James L. Watson (ed.) *Asian and African Systems of Slavery*. Oxford: Blackwell, pp. 1–15.

Weber, Max. 1946. *From Max Weber: Essays in Sociology*. Edited by H. H. Gerth and C. Wright Mills. New York: Oxford University Press.

_____.1950. *General Economic History*. Glencoe, IL: Free Press.

_____.1978. *Economy and Society*. 2 vols. Edited and translated by Guenther Roth and Claus Wittich. Berkeley, CA: University of California Press.

_____.1989a. "The National State and National Economic Policy." In Keith Tribe (ed.), *Reading Weber*. London: Routledge, pp. 188–209.

_____.1989b. "Germany as an Industrial State." in Keith Tribe (ed.), *Reading Weber*. London: Routledge, pp. 210–220.

Weinberg, Steven. 1992. *Dreams of a Final Theory.* New York: Knopf.

Weiner, Myron. 1995. *The Global Migration Crisis.* New York: HarperCollins.

White, Kevin M., and Samuel H. Preston. 1996. "How Many Americans Are Alive Because of Twentieth-Century Improvements in Mortality?" *Population and Development Review* 22, no. 3 (September): 415–429.

White, Leslie A. 1969. *The Science of Culture: A Study of Man and Civilization.* New York: Farrar, Straus and Giroux.

Wilford, John Noble. 1995. "Believers in African Eve Think They Have Found Adam(s)." *The New York Times*, May 26, p. A16.

_____.1996. "Geologists Link Black Sea Deluge to Farming's Rise." *The New York Times*, December 17, pp. C1, C10.

Willey, Gordon R., and Jeremy A. Sabloff. 1980. "General Introduction." In Gordon R. Willey and Jeremy A. Sabloff (eds.), *Pre-Columbian Archaeology: Readings from Scientific American.* San Francisco: Freeman.

Williamson, Joel. 1980. *New People.* New York: Free Press.

Wilson, Edward O. 1971. *The Insect Societies.* Cambridge, MA: Harvard University Press.

_____.1975. *Sociobiology.* Cambridge, MA: Harvard University Press.

_____.1992. *The Diversity of Life.* Cambridge, MA: Harvard University Press.

Wilson, William Julius. 1978. *The Declining Significance of Race.* Chicago: University of Chicago Press.

_____ 1987. *The Truly Disadvantaged.* Chicago: University of Chicago Press.

_____.1996. "Work." *The New York Times Magazine*, August 18, pp. 26–52.

Wirth, Louis. 1945. "The Problem of Minority Groups." In Ralph Linton (ed.), *The Science of Man in the World Crisis.* New York: Columbia University Press.

Wolpoff, Milford H., Wu Xin Zhi, and Alan G. Thorpe. 1984. "Modern Homo sapiens Origins: A General Theory of Hominid Evolution Involving the Fossil Evidence from eastern Africa." In Fred H. Smith and Frank Spencer (eds.), *The Origins of Modern Humans: A World Survey of the Fossil Evidence.* New York: Alan R. Liss, pp. 411–483.

Wriston, Walter B. 1992. *The Twilight of Sovereignty.* New York: Scribner's.

Wuthnow, Robert. 1987. *Meaning and Moral Order.* Berkeley, CA: University of California.

_____.1991. "International Realities: Bringing the Global Picture into Focus." In Wade Clark Roof (ed.), *World Order and Religion.* Albany: State University of New York, pp. 19–37.

Yette, Samuel F. 1971. *The Choice: The Issue of Black Survival in America.* New York: Berkeley.

Yom, Sue Sun. 1996. "The Internet and the Future of Minority Health." *JAMA, The Journal of the American Medical Association* 275, no. 9: 735.

Zolberg, Aristide R. 1995. "Response: Working-Class Dissolution." *International and Working-Class History* no. 4 (Spring):28–38.

INDEX

About the Author

WALTER L. WALLACE is Professor of Sociology at Princeton University. He is author of seven books, including *A Weberian Theory of Human Society* (1994) and *Principles of Scientific Sociology* (1983), as well as numerous articles and book chapters.

ISBN 0-275-95831-0

EAN

9 780275 958312

90000>

HARDCOVER BAR CODE